MasterChef™

THE ULTIMATE COOKBOOK

MasterChef™
THE ULTIMATE COOKBOOK

The Contestants and Judges of *MasterChef*

RODALE

Rodale books may be purchased for business or promotional use or for special sales. For information, please write to:

Special Markets Department, Rodale Inc., 733 Third Avenue, New York, NY 10017

Printed in the United States of America

Rodale Inc. makes every effort to use acid-free ♾, recycled paper ♻.

Food photographs by Tara Donne
Show photographs courtesy of FOX Broadcasting Company

Book design by Mike Smith

Recipe Copywriter and Tester—Rochelle Palermo Torres

Library of Congress Cataloging-in-Publication Data

MasterChef, the ultimate cookbook / the contestants and judges of MasterChef.
    p.   cm
Includes index.
ISBN 978-1-60961-512-3   hardcover
1. Cooking, International.   2. Television cooking shows.   I. MasterChef (Television program)
TX725 .A1M3665   2012
641.5—dc23   2012026711

Distributed to the trade by Macmillan

2 4 6 8 10 9 7 5 3 1   hardcover

We inspire and enable people to improve their lives and the world around them.
rodalebooks.com

Contents

Chapter One: Breakfasts

Chapter Two: Soups, Salads, and Starters

Chapter Three: Pastas and Rice Dishes

Chapter Four: Vegetables and Sides

Chapter Five: Seafood

Chapter Six: Poultry

Chapter Seven: Meats

Chapter Eight: Desserts

Foreword

BY GRAHAM ELLIOT

MasterChef: Take a moment to think of that word, and the two parts that make it up. Master, defined as "an artist, performer of consummate skill." Chef, defined as "the chief cook."

Now, throw in the word *amateur* and you start to get a sense of how amazing this show is! Scouring all four corners of the country in search of the rare home cook that possesses the technical know-how, the passion, determination, palate, skill set—that is what this show and this book are all about.

Having personally been to all fifty states, I can truly say without a doubt that everything that is great about this country of ours is represented. The melting pot of ethnicities, styles, ideas, flavors—all are highlighted by people simply cooking from their hearts and using their personal histories and life experiences to guide them in their quests for culinary excellence.

I'm not only speaking about the cuisine of the Pacific Northwest or New England. I'm talking about Indian, Thai, Korean, Cajun, Italian, French—the flavors that weave this country and its varied people and cultures together.

Once the contestants have presented their dishes and stories to Joe and me, we decide if they're ready to put on an apron and enter the *MasterChef* kitchen. After that, their destinies rest more in their hands than in ours. Great dishes generally consist not only of delicious ingredients, but also blood, sweat, and tears.

This season, we encountered myriad personalities and cooking styles, and I can tell you that I've never been so excited to be surrounded by such talented and passionate individuals—be it Christine, a blind contestant who inspired every one of us by cooking armed only with her palate and sense of touch; or Joshua, a seven-foot consummate athlete and army contract specialist who surprised his friends with his passion for cooking; or Monti, a single mom who was able to create amazingly complex dishes on a tight budget.

Each and every one of the amateur home cooks proved that they possessed the skills to follow their dreams, be it in a professional kitchen, a catering business, or a TV show. Their stories, skills, and creative, unique recipes are all on display in this gorgeous book. I am humbled to be part of such an amazing show and look forward to seeing what the next season of *MasterChef* brings. Until then, keep cooking with all your heart!

Introduction

BY JOE BASTIANICH

This year brings another fantastic edition of the *MasterChef* cookbook! Here is an ambitious compilation of the best recipes to come out of Season 3, by some of the most promising contestants the show has seen to date. We hope this book inspires you as much as they have inspired us!

MasterChef got its start in the UK in 1990 and evolved into its current format in 2005. It has gone on to become the most successful culinary TV show in the world, with franchises currently in over 35 countries and has been seen by more than 200 million people worldwide. Beloved the globe over, *MasterChef* is about more than just another cooking competition; it is about creating the opportunities that will change lives forever. The last three seasons of *MasterChef USA* alone brought out tens of thousands of amateur home cooks from all over the country, each vying for a coveted spot at the Los Angeles auditions. They have but one chance to make it or break it, and the energy—even at the casting events—is astounding. Competing on *MasterChef* is a chance to pursue a life immersed in the exhilarating, innovative, dramatic, thriving world of food and wine.

It isn't easy to pack up life as you know it—these amateur home cooks make huge sacrifices in order to compete. Being chosen means dropping out of their daily lives—literally overnight—and devoting themselves to the mentally and physically grueling twelve-hour-plus days of a fierce competition. It means leaving one's home, spending time away from family and friends (when you probably need them most), giving up income—and in some cases jobs—all for the chance to be fast-tracked into a career where starting at the bottom is the usual prerequisite. It's a huge gamble, and one that I know all too well.

I made a decision early in life to leave a promising and

lucrative career on Wall Street for a line of work notorious for failure, where those who do emerge victorious are rewarded a mere ten-percent profit—at best. Most would say that's downright crazy, or just plain stupid, but I knew where my heart was. I wanted to wake up each morning happy to face each day not dreading how I earned my living, and I am proud to be a part of something that empowers so many others to do the same.

Each year we see the competition get fiercer, and Season 3 was no exception. The promise of $250,000 to fuel your culinary ambitions and a cookbook deal can really heat things up. It is truly a thrill to watch as we whittle down the contestants from tens of thousands to one triumphant winner. The first few days of auditions are intense, as the top one hundred present us with their signature dish: their one shot at advancing into the next round. Emotions are high, family and loved ones are present—it is an exciting, albeit nerve-wracking start to what will be a whirlwind three-month-long journey. As the competition forges ahead, front-runners emerge, and we judges get a chance to get to know the remaining contestants on a much more personal level. Although we are known for being tough—good mentoring usually is—we aren't afraid to push those who we know can do better.

Contestants came out from all walks of life and varying ethnicities—this season had a real international flair, illuminating the incredible diversity of our country. America's Chinatowns and Little Italies certainly sent their best. We met everyone—a Chinese-American college freshman, defying his parents to pursue the culinary arts, a Brazilian artist who brought flair to the plate, cowboys from the Midwest, a Jamaican-American marine, and even a husband-and-wife team competing against each other—as well as the competition's first visually impaired home cook. This show really has its finger on the pulse of what is happening in America's kitchens today, and it is evident in every page of this book. Inside you'll find the best from the top eighteen competitors of Season 3, including Becky Reams's tempura-fried shrimp, Felix Fang's succulent five-spice duck, Frank Mirando's Meyer lemon tiramisu, and Michael Chen's delectable pork dumplings that wowed the judges on the first day of auditions, just to name a few.

Included you'll also find step-by-step instructions to guide you through some culinary basics. No matter what your level of prowess is in the kitchen, we know you'll find something amazing and manageable to create at home for every occasion. And since no meal can ever really be complete without wine, I've also provided some great wine pairings to set your meal to perfection.

We would like to send out a huge thank-you to everyone who came out for the show, and we hope your experience with us only further inspires your love for the culinary arts and that you continue cooking if that is where your heart is.

So what will be served on your dining room table tonight? Christine Ha's stir-fry noodles with scallops, Mike Hill's pan-seared rabbit leg, followed by Stacey Amagrande's Italian trifle, or perhaps one of your own family favorites—whatever it may be, we hope you enjoy creating, sharing, and eating it. Buon appetito!

MasterChef Kitchen Equipment Basics

Pantry contents ebb and flow, but your kitchen equipment remains constant. So while you may spend some time seeking out sea urchins or lamb saddles to recreate some of your favorite *MasterChef* dishes, hold off until you have your kitchen stocked with the basic tools for the job. It's likely easier than you think: The primary items you need are some high-quality knives and a few pots and pans.

The Sharper the Knife...

One of the most important tools in the kitchen is the knife. Professional chefs will use whatever pans they find in the kitchens where they're cooking, but they always travel with their own knives, because once a knife fits your hand with comfort and grace, and you've honed the blade to an ideal sharpness, you won't want to use anyone else's tools. This is merely practical. All pros know that a sharp knife is much safer than a dull one that requires excessive force. But a good knife is also a joy to use. If you've ever owned one of those knives that says it never needs sharpening, a proper knife will be a real revelation. A well-made knife has weight and heft and balance, and after you learn a few basic techniques, it practically does the job for you.

What's It Made Of?

The knives that take and hold the best edge are carbon steel, but carbon steel has the unfortunate tendency to rust if you so much as breathe on it, much less cut food with it. Carbon steel quickly turns dark with use and easily stains, and it can transfer a metallic flavor to foods such as tomatoes when they are cut. However, it takes a razor-sharp edge that is a joy to use. But most cooks want something more practical for everyday use when investing in knives, and fortunately for them, high-carbon stainless was created.

High-carbon stainless is a durable alloy, a compromise between the easily rusted carbon steel and regular old stainless steel, which is alloyed with nickel or chromium to make it durable and flexible. Sure, stainless will never rust, but it will always be dull and never take an edge; and as a knife, stainless steel is not worth even the small amount it would cost you. High-carbon stainless (sometimes called high-carbon no-stain), is generally made of carbon, chromium, molybdenum, and vanadium. It will take and hold an edge and won't rust, uniting the best of the qualities of carbon and stainless.

Forging Ahead: What Knives Do You Need?

You can cook happily and successfully with only three knives. As you increase your knife skills and your confidence, and if you want to spend the money, you may want to branch out into the exact knife for the job. (It's surprising the differences you'll find, for example, when using a proper boning knife to bone out a chicken, for example, instead of making do with a utility knife.) For nearly all other cooks, however, a basic three-knife set will do all your kitchen jobs. Whatever brand you buy, these are the three you need:

1 **CHEF'S KNIFE** *(7- or 8-inch blade)*
If you're buying only one good knife, make it this one. It's the workhorse of the kitchen, the knife you'll automatically reach for every time. Your main tool for chopping and slicing, use it for cutting up vegetables, meats, and herbs. You can use the butt of the knife for a pestle and the flat of the blade to crush cloves of garlic.

2 **UTILITY KNIFE** *(4½- or 5-inch blade)*
This is a small knife to be used when the chef's knife is too big. Use for trimming or for small slicing or chopping jobs (such as a clove of garlic to toss in a stew). Sharp and flexible with a fine point, it can be pressed into service for boning or filleting if necessary.

3 **PARING KNIFE** *(3- or 3½-inch blade)*
This knife is commonly used for paring or scraping, fruit cutting, or quick and small vegetable cutting jobs.

Other Knives You May Want

SERRATED BREAD KNIFE
A serrated knife with its long blade hacks through chewy, crisp-crusted bread or can thinly slice tomatoes, kiwifruit, and other soft fruits because the sharp teeth prevent the soft inside from being crushed.

CARVING KNIFE
A carving knife has a long, narrow, flexible blade that is very thin and sharp. It allows you to smoothly cut through large joints of meat.

FILLETING KNIFE
Mainly used for filleting fish or also for cutting meat into thin slices across the grain, a filleting knife has a thin, flexible blade that allows you to follow the contours of the fish or meat.

BONING KNIFE
This type of knife has a narrow blade that curves into a thicker heel and bolster for leverage, and it has a larger handle. Used a great deal by butchers to cut the meat off bones in raw roasts. Good for separating ribs, removing larger pieces of bone (such as backbone) from roasts, or for Frenching chops.

CLEAVER
Chinese cooks use a cleaver for everything the way Western cooks use a chef's knife. But in Western kitchens, a cleaver is good to have if only for hacking bones. Bones can leave a nick in the edge of a regular knife blade—they're meant for cutting, not hacking—and you can ruin an expensive knife with one swipe at a drumstick.

Care and Use: Techniques for Handling Your Knives

Use whichever of the grips below is most comfortable for you, but remember that all the fingers of the hand holding the knife should be curved around the knife. Any other method of holding the knife will result in unnecessary muscle strain and a less effective technique. Avoid laying the index finger along the spine of the knife; although this offers the illusion of control, you actually have less control of that finger. All four fingers should encircle the handle; the difference in grips lies in where the forefinger and thumb hold the blade.

For smaller hands: The thumb and forefinger are below the bolster. With the thumb and forefinger, grasp the handle below the ferrule, letting the thumb just touch the bolster for control. Loosely wrap your other fingers around the handle. With this grip, extended use is less likely to cause calluses.

For bigger hands: The thumb and forefinger touch the heel of the blade. With the thumb and forefinger, grasp the knife on the heel just above the ferrule, allowing the front joint of the index finger to lie roughly parallel to the bolster. Loosely wrap the other three fingers around the handle. For men with big hands, the blade grip keeps their hands from feeling cramped up below the handle. For professionals who must use knives all day, this grip often results in knife calluses, which are not a bad thing to serious cooks.

The hand not holding the knife guides the knife—always move the hands and the knife, not the food. Many chefs swear by the curled finger method, whereby the fingers of the guiding hand are actually curled under so that the fingernails rest on the food being cut. It's very safe for those practicing their cutting techniques, but the thumb and little finger are also angled under, meaning that most of the guiding is done by the three middle fingers. The knife blade rests against the knuckles, and the blade moves along as the fingers back away from the knife along the food, so the knife is guided with no chance of cutting off your fingertips.

How to Cut: The Techniques

There are three techniques to cutting, and some cutting jobs require variations of each. You need to be comfortable with each basic method for the safest, most efficient cutting.

CHOPPING
Carrots, onions, celery, potatoes, vegetables to be diced or cubed

Using the largest part of the blade, between the heel and the middle, repeatedly raise the blade and lower it with a forward and downward motion through the food to be cut. The guiding hand should move along the food, guiding the blade along but not moving the food.

MINCING
Garlic, fresh herbs

The guiding hand holds the tip of the blade on the board, and the heel of the blade is raised and lowered rapidly in a fanwise motion across the food. The food to be finely minced, such as garlic or herbs, has already been chopped into slightly smaller pieces. You want to rock the curved edge of the knife back and forth along the food, always holding the tip to the cutting surface.

SLICING
Larger fruits and vegetables such as cabbage, eggplant, zucchini; meats

The whole blade is used in a longer, piston-like

motion. Using the guiding hand, hold the food to the board, and angle the tip of the knife downward to the food. Push the knife forward, allowing the weight of the knife to make the cut. Keeping the edge in contact with the board, pull back through the food, and follow the guiding hand to move the tip to the start of the next cut.

When slicing, do not let the blade rest against the knuckles, but keep the guiding hand at least an inch away from the cutting edge. The cutting motion is too swift and long to keep the fingers safely close to the blade—a moment's distraction could be dangerous.

Keep the Edge: Steeling and Sharpening

A dull knife is a dangerous one. It requires more force and makes it more likely that you'll cut yourself—even a dull knife is still going to go through skin. You should habitually give your knife a few swipes of the steel every few uses. This will keep your knives in peak condition. Always avoid putting your good knives in an electric sharpener. Most of them grind away your blade between disks and will shorten the life of the knife.

Your steel is your main tool for keeping a sharp edge. A sharp blade is a delicate thing, even on a carbon steel knife. Steeling does not sharpen the edge but instead hones it, removing the invisible burrs created by everyday use and returning the edge to pristine condition. Steels are long metal cylinders with a ridged surface that the knife is drawn against to true the knife's edge. A magnetized steel will also pull the molecules of the blade back into alignment.

If you're right-handed, hold the steel rigidly in your left hand and, using moderate pressure and holding the knife at a constant 20-degree angle to the steel, swiftly swipe the knife from heel to tip along the length of the steel. Repeat on the other side of the blade, pulling it along the other side of the steel. Steel each side three or four times.

Ideally, you'll have your knives professionally sharpened every couple of years, only when the edge noticeably dulls.

You can also sharpen using a whetstone. To do this, buy a professional-quality carborundum stone that you lubricate with oil. Very carefully, pull your blade, always at a constant 20-degree angle, along the entire length of the knife. You're actually removing metal here, so don't oversharpen. If the knife is badly nicked or very dull, it may take you more than 10 minutes to sharpen, but test the edge frequently so as not to overdo it. Be sure to sharpen the blade evenly along its whole length—you don't want to take more metal off the tip than the heel, for example. There are tools available that will hold the knife at a constant angle while you sharpen.

Cutting Surfaces

Do not cut against hard surfaces such as metal, porcelain, or even countertops, or you might nick the blade and permanently damage it. Wood is considered best, but to avoid cross-contamination, it should be thoroughly cleaned after slicing meat, poultry, or fish. Molded propylene boards are also excellent and can be run through a dishwasher after use. There has been a lot of debate in recent years over whether wooden boards store germs, but recent studies have shown that bacteria can grow even in the molded plastic, because grooves are cut into the plastic with each use. After using, always wash your board thoroughly with hot soapy water and dry it well.

Storing: There's No Such Thing as a Knife Drawer!

Knives should never be stored in a drawer. Don't let them touch each other or anything else besides food, a cutting surface, and a damp sponge.

Wooden knife blocks look good, but be careful how you remove the knives so you don't drag the blades against the wooden sheath as you remove them. Your best bet is to mount a magnetic knife rack on the kitchen wall (high enough to keep it away from small, interested hands).

Pots and Pans: The Basics

Heavy-weight stainless steel cookware with an aluminum core is ideal for home cooks. The aluminum sealed into the base ensures that the heat will spread evenly underneath the pans but does not come into contact with the food. Aluminum reacts negatively with acid-based foods like tomato or wine. At the very least, you should own a 1-quart, 2½-quart, and 4-quart saucepan, as well as an 8-quart Dutch oven and a 10- or 12-inch sauté pan with a lid. Other useful pans to have in the kitchen are as follows:

How to Season Your Cast-Iron Pan

Preheat the oven to 300°F. Wash and dry the new pan thoroughly, completely removing any labels or stickers. Rub the pan inside and out with corn oil, and place it in the oven for 30 minutes. Remove the pan and rub it only inside with oil; put it back in the oven for another 30 minutes. The pan may smoke a bit, and this is perfectly fine. Turn off the oven, and let the pan cool inside the oven to room temperature. You can now use it for regular cooking.

After every few uses, while the seasoning is still darkening, heat the skillet over a high flame or on high heat for several minutes until the pan is very, very hot. It may even smoke a bit if there are any particles on the inside. Remove it from the heat for a moment, pour in a couple tablespoons of cooking oil, and spread the oil around with a wadded-up paper towel. Return the pan to the heat for a few minutes more before turning it off and leaving the pan to cool. Keep in mind that cast iron is used mostly for frying. Don't make a lot of wet dishes in it. If you already have a cast-iron skillet that doesn't get much use, you can reseason it in the oven for an hour.

When you clean your seasoned skillet—always by hand—don't use any sort of cleanser or dishwashing liquid. You can run it under hot water for a couple of seconds and wipe it with a sponge. Any food that sticks can be scrubbed off with a handful of kosher salt applied to the sponge or with a plastic scrubber. Never use steel wool. Avoid removing the blackened patina of oil that you're building up.

CAST-IRON SKILLET

A seasoned cast-iron pan is a durable and high-performing cooking utensil. It is perfect for nearly every kind of cooking, except for anything acid-based, like tomatoes or wine. In a seasoned pan, the microscopic peaks and valleys of the cast iron are filled with the oil, which not only leaves a slick surface for cooking but leaves the pan's surface airtight and protects it from rust. The heat helps drive the oil deeper into the iron and creates a more durable finish. You're essentially shellacking the bottom of the pan with a smooth, hard, nonstick coating.

WOK

A wok should be hand-beaten carbon steel, at least 14 inches in diameter. A brand-new wok needs to be scrubbed with a gentle cleanser or with baking soda to remove the oil from manufacturing, dried thoroughly, and then never washed with soap again. Once the wok is scrubbed the first time, dry it and set it over a low flame on the stove. Pour in 2 tablespoons of vegetable oil, and rub it all over the inside of the wok with a paper towel. Continue heating for about 10 minutes, and then wipe it out with a paper towel, which will be black. Repeat this process several times until the paper towel is clean. The wok will become further darkened and seasoned with each use. Wash it in plain water, and don't scrub with anything rougher than a plastic scrubber.

GRILL PAN

These cast-iron pans can be round or square, deep or flat, but their distinguishing marks are the raised ridges on the bottom. The ridges allow the fat to drain away from the cooking meat and make the black grill marks on the meat.

STOCKPOT

A stockpot is a large, deep, straight-sided pot with a lid and is used for making stock or boiling large quantities of liquid. They range in size from 6 quarts to bathtub size.

GRATIN DISH

This is a shallow, flat casserole that leaves a wide surface area for baking a browned crust on dishes with cheese or bread crumbs.

CLAY POT

An unglazed clay dish, available in many Asian or Middle Eastern markets, the clay pot is soaked in water and sealed with a lid for long, slow cooking.

ROASTING PAN

A very large, deep, lidded pan, generally rectangular or oval, the roasting pan is used for cooking very large cuts of meat and poultry such as turkeys.

TERRINE

The terrine is a narrow, tall-sided loaf pan, usually made of glazed earthenware, with a lid used for cooking pâtés and terrines.

OMELET PAN

A small, slope-sided carbon-steel skillet, the omelet pan needs to be very well seasoned (see cast-iron skillet at left) before cooking omelets over high heat.

SPRINGFORM PAN

This is a round pan with a metal clasp that locks the base of the pan into the sides. When unlocked, it allows easy removal of baked goods such as flans or, more important, cheesecakes.

The Four Main Challenges

There are four types of challenges that the *MasterChef* producers set for the contestants, and each episode features two challenges. They are:

1   **The Mystery Box:** *Each contestant gets a box containing a set of mystery ingredients. The box may contain something as simple as one sea urchin, an aquarium containing spot prawns, or a whole raft of Southern ingredients. Contestants don't have to use every ingredient in the box. They can use whatever inspires them, backed by the Mystery Box Staple Pantry of eggs, milk, flour, butter, sugar, lemons, and baking powder. It is important that they do their best, because the winner gets a huge advantage in the following Elimination challenge!*

2   **Elimination:** *This challenge is dictated by the winner of the Mystery Box. They will usually have a choice between three or more items, and they'll get to decide what everyone is cooking or what everyone is cooking with. For instance, the contestants may each get assigned a different fish that has to be a star of their dish. Or they may have to cook a version of a highly sophisticated dish they've seen and tasted, but they may not be allowed to ask further questions. Other Eliminations have featured using a single piece of equipment, such as a pizza stone—all of these chosen by the winner of the Mystery Box. One or more contestants are eliminated each time.*

3   **The Team Challenge:** *The contestants are split into two and, on the rare occasion, three teams. They are selected schoolyard-style by the contestants that performed the best in the previous Elimination challenge. The contestants are then taken to a location, such as a Marine Corps base camp, a hotel, an offsite restaurant, or a dude ranch. They never know quite where they're going, even if they think they do, and when they get there, they generally have to cook for a lot of people. At one point, they ran three competing food trucks and ended up serving lunch to hundreds of locals and tourists in Venice, California.*

4   **Pressure Test:** *The losing team from the Team Challenge must face the Pressure Test. Judges choose one particular dish or item that the contestants must cook to perfection in a certain amount of time, with no second chances and no extra ingredients. Anxiety is at an all-time high for the contestants, who might have to turn out three soufflés at the same time, cook six eggs three different ways, make an ideal apple pie, or sear a perfect steak.*

MICHAEL CHEN
20 AUSTIN, TX

Michael grew up loving his father's cooking, and despite the lack of support from his parents, wants to pursue it as a career.

BECKY REAMS
27 STILWELL, KS

A "make it happen" girl who put herself through college and taught herself to cook, Becky makes her own fruit and vegetable pickles.

JOSHUA MARKS
24 CHICAGO, IL

At 7'0", Joshua may look intimidating, but he is warm, charming, and can "shoot onions into the skillet" as well as he slam-dunks a basketball.

FELIX FANG
25 PUNA, HI

From an early age, Felix broke all the rules and challenged her parents' expectations of her. She cooks to make her parents proud.

TANYA NOBLE
22 JAKARTA, INDONESIA

A self-proclaimed "oil brat" who has lived all over the world, Tanya uses cooking to prove that she can strike out on her own.

CHRISTINE HA
33 HOUSTON, TX

Legally blind, Christine wants her skill to inspire others with disabilities that anything is possible.

FRANK MIRANDO
28 HOLBROOK, NY

Frank is the quintessential Italian New Yorker. He auditioned to show his daughter that she should pursue her dreams, no matter the risk.

ANNA ROSSI
29 BOSTON, MA

Anna beat out her husband in the *MasterChef* auditions and discovered her love for cooking when she rented a room with an extensive culinary library.

HELENE LEEDS
36 FAIRFAX, VA

A former plus-size model, Helene has lived all over the world and is eager to bring her cooking to new places.

DAVID MACK
28 FORT LAUDERDALE, FL

Having traveled over 40 states in a custom motorhome, David wants to catapult from the family catering business and cook on his own.

STACEY AMAGRANDE
30 APPLE VALLEY, CA

Vegetarian at 12, Stacey works with her local farmers' market to teach her community how to eat sustainably.

SCOTT LITTLE
39 ANNANDALE, VA

With $30 to his name, Scott found out he had a baby girl. Cooking and a talent for homemade pasta inspire him to change his life to provide for his daughter.

DAVID MARTINEZ
32 CHICAGO, IL

A former gang member and dropout, David turned his life around. He's pursuing multiple higher degrees and loves to cook new dishes.

MIKE HILL
41 POWDER SPRINGS, GA

A good ol' cowboy, Mike competes in rodeos as a team roper—and is passionate about smoking and curing meats.

RYAN UMANE
27 NEW YORK, NY

Ryan is serious about cooking and aspires to own his own food truck so he can change the menu.

MONTI CARLO
37 MAYAGUEZ, PUERTO RICO

A recent divorcee and single mom, Monti found that cooking got her through the pain and gave her a new way to bond with her son.

TALI CLAVIJO
29 CHICAGO, IL

Modernist foodie with a passion for "blowing stuff up" in the kitchen, Tali creates simple dishes from unconventional ingredients.

SAMANTHA DE SILVA
28 MOUNT LAVINIA, SRI LANKA

Samantha loves to be in control in the kitchen. Cooking was not her first love, but she wants to open a bistro with a staff of all women.

FRUIT CUP

The sheer variety of fruits in the bowl makes this fruit cup an elegant morning treat or even a wonderful dessert for later in the day. You can mix and match the fruits depending on what's fresh and available at your local market. Be sure to use equal proportions of all the fruits, cutting or slicing them into similarly shaped pieces, to keep your version true to the original recipe, with no one fruit predominating. If you can't find dragon fruit, try to add at least one dramatic fruit to mix it up a bit, such as carambola, also called star fruit.

For the competition, the team members used precisely equal amounts of fruit for each serving, but you may prefer to just use an appropriate quantity to avoid waste. If you like, try the recipe using one dragon fruit, a quarter each of the melons and pineapple, and a cupful of each type of berry.

- 6 ounces cubed cantaloupe
- 6 ounces cubed honeydew
- 6 ounces cubed pineapple
- 6 ounces cubed watermelon
- 6 ounces sliced dragon fruit
- 6 ounces sliced fresh strawberries
- 6 ounces fresh blackberries
- 6 ounces fresh blueberries
- 6 ounces fresh raspberries
- 4 whole strawberries

Divide the fruit, except for the whole strawberries, equally among 4 serving bowls. Slice the whole strawberries without cutting through the stem ends, then fan the strawberries on top of the fruit and serve.

SERVES 4

Recipe courtesy of
THE RED TEAM
(Christine Ha, Becky Reams, Felix Fang, Mike Hill, Scott Little, Stacey Amagrande, Tanya Noble)

Dragon fruit is the fruit of a cactus. It has knobby skin that's bright fuchsia or yellow and a seed-speckled interior that's either pink or white, depending on the variety. It has long been popular in Southeast Asia, and now it's becoming increasingly available in American stores. Dragon fruit is also grown in South America and Israel, but wherever your dragon fruit originated and no matter what its color, be sure that the one you're buying is in top condition: firm flesh, evenly colored, and just ripe enough to give very slightly to the pressure of your thumb, like a perfectly ripe avocado. The stem and the little leaves that protrude from the surface should still be soft and flexible, not dry and brittle. A soft fruit with brown spots on the skin is past ripe and should be avoided.

The flavor is mild and creamy, not at all tart, with a texture sort of like a medium-crisp apple, such as a Golden Delicious. The tiny black seeds have a gentle crunch that's reminiscent of the tiny seeds in a kiwifruit.

To cut up a dragon fruit, halve the fruit from end to end with a knife, and then use the sharp edge of a teaspoon to scoop the fruit from the tough skin. It will come out of each half in one domed piece that can then be evenly diced.

OATMEAL
WITH BROWN SUGAR AND GOLDEN RAISINS

For a team challenge, the contestants thought they were flying to Hawaii. They were transferred to an airport hotel and woke up to find that instead of boarding a plane to a tropical paradise, they were expected to serve room-service breakfast to an entire hotel! The teams managed admirably to perk up some classics with new twists, but it wasn't exactly a holiday.

Nevertheless, ordinary oatmeal became a luxurious morning treat, thanks to a simple but novel technique: cooking the oats with golden brown sugar. It adds a caramel-like note to the nutty flavor of the oats and elevates them from everyday cereal. Be sure to use traditional rolled oats here, not quick-cooking oats. Golden raisins and milk stirred in at the end add chewy sweetness and creaminess.

4 cups water

¼ teaspoon kosher salt

2 cups old-fashioned rolled oats

½ cup packed light brown sugar

6 tablespoons golden raisins

About 1 cup whole milk

Additional light brown sugar

Combine the water and salt in a medium, heavy-bottomed saucepan, and bring to a boil over high heat. Stir in the oats and the brown sugar and return to a simmer. Reduce the heat to medium and simmer until the oats are tender and the oatmeal is thick, stirring occasionally, about 10 minutes. Stir in the raisins and cook until they're plump, about 2 minutes.

Just before serving, stir enough milk into the oatmeal to thin it to the desired consistency. Divide the oatmeal among 4 bowls. Sprinkle with more brown sugar and serve immediately.

SERVES 4

Recipe courtesy of
THE RED TEAM
(Christine Ha, Becky Reams, Felix Fang, Mike Hill, Scott Little, Stacey Amagrande, Tanya Noble)

EGGS FOUR WAYS

For a Pressure Test, Monti Carlo found herself required to do nothing more than cook eggs—but to utter perfection. Cooking eggs is simple, right? But doing it without a single flaw is a challenging matter. Monti was really feeling the pressure because she had one shot to get each one right.

But she did it, and so can you. For example, if your poached eggs never seem to come out as delicate ovals with tender whites and perfectly runny yolks and without any trailing strands, try Monti's method. It's a winner.

OMELETS

2 tablespoons unsalted butter

12 large eggs

Kosher salt and freshly ground black pepper

Heat an 8- to 10-inch nonstick omelet pan over medium heat until hot. Add ½ tablespoon of the butter and cook until it melts, swirling the pan to coat. Beat 3 of the eggs in a large bowl until frothy, and season with salt and pepper. Pour the beaten egg mixture into the pan. Cook, lifting the edges with a silicone spatula and allowing the uncooked eggs to run onto the pan until the bottom is set and just beginning to brown and the top begins to set, about 3 minutes. Using the spatula, fold over one-third of the omelet (the edge closest to the pan handle) onto the center of the omelet, then tilt the pan and slide the opposite edge of the omelet onto a plate, rolling the center of the omelet onto the unfolded portion to create a trifold. Repeat to make 3 more omelets.

MAKES 4

POACHED EGGS

1 tablespoon distilled white vinegar

2 teaspoons kosher salt

4 large eggs

Bring 4 inches of water to a boil in a deep saucepan. Stir in the vinegar and salt. Reduce the heat so that the water just barely simmers. Using a slotted spoon, stir the water to create a slow-moving vortex in the center. Break 1 egg into a cup and slide it into the vortex. Poach until the white is firm and the yolk thickens slightly but is still runny, about 3 minutes. Using a slotted spoon, lift the egg out of the poaching liquid and drain it briefly in the spoon on paper towels before serving. Repeat with the remaining eggs.

MAKES 4

SOFT-BOILED EGGS

4   large eggs

Bring 4 inches of water to a boil in a deep saucepan. Add the eggs (still in the shells) and cook for 5 minutes. Remove the eggs from the water, place them into egg cups, and set them aside for 2 minutes. Cut off the tops of the eggs and serve immediately. Or, to serve them later, transfer the eggs to a bowl of ice water to stop them from cooking, then rewarm them in the boiling water for 1 minute before serving.

MAKES 4

SUNNY-SIDE-UP EGGS

2   tablespoons canola oil

4   large eggs

Kosher salt and freshly ground black pepper

Heat 1 tablespoon of the oil in a large nonstick skillet over medium heat. Spray two 4-inch-diameter ring molds with nonstick cooking spray, and set the rings in the skillet. Crack 1 egg into each ring, and fry until the whites are cooked through and the yolks are thick but still fluid, about 3 minutes. Remove the rings, then transfer the eggs to 2 plates. Repeat with the remaining oil and eggs.

MAKES 4

Recipes courtesy of
MONTI CARLO

LEMON PANCAKES
WITH MIXED BERRIES

L eave out the lemon zest, and you have a mile-high buttermilk pancake that's both tender and fluffy, a recipe you'll use all year to top with a slather of butter and a hefty drizzle of maple syrup. Add the lemon zest, and turn them into a gourmet treat, a pancake that's destined for more. The bright lemony flavor makes them an ideal base for mixed fresh raspberries, blueberries, and blackberries. Dust them generously with confectioners' sugar, and serve them for an elegant brunch.

1   cup all-purpose flour

1   tablespoon granulated sugar

1   teaspoon baking powder

½   teaspoon baking soda

¼   teaspoon salt

1   cup buttermilk

3   tablespoons whole milk

1   large egg

2   tablespoons melted unsalted butter, plus about 2 tablespoons for frying

2   teaspoons finely grated lemon zest

½   cup fresh blackberries

½   cup fresh blueberries

½   cup fresh raspberries

About ½ cup confectioners' sugar

Whisk the flour, granulated sugar, baking powder, baking soda, and salt in a large bowl to blend. Whisk the buttermilk, milk, egg, melted butter, and lemon zest in a medium bowl to blend. Keep the two mixtures separate until you are ready to cook.

Heat a heavy griddle or skillet over medium heat. Once hot, coat the griddle or pan with some butter. Pour the wet mixture into the dry mixture and stir until a slightly lumpy batter forms. Using about ½ cup of the batter for each pancake, pour the batter onto the griddle, evenly spacing the pancakes. Cook until golden brown and puffed, about 2½ minutes per side. (You should be able to make 8 pancakes.)

Divide the hot pancakes among 4 plates, top with the berries, dust with the confectioners' sugar, and serve immediately.

SERVES 4

Recipe courtesy of
THE RED TEAM
(Christine Ha, Becky Reams, Felix Fang, Mike Hill,
Scott Little, Stacey Amagrande, Tanya Noble)

EGG WHITE OMELET
WITH SAUTÉED MUSHROOMS AND SPINACH

Think that a "healthy" omelet is by nature a dull omelet? Think again. With thick-sliced mushrooms seared into meaty flavorfulness in a hot pan, and tender baby spinach, flash-cooked and well seasoned, you'll forget any hint of virtue when you take the first bite. The quick-cooking technique lets you turn out four omelets so fast that everyone can get their breakfast cooked to order while still sitting down to eat together. Ideally, use only ripe, summer-fresh tomatoes, and slice them thick to accompany each omelet.

3 tablespoons plus 8 teaspoons olive oil

12 ounces button mushrooms, thickly sliced

12 ounces fresh baby spinach leaves

Kosher salt and freshly ground black pepper

8 teaspoons canola oil

12 large egg whites

12 tomato slices

6 ounces watercress, stems removed

Heat 3 tablespoons of olive oil in a large, heavy-bottomed sauté pan over high heat. Add the mushrooms and sauté until they are tender and golden brown, about 7 minutes. Add half of the spinach and sauté just until it begins to wilt, about 1 minute. Add the remaining spinach and sauté until all the spinach has wilted, about 2 minutes. Season the mushrooms and spinach to taste with salt and pepper. Set aside and keep hot.

Heat a 10-inch nonstick sauté pan over medium heat until hot. Spray the pan with nonstick cooking spray. Add 2 teaspoons of the canola oil and swirl the pan to coat. Beat 3 of the egg whites in a large bowl to blend, and season to taste with salt and pepper. Pour the beaten egg mixture into the pan and cook, swirling the pan to distribute the eggs evenly, until the bottom is set and just beginning to brown and the top begins to set, about 2 minutes. Spoon one-fourth of the hot sautéed mushrooms and spinach over the eggs. Using the spatula, fold one-third of the omelet (the edge closest to the pan handle) over onto the center of the omelet, then tilt the pan and slide the opposite edge of the omelet onto a plate, rolling the center of the omelet onto the unfolded portion to create a trifold. Repeat to make 3 more omelets.

Arrange the tomato slices alongside the omelets on the plates. Top with the watercress and serve immediately.

SERVES 4

Recipe courtesy of
THE RED TEAM
(Christine Ha, Becky Reams, Felix Fang, Mike Hill, Scott Little, Stacey Amagrande, Tanya Noble)

Nobody who watched Season 2 of *MasterChef* is likely to forget Ben Starr's amazing Pumpkin Carrot Cake. In its lush, rich, over-the-top preparation, replete with six layers of moist, fragrant cake, it was a fantasy version of a classic American dessert. But Ben took away more from the experience than a nation's gratitude for his cake!

Ben says, "*MasterChef* was a life-changing experience, to say the least. Perhaps the biggest thing to come out of the experience, for me, were the relationships with my fellow contestants. Six months after filming, I had already been to visit almost all of the top 18 contestants in their homes. I talk to many of them on an almost daily basis. They have become my family.

"In the year before *MasterChef,* I had decided I wanted to move to Hawaii to start a guest farm and restaurant there. So many residents in Hawaii have reached out to me since the show that I have developed a solid network there that would have taken me years to develop on my own. I've been to Hawaii twice in the past few months alone to cook for homeless charities, visit schools and organic farms, and get involved in community development projects. It looks like my Hawaiian dream will come true sooner than I could have ever hoped before *MasterChef.*

"And last but not least are the thousands of amazing fans who are still with me, long after the show initially aired, sharing recipes and stories through social media and e-mail, begging me to return to their television screens, and helping me spread the message of love and peace around the world through food. I have never felt more loved in my life, thanks to the wonderful friends and fans that *MasterChef* brought me."

PUMPKIN-CARROT PANCAKES

"After the six-layer cake episode aired, I was inundated with requests for the recipe for my Pumpkin Carrot Cake with Cream Cheese Frosting and Candied Hazelnuts," says Ben Starr, a contestant from Season 2. "Still, about once a week, someone will e-mail me a photo of their family with the cake. I've been so overwhelmed by the response, and it warms my heart to think of people venturing beyond their comfort zone to bake my fairly complex cake to share with their family and friends. "Eventually, though, so many people said, 'I just don't know how you pulled that off in 2 hours—it's way too complicated for me,' that I decided to make a simplified pancake version that anyone could throw together in the morning for a special breakfast."

FOR THE PANCAKES

- 1 cup old-fashioned rolled oats (not quick-cooking oats)
- 1 cup whole milk
- 1 large carrot, peeled and grated
- ¾ cup pumpkin puree
- ½ cup firmly packed light brown sugar
- 2 teaspoons ground cinnamon
- 1 teaspoon ground cardamom
- 1 teaspoon ground ginger
- 1 teaspoon kosher salt
- ⅔ cup buttermilk
- 2 large eggs
- 2 tablespoons canola oil
- 1 teaspoon vanilla extract
- 1 cup all-purpose flour
- 1 tablespoon baking powder
- ½ teaspoon baking soda
- 6 tablespoons unsalted butter

FOR THE ORANGE-GINGER SYRUP

- ½ cup honey
- ½ cup packed light brown sugar
- ½ cup orange juice
- 1½ teaspoons grated orange zest
- 1½ teaspoons peeled, grated fresh ginger

Preheat the oven to 200°F.

Stir the oats, milk, and carrot in a large microwave-safe bowl, then microwave on high for 5 minutes, stirring every minute. Cool slightly. Stir in the pumpkin, brown sugar, cinnamon, cardamom, ginger, and salt. Mix in the buttermilk, eggs, oil, and vanilla.

Whisk the flour, baking powder, and baking soda in a medium bowl to blend, then stir the flour mixture into the oatmeal until all the flour has disappeared but a few lumps still remain.

Heat a large ungreased nonstick or cast-iron skillet over medium-low heat. Using about ½ cup of the batter for each pancake, spoon the batter into the hot pan and cook until the edges look dry and the bottom is lightly browned, about 4 minutes per side.

To make the syrup: Combine the honey, brown sugar, orange juice, zest, and ginger in a small, heavy-bottomed saucepan and simmer over medium heat, stirring often, until the syrup is reduced to 1 cup, about 5 minutes.

Transfer the hot pancakes to plates and serve with the butter and syrup.

SERVES 4

AMERICAN BREAKFAST

W hy are Americans so addicted to breakfast in diners? It's the fried potatoes. That's what makes this all-American breakfast an all-star breakfast, too. Fried eggs, bacon or sausage (or, you know, both), even the caramelized tomatoes, they're all just the frame on the plate for the real masterpiece: thin-skinned red potatoes fried in butter until they're crisp and golden-edged. The *MasterChef* technique that this team used to get the potatoes good and crisp is to leave them alone! If you flip and flip, they won't have time to develop a golden crust. Let them sizzle quietly in the butter, and make sure they're browned on one side before turning.

FOR THE POTATOES

- 1 pound red-skinned potatoes, quartered
- 1 tablespoon olive oil
- 2 tablespoons unsalted butter, melted

  Kosher salt and freshly ground black pepper

FOR THE EGGS AND BACON OR SAUSAGE

- 4 tablespoons canola oil
- 8 large eggs
- 8 bacon slices or breakfast sausages

FOR THE TOMATOES

- 4 tomatoes, halved
- ½ cup olive oil

  Kosher salt and freshly ground pepper

Recipe courtesy of
THE RED TEAM
(Christine Ha, Becky Reams, Felix Fang, Mike Hill, Scott Little, Stacey Amagrande, Tanya Noble)

TO MAKE THE POTATOES: Cook the potatoes in a large pot of boiling salted water just until partially tender and still holding their shape, about 10 minutes. Drain in a colander. Place the potatoes in a bowl of ice water to cool completely. Drain well and pat dry with paper towels.

Heat the oil in a large, heavy-bottomed nonstick skillet over medium heat. Add the potatoes and butter and cook until tender and golden, turning as necessary, about 10 minutes. Season with salt and pepper.

TO MAKE THE EGGS AND BACON OR SAUSAGE: Heat 1 tablespoon of the oil in a large nonstick skillet over medium heat. Crack 2 eggs into the skillet and fry until the whites are cooked through and the yolks are thick but still fluid, about 3 minutes. Transfer the eggs to a plate. Repeat with the remaining oil and eggs.

Meanwhile, cook the bacon or sausage in a large skillet over medium-high heat until the bacon is crisp and golden or the sausages are browned and cooked through, about 5 minutes.

TO MAKE THE TOMATOES: While the eggs and bacon cook, arrange the tomatoes on a baking sheet and drizzle the oil over them. Season with salt and pepper. Heat a large, heavy-bottomed sauté pan over high heat. Place the tomatoes cut side down in the pan and cook until caramelized, about 5 minutes. Turn the tomatoes over and cook until they soften slightly and caramelize on the bottom, about 3 minutes.

TO SERVE: Place 2 bacon slices or sausages and 2 tomato halves on each plate alongside the eggs. Divide the potatoes among the plates and serve immediately.

SERVES 4

EGGS BENEDICT

H ome cooks are often worried about making hollandaise sauce because cookbooks are always so full of dire warnings about how difficult it is. Follow the straightforward directions below and don't be intimidated. It helps that the *MasterChef* hollandaise begins with clarified butter (directions below), which makes it easier to emulsify the sauce and also easier to let it sit on the back of the stove without "breaking" as you finish the eggs. Once you've mastered hollandaise, throwing together a restaurant-worthy version of Eggs Benedict is fast and easy.

FOR THE CLARIFIED BUTTER

1   cup (2 sticks) unsalted butter

FOR THE HOLLANDAISE SAUCE

3   large egg yolks

2   tablespoons fresh lemon juice

About 4 tablespoons water

¾   cup hot Clarified Butter

Kosher salt

FOR THE POACHED EGGS

2   tablespoons distilled white vinegar

2   teaspoons kosher salt

8   large eggs

FOR THE BACON

1   tablespoon unsalted butter

8   slices Canadian bacon

4   English muffins, split and toasted

2   tablespoons chopped fresh chives, for garnish

TO MAKE THE CLARIFIED BUTTER: Cook the butter in a small, heavy-bottomed saucepan over medium heat until melted and beginning to simmer (do not stir). Remove from the heat. Spoon off the foam from atop the butter. Carefully pour the clarified butter into a small bowl, leaving the liquid whey and milk solids behind. Cool the clarified butter. Cover tightly and refrigerate.

TO MAKE THE HOLLANDAISE SAUCE: Whisk the yolks, lemon juice, and 2 tablespoons of the water in a medium bowl to blend. Set the bowl over a saucepan of barely simmering water, and whisk until light in color and beginning to thicken slightly, about 1 minute. Do not allow the water to boil. Whisk the eggs constantly so they don't curdle. Slowly add the clarified butter in a thin, steady stream, whisking constantly until the sauce is well blended and thick. Add enough of the remaining water to the sauce to thin it to the desired consistency. Season the sauce to taste with salt. To keep the sauce warm, set the bowl over the pan of hot water (off the heat), then cover and set aside, whisking occasionally.

EGGS BENEDICT

(continued)

TO MAKE THE POACHED EGGS: Bring 4 inches of water to a boil in a deep saucepan. Stir in the vinegar and salt. Reduce the heat so that the water just barely simmers. Using a slotted spoon, stir the water to create a slow-moving vortex in the center. Break 1 egg into a cup and slide the egg into the vortex. Poach until the white is firm and the yolk thickens slightly but is still runny, about 3 minutes. Using a slotted spoon, lift the egg out of the poaching liquid and set it in a baking dish of ice water to stop the cooking. Repeat with the remaining eggs. Reserve the boiling water.

To rewarm the eggs before serving, submerge them in the reserved saucepan of hot water just until they are hot. Using a slotted spoon, lift the eggs out of the water and drain them briefly in the spoon over paper towels.

TO MAKE THE BACON: Meanwhile, melt the butter in a large, heavy-bottomed skillet over medium-high heat. Add the Canadian bacon and cook just until beginning to brown, about 1 minute per side. Place the bacon on the toasted English muffin halves.

TO ASSEMBLE AND SERVE: Place 2 muffin halves on each of 4 plates, then gently place 1 egg on top of the bacon on each muffin half. Sprinkle with salt and spoon on a generous amount of hollandaise sauce. Garnish with the chives and serve immediately.

SERVES 4

Recipe courtesy of
THE RED TEAM
(Christine Ha, Becky Reams, Felix Fang, Mike Hill,
Scott Little, Stacey Amagrande, Tanya Noble)

Similar to mayonnaise, an emulsion of egg yolks and oil,

hollandaise is an emulsion of egg yolks and butter. While mayonnaise is made at room temperature, however, hollandaise is very sensitive to the heat it's cooked on. If it gets too warm, the beautiful golden sauce will split, or break, into oily-looking melted butter and clumps of egg protein—a real downer for a cook who's waiting to spoon it over perfect poached eggs nestled on rounds of Canadian bacon and toasted English muffins. Ideally, avoid breaking it in the first place by using a double boiler and keeping the heat low. If the sauce does break, try these quick fixes:

1	2	3	4
Whisk as fast as you can! If the sauce has just broken, sometimes you can simply whisk it back together. You can also try pouring the sauce into a blender and pulsing until it's creamy again.	If the sauce feels cool to your finger, add 1 or 2 teaspoons of boiling water and whisk until the sauce recombines.	If the sauce feels very warm, add an ice cube to the sauce and whisk vigorously until it recombines, then remove any remnant of the ice cube.	If all else fails, whisk an egg yolk in a bowl and then gradually whisk in the broken sauce, a little at a time. Set this over the double boiler and use the sauce promptly.

BOMBAY FLATBREAD

Think of a flatbread as a highly refined pizza, one that skips the tomato sauce, rubbery mozzarella, and the pepperoni. The hallmark of a good flatbread is the thin crust made without leavening. This elegant crust has a secret ingredient—a cup of cold beer, resulting in a vaguely yeasty flavor and a crispness that's almost crackerlike. You can use it as a base for any toppings you like.

Christine Ha covered it with a fragrant cilantro cream and chicken brightened with fresh ginger and the warm flavor of curry powder and garam masala. She scattered on crumbled feta for some sharpness and fresh mozzarella for a creamy undertone, and then topped each flatbread with a fried egg. This is like Indian street food taken to a whole new level.

FOR THE BREAD

- 2¾ cups all-purpose flour
- 1 teaspoon kosher salt
- 1 teaspoon sugar
- 2 tablespoons olive oil
- 1 cup chilled beer

FOR THE CHICKEN

- 1 teaspoon peeled, minced fresh ginger
- 1 clove garlic, minced
- 1 teaspoon kosher salt
- ¼ teaspoon curry powder
- ¼ teaspoon garam masala
- ¼ teaspoon turmeric
- 12 ounces boneless, skinless chicken breasts, cut into ¾-inch pieces
- 1 tablespoon olive oil
- 1 tablespoon unsalted butter

FOR THE CILANTRO CREAM

- 1 cup heavy cream
- ½ cup packed fresh cilantro
- 1 teaspoon kosher salt

FOR THE TOPPINGS

- 4 ounces feta cheese, crumbled
- 6 ounces fresh mozzarella cheese, torn into bite-size pieces
- 8 teaspoons canola oil
- 4 large eggs
- ¼ cup chopped fresh cilantro

BOMBAY FLATBREAD

(continued)

TO MAKE THE BREAD: Whisk the flour, salt, sugar, and oil in the bowl of an electric stand mixer. Fit the mixer with the dough hook attachment and position the bowl on the stand. Mix on low speed. Add the beer and mix on medium speed until the dough pulls away from the sides of the bowl and forms a smooth, elastic ball, scraping down the sides and bottom of the bowl as needed, about 5 minutes. Cover the bowl and set the dough aside for 20 minutes.

TO MAKE THE CHICKEN: Mix together the ginger, garlic, salt, curry powder, garam masala, and turmeric in a medium bowl. Add the chicken pieces and toss to coat.

Heat a large, heavy-bottomed sauté pan over high heat. Once the pan is hot, add the oil and butter. When the butter has melted, add the chicken and cook just until golden brown, turning as needed, about 3 minutes. Set the chicken aside to cool completely.

TO MAKE THE CILANTRO CREAM: Combine the cream, cilantro, and salt in a blender and pulse until smooth and pale green. Do not overblend or the cream will curdle. Set aside.

TO MAKE THE FLATBREADS WITH TOPPINGS: Place 2 baking stones on the bottom rack of the oven and preheat the oven to 500°F.

Divide the dough into 4 pieces. Working with one piece at a time, roll out the dough into thin 12 x 6-inch ovals. Spread ¼ cup of the cilantro cream over each flatbread. Top each with the feta, mozzarella, and chicken. Transfer the flatbreads to the baking stones and bake until the breads are brown on the bottom and the cheese is melted, about 8 minutes.

Meanwhile, set a small, heavy-bottomed nonstick sauté pan over medium heat until hot. Add 2 teaspoons of the canola oil and crack 1 egg into the pan. Cover and cook until the egg white is set and golden brown on the bottom and the yolk thickens but is still fluid, about 3 minutes. Transfer the fried egg to a plate and repeat with the remaining oil and eggs to fry 4 eggs total.

Sprinkle the cilantro over the flatbreads, then set the fried eggs on top and serve immediately.

MAKES 4

Recipe courtesy of
CHRISTINE HA

TOM KHA KAI

When contestants were each given an empty Mystery Box and told they could "shop" in the pantry to fulfill the challenge, they were delighted. Finally, a break! Each person hand-selected a boxful of ingredients, crafting a dish in their heads as they made their decisions.

But nothing is ever that easy during competition. When they returned to the kitchen, each contestant was instructed to give the box they were holding to the person in front of them. When Monti Carlo found herself in possession of Christine Ha's box, she was terrified. But the classic Southeast Asian soup she crafted from the contents was a lesson in the flavors of Thai cooking: hot, salty, sour, and also creamy-sweet from the coconut milk. Serve it as soon as you stir in the cilantro and fresh lime juice, while the tanginess of the fresh herb and citrus is most pronounced.

- 6 **cups chicken stock**
- 1 **can (13.5 ounces) unsweetened coconut milk, whisked to blend**
- 2 **lemongrass stalks, thinly sliced on a bias**
- 1 **kaffir lime leaf**
- 2 **tablespoons peeled, minced fresh ginger**
- ¼ **cup fish sauce**
- 1 **tablespoon Thai red curry powder**
- 5 **bone-in chicken thighs**
- 3 **medium carrots, peeled and thinly sliced into rounds**
- 1 **red jalapeño chile pepper, thinly sliced into rounds (wear plastic gloves when handling)**
- ½ **cup fresh cilantro**
- ¼ **cup fresh lime juice**

Combine the stock, coconut milk, lemongrass, lime leaf, ginger, fish sauce, and curry powder in a large, heavy-bottomed saucepan. Bring to a simmer over high heat. Add the chicken and reduce the heat to medium-low. Simmer gently until the chicken is cooked through and tender, about 20 minutes. Transfer the chicken to a plate and set aside until cool enough to handle, about 10 minutes. Cover the soup and set it aside while the chicken cools.

Remove the skin and bones from the chicken and coarsely tear the meat into bite-size pieces. Strain the soup through a fine-mesh sieve and into another saucepan. Spoon off the excess oil from the top of the soup.

Add the carrots and jalapeño to the soup and simmer gently over medium heat, until the carrots are tender, about 3 minutes. Stir in the chicken pieces and return the soup to a simmer. Stir in the cilantro and lime juice.

Ladle the soup into 4 to 6 bowls and serve.

SERVES 4 to 6

Recipe courtesy of
MONTI CARLO

WHITE CLAM PIZZA
WITH BLOODY CAESARS

F resh clams have a delicate sweetness that can't compete with too many overbearing ingredients. And who knows how to handle a fresh clam better than a cook from Massachusetts? Anna Rossi was careful not to overwhelm the flavor of fresh littleneck clams by keeping the complements light, bright, and classic: garlic, lemon zest, a little fresh oregano. And no heavy, creamy cheese here—coarsely shredded Parmigiano-Reggiano adds a salty savor without hiding the clams.

When shucking the clams, be careful to keep every drop of their sweet briny liquid for the Bloody Caesars (below). They're an innovative take on a Bloody Mary, using homemade tomato juice spiked with a hefty dose of lime. These pizzas and a Bloody Caesar are the perfect New England brunch!

FOR THE DOUGH

- 2¾ cups lukewarm water (about 110°F)
- 1½ packages (¼ ounce each) active dry yeast
- ¾ cup (or more) olive oil
- 5½ cups unbleached all-purpose flour
- 1 tablespoon sugar
- 1½ teaspoons salt

FOR THE GARLIC-LEMON OIL

- ½ cup olive oil
- 12 cloves garlic, minced
- 4 teaspoons grated lemon zest

FOR THE TOPPINGS

- 8 dozen littleneck clams, shucked, juices reserved for Bloody Caesar
- 8 tablespoons fresh oregano, finely chopped

  About 4 cups freshly shredded Parmigiano-Reggiano cheese

  Extra-virgin olive oil
- ½ lemon

FOR THE BLOODY CAESARS

- 4 pounds tomatoes, chopped
- 1 large red onion, peeled and halved
- 1 large celery stalk plus 4 small celery stalks with leaves, for garnish
- 2 teaspoons sugar
- 2 teaspoons kosher salt
- ¾ cup (or more) vodka
- 4 teaspoons fresh lime juice

- 1½ teaspoons prepared horseradish
- 1 teaspoon Worcestershire sauce
- ¾ teaspoon Tabasco sauce
- 1 teaspoon freshly ground black pepper

  About ½ cup reserved clam juices
- 2 tablespoons coarse salt
- 1 tablespoon celery salt

  Ice cubes
- 4 lime wedges

WHITE CLAM PIZZA
(continued)

TO MAKE THE DOUGH: Mix the water and yeast in a small bowl, then set aside until bubbles form on top of the mixture, about 5 minutes. Mix in ¾ cup oil.

Combine the flour, sugar, and salt in the bowl of an electric stand mixer. Set the bowl on the mixer stand and fit it with the paddle attachment. With the machine running on low speed, pour the yeast mixture into the dry ingredients and mix until the dough forms into a ball. If the dough is dry, mix in more oil. Transfer the dough to a floured work surface and knead until smooth and elastic, about 2 minutes. Divide the dough into 4 equal pieces. Shape each piece into a ball and set on a lightly floured baking sheet. Cover the dough with a slightly dampened towel and let rise in a warm, draft-free place until doubled in size, about 35 minutes.

TO MAKE THE GARLIC-LEMON OIL: Combine the oil, garlic, and lemon zest in a small saucepan. Simmer over low heat for 5 minutes to infuse the oil. Set aside.

TO MAKE THE PIZZAS WITH TOPPINGS: Place a baking stone on the bottom rack of the oven and preheat the oven to 500°F. On a lightly floured surface, roll out 1 dough ball as thin as possible into an irregular-shaped oval. Transfer the dough to the baking stone and bake until it puffs and looks a bit dry on top, but is still pale, about 5 minutes. Remove the partially baked pizza dough from the oven and brush with the garlic-lemon oil. Set aside and repeat with the remaining 3 dough balls.

Scatter the clam meats, oregano, and then the Parmigiano-Reggiano over the partially baked pizzas. Bake until the cheese melts and the pizzas are golden brown on the top and bottom, about 4 minutes.

Transfer the pizzas to a cutting board. Drizzle with some extra-virgin olive oil and squeeze the juice from the lemon half over the pizzas. Cut the pizzas into pieces and serve immediately with the Bloody Caesars.

TO MAKE THE BLOODY CAESARS: Combine the tomatoes, onion, and large stalk of celery in a large, heavy-bottomed pot over medium heat. Cook until juices form and begin to simmer. Continue simmering to allow the flavors to blend and the tomatoes to soften, stirring often, about 25 minutes. Discard the onion and celery.

Working in batches, press the tomato mixture through a food mill to extract 3 cups of juice. Transfer the tomato juice to a small, heavy-bottomed saucepan. Add the sugar and kosher salt and simmer just until dissolved. Transfer the tomato juice to a bowl and refrigerate until cold.

In a blender, combine the tomato juice, vodka, lime juice, horseradish, Worcestershire, Tabasco, and ½ teaspoon of the black pepper. Blend well. Add the clam juice to taste.

Mix the coarse salt, celery salt, and the remaining ½ teaspoon black pepper on a small plate. Moisten the rims of four 8-ounce glasses with water, then dip the rims into the salt mixture to coat lightly. Fill the glasses with ice. Divide the Bloody Caesar mixture among the glasses. Garnish with the small celery stalks and lime wedges and serve immediately.

SERVES 4 (makes 4 pizzas)

Recipe courtesy of
ANNA ROSSI

CHEDDAR CHEESE SOUFFLÉS

A successful soufflé is still considered evidence of a cook's prowess because it is so likely to fall between the oven and the table. But it doesn't have to be difficult. A soufflé is mainly a thick, cheese-enriched white sauce leavened with egg whites. Follow the instructions precisely and be sure to beat your egg whites until they're stiff, but not dry. Getting the soufflé to rise is not that hard; keeping it risen, however, is nearly impossible, so the trick is not to let the soufflés hang around after they have baked. These individual soufflés only take about 10 minutes to cook, so put them in the oven when your guests are actually moving toward the table so you can serve the soufflés the instant they come out of the oven. And for best flavor, use the sharpest cheddar you can find.

4   **tablespoons (½ stick) unsalted butter**

⅓   **cup finely grated Parmesan cheese**

1   **teaspoon kosher salt**

½   **teaspoon sweet paprika**

  Pinch of grated nutmeg

2   **cups whole milk**

6   **large eggs, separated**

¼   **cup cornstarch**

5   **ounces sharp cheddar cheese, grated (about 1¼ packed cups)**

Preheat the oven to 425°F. Using 1 tablespoon of the butter, coat four 12-ounce soufflé dishes, then sprinkle with the Parmesan cheese, tilting the dishes to coat completely and tapping out any excess. Arrange the prepared soufflé dishes on a large baking sheet.

In a medium, heavy-bottomed saucepan, combine the salt, paprika, nutmeg, 1 cup of the milk, and the remaining 3 tablespoons butter. Bring to a simmer over medium-high heat.

Meanwhile, whisk the egg yolks, cornstarch, and the remaining 1 cup milk in a large bowl to blend. Whisk into the simmering milk mixture and return to a simmer, whisking constantly. Simmer until the mixture thickens, about 1½ minutes. Whisk in the cheddar cheese. Pour the cheese mixture into the large bowl and set aside to cool slightly, whisking occasionally.

Meanwhile, using an electric mixer, beat the egg whites in a large bowl until stiff peaks begin to form. Fold the egg whites into the cheese mixture. Divide the mixture among the prepared soufflé dishes, filling the dishes completely.

Bake until the soufflés puff and the tops feel firm, 10 to 12 minutes. Serve immediately.

SERVES 4

Recipe courtesy of
JOSHUA MARKS

CHICKEN TIKKA MASALA WRAP

W hen the Blue Team had to staff a food truck, it made sense to create handheld food. Wraps are ideal to hand out a window to hungry folks on their feet.

Marinating chicken in yogurt results in a lush, velvety texture, thanks to the yogurt's natural enzymes. The chicken can be left in the marinade for as little as 30 minutes, which will let the potent spices begin to penetrate the flesh, or as long as 24 hours. If you can, plan ahead to let the chicken marinate overnight so that, when grilled, each piece will be full of flavor and incredibly tender. The grilled chicken is then stirred into a fragrant tomato sauce enriched with cream and butter. Wrapped in warm naan bread and topped with tangy slaw, it's a divine lunch.

FOR THE SAUCE

- 4 tablespoons (½ stick) unsalted butter
- 1 small onion, thinly sliced
- 1 small jalapeño chile pepper, finely diced (wear plastic gloves when handling)
- 1½ cups tomato sauce
- ¾ cup heavy cream
- 1½ teaspoons kosher salt
- 1½ teaspoons cayenne
- ⅓ cup chopped fresh cilantro
- 2 tablespoons fresh lemon juice

FOR THE SLAW

- ¼ cup plain Greek yogurt
- 2 tablespoons fresh lemon juice
- 1 teaspoon sugar
- ½ teaspoon cayenne
- ½ teaspoon curry powder
- ½ teaspoon ground cumin
- ⅛ teaspoon ground cinnamon
- ¼ head red cabbage, thinly sliced

  Kosher salt

FOR THE CHICKEN

- ½ cup plain Greek yogurt
- 2 tablespoons fresh lemon juice
- 2 tablespoons peeled, minced fresh ginger
- 2 cloves garlic, minced
- ½ habanero chile pepper, minced (wear plastic gloves when handling)
- ½ teaspoon cayenne
- ½ teaspoon garam masala
- ½ teaspoon ground cumin
- ½ teaspoon paprika
- ½ teaspoon kosher salt
- ½ teaspoon freshly ground black pepper
- 2 pounds boneless, skinless chicken thighs

  Canola oil
- 4 store-bought breads, warmed

TO MAKE THE SAUCE: Melt the butter in a large, heavy-bottomed saucepan over medium-high heat. Add the onion and jalapeño chile pepper and sauté until the onion begins to soften, about 3 minutes. Stir in the tomato sauce, cream, salt, and cayenne. Bring the sauce to a simmer, then reduce the heat to medium-low. Cover and simmer gently until the sauce thickens slightly and the flavors blend, about 45 minutes. Stir in the cilantro and lemon juice and simmer for 1 minute to blend the flavors.

TO MAKE THE SLAW: Whisk the yogurt, lemon juice, sugar, cayenne, curry powder, cumin, and cinnamon in a large bowl to blend. Add the cabbage and toss to coat. Set the slaw aside for 20 minutes to allow the flavors to blend. Season to taste with salt. Toss the slaw again before serving with the chicken.

TO MAKE THE CHICKEN: Meanwhile, whisk the yogurt, lemon juice, ginger, garlic, habanero chile pepper, cayenne, garam masala, cumin, paprika, salt, and black pepper in a large bowl to blend. Add the chicken thighs and toss to coat well. Cover and refrigerate for at least 30 minutes and up to 1 day.

Brush the rack of a barbecue grill with the oil and prepare the grill for medium-high heat. Remove the chicken from the marinade and grill until grill marks form and the chicken is just cooked through, about 5 minutes per side. Transfer the chicken to a cutting board and let rest for 5 minutes, then cut the chicken into bite-size pieces.

Add the chicken to the sauce and simmer over medium-high heat until the chicken is heated through and the sauce is hot.

Lay 1 warm naan bread on each of 4 plates. Divide the chicken and sauce among the naan.

SERVES 4

Recipe courtesy of
THE BLUE TEAM
(Christine Ha, Joshua Marks, Felix Fang, Mike Hill)

MADE-FROM-SCRATCH PORK DUMPLINGS

Y ou can buy dumpling wrappers ready-made, but Michael Chen's recipe will make you wonder why anyone bothers. Simply combine flour and water into a smooth dough and roll it under your palms into a rope. To make each wrapper, pinch off a lump of dough and roll it into a circle. It's so easy, and the cooked wrapper tastes fresher and more tender than a commercial wrapper, which can sometimes be a little tough. For the best results, pull off about half an inch of dough for each wrapper and roll it into a 4-inch circle.

Be sure not to add too much chicken broth to the filling. It should be moist but still quite firm. If it's too damp, the dumpling won't close up tight, and when you drop it in the boiling water, the seal won't hold.

The garlic-chili oil for drizzling over the finished plates calls for both regular red-pepper flakes, which provide heat, and Korean red-pepper flakes, which are much milder and provide a more rounded, fruity flavor. If you can't find the Korean pepper at an Asian market, it's fine to leave it out, but don't double the regular pepper flakes to make up the difference. It will be far too hot for comfort.

FOR THE DUMPLINGS

- 1¾ cups all-purpose flour plus more for dusting
- ½ cup water
- ½ pound ground pork
- ¼ cup chicken broth
- 7 fresh shiitake mushrooms, stemmed and minced
- ½ cup minced napa cabbage
- 3 scallions, minced
- 1½ teaspoons peeled, minced fresh ginger
- 1 tablespoon soy sauce
- 1½ teaspoons vegetable oil
- ½ teaspoon salt
- ¼ teaspoon freshly ground black pepper

FOR THE GARLIC-CHILI OIL

- 3 tablespoons vegetable oil
- 1 tablespoon toasted sesame oil
- ½ teaspoon red-pepper flakes
- ½ teaspoon Korean red-pepper flakes
- 1 clove garlic, peeled

FOR THE DIPPING SAUCE

- 1 tablespoon Chinese black vinegar
- 1 tablespoon soy sauce
- 1 teaspoon toasted sesame oil

FOR THE GARNISH

- 1 cup cilantro
- 3 scallions, thinly sliced

  Coarsely chopped roasted peanuts

TO MAKE THE DUMPLINGS: Mix the flour and water in the bowl of a stand mixer fitted with a paddle attachment until the dough is smooth, elastic, and not sticky. Cover and set aside.

Place the pork in a medium bowl and stir in enough broth, 1 tablespoon at a time, until the mixture has the consistency of thick pudding. Add

MADE-FROM-SCRATCH PORK DUMPLINGS

(continued)

the mushrooms, cabbage, scallions, ginger, soy sauce, vegetable oil, salt, and pepper and mix well. The mixture should be very moist and shiny, but should hold its shape when scooped out of the bowl.

Using your hands, roll out the dough on a floured surface into a long rope between ½ inch and 1 inch in diameter. Cut the rope crosswise into 24 cylinders. Working with one dough cylinder at a time, flatten it into a small quarter-size disk in the palm of your hand, then roll it out into a circle that is 3 to 4 inches in diameter.

Place a spoonful of the pork mixture in the center of each dough round. Moisten the dough edges with water and pinch the edges to enclose the filling and seal. Place the dumplings on a baking sheet, not touching. Cover the dumplings and refrigerate until ready to cook.

Bring a large pot of water to a boil. Cook the dumplings in the boiling water until they are plump and rise to the surface, about 8 minutes.

TO MAKE THE GARLIC-CHILI OIL: Combine the vegetable oil, sesame oil, regular red-pepper flakes, and Korean red-pepper flakes in a small, heavy-bottomed saucepan. Cook over medium-low heat until the oil is infused and aromatic, about 5 minutes. Strain the oil and discard the pepper flakes. Return the oil to the saucepan and add the garlic. Cook over medium-low heat until the garlic loses its pungency, about 5 minutes.

TO MAKE THE DIPPING SAUCE: Mix the vinegar, soy sauce, and sesame oil in a small bowl.

TO SERVE: Toss the cilantro and scallions in a small bowl. Mound the mixture in the center of 6 plates. Divide the dipping sauce among 6 small ramekins. Arrange 4 dumplings on each of the 6 plates. Drizzle the garlic-chili oil over the dumplings and salad. Garnish with the peanuts and serve immediately.

Recipe courtesy of
MICHAEL CHEN

SERVES 4 (makes 24 dumplings)

WINE PAIRING

A Gewürztraminer will complement both the chile pepper and the fat from the pork. A light, easy-drinking wine, Gewürztraminers are generally lower in acidity and won't clash with spicy flavors. Also known for their aromatics, they balance the spices in Asian food. Despite the name, this varietal is actually native to Northeast Italy. Look for one from France, Northeast Italy (Alto Adige), Germany, or Switzerland, where they tend to produce the best bottles.

Chicago native Suzy Singh came to her chef

career from a more unusual path than most: She started as a neural engineer. But her love of food drove her to the full-time pursuit of being a chef. After placing fourth in the second season of *MasterChef*, she has continued working in the food world, and her hope is that her successes will inspire others to follow their dreams as well. Suzy is now:

Creator of the very first Indian food truck in Chicago: Suzy Samosas	National spokesperson for Le Cordon Bleu	Supporting actor in the feature film *Promiseland*	Chef correspondent for Fox's *Good Day Chicago*	Culinary head for Bombay Wraps and for Kulfi & Company

Not only that, but she got to throw out the first pitch for both the Chicago White Sox and the Chicago Cubs.

GARAM MASALA CHICKEN SLIDERS
WITH CHICKPEA AIOLI

Though Suzy Singh was raised just outside of Chicago, her parents are Punjabi, and as with nearly all her MasterChef creations, Suzy works best when she can bring the flavors of her Eastern roots to Western cuisine. She refers to these flavorful sliders as "Indian bar food," and truly, the spicy chicken patties topped with garlicky aioli seem to cry out for a cold beer to accompany them!

FOR THE SLIDERS

- ¼ cup finely chopped fresh cilantro
- 2 tablespoons minced onion
- 2 teaspoons freshly ground black pepper
- 2 teaspoons ground fennel seeds
- 1 teaspoon garam masala
- 1 teaspoon ground cumin
- 1 teaspoon kosher salt
- 1 pound ground chicken
- 4 tablespoons (½ stick) unsalted butter
- 8 slider buns or sesame dinner rolls, split

  Chickpea Aioli (recipe follows)
- 8 small romaine lettuce leaves
- 8 thin slices red onion

FOR THE CHICKPEA AIOLI

- 2 cloves garlic
- ½ cup canned chickpeas, well drained
- 1 teaspoon ground cumin
- 1 teaspoon kosher salt
- ½ teaspoon freshly ground black pepper
- 1 tablespoon fresh lemon juice
- 1 large egg
- ½ cup grapeseed oil

TO MAKE THE SLIDERS: Mix the cilantro, onion, black pepper, fennel seeds, garam masala, cumin, and salt in a large bowl to blend. Add the chicken and mix gently just until blended. Form the mixture into 8 patties that are about 3 inches in diameter (or the diameter of your buns). Lay the patties on a baking sheet, cover, and refrigerate for 1 hour.

Heat a large, heavy-bottomed skillet over medium heat. Add 2 tablespoons of the butter, then the patties, and cook until golden brown on the outside and cooked through, about 3 minutes per side. Transfer the patties to a platter and tent with foil to keep them warm.

Spread the remaining 2 tablespoons butter over the cut sides of the buns and cook in the same skillet until golden brown, about 1 minute.

GARAM MASALA CHICKEN SLIDERS

TO MAKE THE AIOLI: Finely chop the garlic in a small food processor. Add the chickpeas, cumin, salt, and pepper and process until nearly smooth. Blend in the lemon juice. Add the egg and puree to blend well. With the machine on, drizzle the oil into the chickpea mixture in a thin, steady stream and continue blending until the mixture is creamy.

Spoon some of the aioli over the bun bottoms, then place the lettuce and onion on the buns. Add the patties. Spoon a bit more aioli over the patties. Cover with the bun tops and serve.

MAKES 8

LIVE CRAB COCKTAIL

Dungeness crabs inhabit the cold waters off the west coast of the United States, and they're best eaten locally, freshly caught, to get their sweet, distinctive taste. Outside the Pacific Northwest, they're often sold cooked and frozen, but they can also be shipped live overnight. They're one of the meatiest of all varieties of crab, but even so, expect only about 25 percent of the crab's bulk weight to be meat. For this recipe, a crab of roughly 1½ pounds is needed to produce the 6 ounces of meat required.

Picking apart a cooked crab to extract that meat is no mean feat, and that's why Ryan Umane, a contestant from New York, handed this particular challenge on to Christine Ha, a blind chef from Houston. Could a blind chef manage to cook and process a crab—and in a tight amount of time? Not only did she do so, but she made a cocktail that blew the judges away with its bright flavors of fresh chiles and lime.

FOR THE CRAB

- 1   celery stalk, sliced
- ½   red onion, diced
- 2   cloves garlic, sliced
- 1½ teaspoons kosher salt
- 1   live Dungeness crab, about 1½ pounds

FOR THE SAUCE

- 1   cup chilled tomato-vegetable juice (such as V8)
- ¼   cup finely diced red onion
- ¼   cup finely diced celery, plus 4 small celery stalks, for garnish
- ¼   cup finely diced tomato
- 2   tablespoons finely diced scallion
- 1   tablespoon finely diced Fresno chile pepper (wear plastic gloves when handling)
- 1   tablespoon finely diced jalapeño chile pepper (wear plastic gloves when handling)
- 1   tablespoon minced fresh cilantro
  Juice of 2 limes
- 4   dashes hot sauce
  Kosher salt and freshly ground black pepper
- 1   avocado, peeled, pitted, and finely diced

TO MAKE THE CRAB: Combine the celery, onion, garlic, and salt in a large heavy stockpot and fill the pot with water. Bring the water to a boil over high heat. Add the crab with tongs, then cover the pot and cook until the crab's shell is bright red, about 2 minutes. Transfer the crab to a large bowl of ice water and set aside until cold. Remove all the crabmeat from the shells (you should have about 6 ounces of crabmeat). Cover and refrigerate until ready to serve.

LIVE CRAB
COCKTAIL
(continued)

TO MAKE THE SAUCE: Combine the vegetable juice, onion, diced celery, tomato, scallion, chile peppers, cilantro, lime juice, and hot sauce in a large bowl. Season to taste with salt and black pepper. Fold in half of the avocado and the reserved crabmeat.

Divide the mixture among 4 small serving bowls. Garnish with the remaining avocado and small celery stalks, and serve immediately.

SERVES 4

Recipe courtesy of
CHRISTINE HA

Let's assume that, like Christine Ha, you're starting with

a live Dungeness crab—this is really what you want, in terms of freshness and flavor. And ideally, your crab is pretty active, if it's just out of the water. If your crab was shipped to you overnight, it has probably been chilled, and a cold crab is a slow crab. Nonetheless, the thing to remember initially is that crab claws are no joke. If it gets ahold of you with its pincers, it's going to hurt. So use tongs to pick up the crab, or grab it at the very back of the shell, on the opposite side from the claws.

Drop it in the boiling water, with aromatics such as onion, garlic, and celery, which Christine recommends, and cook just until the crab is bright red. If you're going to go to the trouble to source a live crab, don't ruin it by overcooking. Lift it from the boiling water with tongs and drop it in a bowl of ice water to stop the cooking instantly.

When the crab is cool enough to handle, flip it over and pull off the jointed flap called the apron, on the underside of the body. This will expose the interior so that you can put your thumb inside and break off and discard the carapace, the "top half" of the crab shell. Inside it are sticky bits of crab "mustard," as some of the guts are called. If you like to eat these, as crab aficionados do, scrape them from the inside of the carapace with your thumb or a spoon, and put them into a glass bowl where you'll collect the meat.

On the crab's body, pull off and discard the spongy gills that you'll see on either side of the interior, and also discard the mandibles—the loose, slightly fuzzed "mouth" pieces near the head. Break the body in half down the center, along the line where the apron was. Now you should have two halves, both with legs. There will be visible chunks of meat on either side, along with more "mustard" that you can either rinse out or add to your bowl. Pull out the meat and put it in the bowl.

Now, use a pair of heavy kitchen scissors to slice open the legs lengthwise. This allows you to access the meat more easily than cracking the legs, and it also lets you pull it out in bigger chunks, rather than picking it out in shreds. You may need a pick to pull the meat from the very tips, but you can also use the sharp tip of one leg to pick the meat from another. You may need a nutcracker to open the claws, where the biggest chunks of meat are, but strong scissors will do the job, too.

ROASTED CARROT SOUP
WITH GRILLED SODA BREAD

In addition to her formidable cooking skills, California-based Monti Carlo is also an accomplished stand-up comedian who has opened for some of the biggest names in the business, including Bob Saget and Gilbert Gottfried. With her silky voice, it's not surprising that she's also been a radio host and a successful voice-over artist. But her real loves are food and her son, Danger, who is a huge fan of this soda bread.

Given the time limitation, the judges never expected anyone to bake a loaf of bread! But Monti's quick soda bread, which rises solely from the action of the buttermilk and baking soda, bakes up in barely half an hour in a hot oven—leaving her time to slice it and slap it in a grill pan to add flavor. Topped with plenty of butter and a little fresh parsley, it's a hearty accompaniment to her creamy and sophisticated carrot soup, spiked with white wine, shallots, and salt pork.

FOR THE CARROT SOUP

- 4 tablespoons (½ stick) unsalted butter
- 2 large shallots, coarsely chopped
- 2 ounces salt pork, cut into lardons
- 1 cup dry white wine
- 3 cups reduced-sodium chicken broth
- 6 medium carrots (1 pound total), peeled and cut into 1-inch rounds
- ⅓ cup heavy cream
- Kosher salt and freshly ground black pepper
- ¼ cup crème fraîche
- 1 (2-inch) piece fresh ginger, peeled
- 4 small sprigs fresh thyme

SODA BREAD

- 2 cups all-purpose flour
- 1 tablespoon fresh thyme leaves
- ½ teaspoon baking soda
- ½ teaspoon kosher salt
- ¼ teaspoon freshly ground black pepper
- 1 cup buttermilk
- 6 tablespoons (¾ stick) salted butter, at room temperature
- 8 small flat-leaf parsley leaves

TO MAKE THE CARROT SOUP: Set a baking stone at least 4 inches below the broiler and preheat the broiler.

Melt the butter in a large, heavy-bottomed saucepan over medium heat. Add the shallots and sauté until pale golden, about 2 minutes. Add the salt pork and cook until the fat is rendered, stirring often, about 3 minutes. Stir in the wine and simmer 2 minutes. Add the broth and carrots and cook until the carrots soften slightly, about 15 minutes.

Strain the broth into a bowl. Arrange the carrots, lardons, and shallots on the preheated baking stone and broil until the carrots are well browned on all sides and the lardons are crisp, stirring often, about 15 minutes. Transfer the carrots and shallots to a blender and discard

ROASTED CARROT SOUP

(continued)

the lardons. Puree the carrots and shallots with the broth until smooth. Strain the soup through a fine-mesh sieve back into the saucepan. Stir in the heavy cream. Season to taste with salt and pepper.

TO MAKE THE SODA BREAD: Place a baking stone on the middle rack in the oven and preheat the oven to 450°F.

Mix the flour, thyme, baking soda, salt, and pepper in a large bowl to blend. Form a well in the center of the flour mixture and add the buttermilk to the center of the well. Using a fork, gradually stir the flour mixture into the buttermilk until a thick batter forms. Using your hands, gradually mix in the remaining flour mixture to form a very soft dough (do not overwork the dough).

Transfer the dough to a floured work surface and gently shape it into a round that is 6 inches in diameter and about 1½ inches thick. Using a sharp knife, cut a large X into the top of the dough. Transfer to the baking stone and bake 10 minutes. Lower the oven temperature to 400°F and continue baking until the bread is golden brown and crusty on the outside, about 20 minutes. Transfer to a rack and cool.

Preheat a grill pan over medium-high heat. Using a serrated knife, cut the soda bread into ½-inch-thick slices. Grill the bread until grill marks form and the bread is hot, about 3 minutes per side.

Top each slice of grilled bread with butter and a parsley leaf. Serve warm.

TO SERVE: Ladle the soup into 4 bowls. Spoon a dollop of crème fraîche on top. Grate some ginger over the soup, garnish with the thyme sprigs, and serve immediately with the grilled soda bread.

SERVES 4

Recipe courtesy of
MONTI CARLO

WINE PAIRING

Cabernet Franc has a vegetal edge that will harmonize nicely with the carrots, but enough acidity to cut the creaminess of the crème fraîche and heavy cream in the soup base. Choose one that is not too mature and is without a heavy oak influence. Cabernet Franc from cooler climates, such as France and Italy, would do well here, as opposed to one from a warmer climate such as California.

The Offal Trio Part 1

CHICKEN LIVER CROSTINI
WITH PICKLED CHARD STEMS

The secret to making a good pâté is to not overcook the chicken livers. The outside should be beautifully browned and caramelized, but the interior should still be quite pink—otherwise, the finished pate will taste overcooked and "livery." Becky Reams, a food stylist and photographer from Stilwell, Kansas, hit the balance just right to make the topping for these crostini. Follow her instructions: The livers should be nearly ready, and then the quick hit of Madeira in the pan creates enough steam to finish them to perfection. Quick pickles, cleverly made of Swiss chard stems cut into narrow matchsticks, add a sweet-and-sour note that keeps the pâté from being cloying.

This dish was part of an "Offal Trio" that Becky produced in response to the Mystery Box challenge that included sweetbreads among other offal. She served these crostini on a plate with Fried Sweetbreads with Béarnaise (page 50) and Grilled Sweetbreads with Salsa Verde and Roasted Onions and Shiitake Mushrooms (page 52).

FOR THE PICKLED CHARD STEMS

- 1 cup apple cider vinegar
- ½ cup water
- ¾ cup packed brown sugar
- 1 tablespoon kosher salt
- 1 fresh bay leaf
- 1 bunch red Swiss chard, cut into matchsticks

FOR THE LIVER PÂTÉ

- 2 ounces pork fatback
- ½ onion, diced
- 1 pound chicken livers, cleaned of connective tissue and spots
- 3 tablespoons Madeira
- ½ teaspoon fresh lemon juice

  Kosher salt and freshly ground black pepper

FOR THE CROSTINI

- 2 ciabatta rolls
- 3 tablespoons unsalted butter

TO MAKE THE PICKLED CHARD STEMS: Combine the vinegar, water, brown sugar, salt, and bay leaf in a medium, heavy-bottomed saucepan and bring to a boil over high heat. Cut the chard stems crosswise to fit in the saucepan, reserving the leaves for another use. Add the stems to the boiling liquid and cook until tender, about 5 minutes. Transfer the stems to a baking sheet to cool and set the pickling liquid aside to cool separately. Once cooled, cut the chard stems into small batons and submerge them in the cooled pickling liquid.

TO MAKE THE LIVER PÂTÉ: Cook the fatback in a medium, heavy-bottomed sauté pan over medium heat until about 2 table-spoons of the fat is rendered, about 5 minutes. Remove the fatback from the pan and discard it. Add the onion to the rendered fat in the pan over medium-high heat and stir until the onion begins to caramelize, about 5 minutes. Add the chicken livers and sauté until browned, about 5 minutes. Add the Madeira and simmer until the liquid evaporates, about 2 minutes.

Transfer the mixture to a food processor and blend until smooth. Add the lemon juice. Season to taste with salt and pepper. Transfer the pâté to a glass bowl and press a sheet of plastic wrap directly on the surface of the pâté. Refrigerate until cold, about 30 minutes.

TO MAKE THE CROSTINI: Cut the ciabatta into ½-inch-thick slices (like small bruschetta). Melt the butter in a large, heavy-bottomed sauté pan over medium heat. Lay the ciabatta slices in the pan and cook until they are golden brown, about 2 minutes. Set aside to cool.

To serve, preheat the oven to 400°F. Line a small baking sheet with parchment paper.

Spread an even layer of the pâté over the crostini. Arrange the crostini in a single layer on the prepared baking sheet. Bake until the tops just start to brown, about 5 minutes. Transfer the crostini to plates, garnish with the chard stems, and serve immediately.

SERVES 4

Recipe courtesy of
BECKY REAMS

FRIED SWEETBREADS
WITH BÉARNAISE

I f you've never cooked (or eaten) sweetbreads before, this recipe is an excellent way to introduce yourself to a beloved gourmet delicacy. The cooking method is extremely simple, and deep-frying them with a chile-spiced coating results in golden, crisp strips that are amazingly delicious when topped with a creamy béarnaise sauce. The beauty of Becky Reams's presentation is that it moves from crunchy (those toasty crostini) to creamy (with this unctuous béarnaise), a seductive introduction to offal for any dubious diners.

FOR THE SWEETBREADS

- 1 **pound sweetbreads, membranes removed**
- 2 **cups all-purpose flour**
- 2 **teaspoons ground dried árbol chile pepper**
- **Kosher salt**
- **Vegetable oil**

FOR THE BÉARNAISE

- ½ **cup (1 stick) unsalted butter**
- 1 **small shallot, minced**
- 1 **tablespoon (or more) fresh lemon juice**
- 1 **teaspoon (or more) Madeira**
- 2 **large egg yolks**
- 2 **tablespoons chopped fresh tarragon**
- **Large pinch of kosher salt**

FOR THE GARNISH

- **Red-pepper flakes**
- **Sea salt**

TO MAKE THE SWEETBREADS: Bring a large pot of salted water to a boil over high heat. Add the sweetbreads and cook for 1 to 2 minutes. Remove the sweetbreads and place them in a resealable plastic bag, but do not seal the bag. Place the bag in a large bowl of ice water and submerge just enough to keep the meat below the surface, being careful not to allow water to enter through the top. Set aside until the sweetbreads are completely cooled, about 20 minutes.

Remove the sweetbreads from the bag and pat them dry with a towel. Cut them into long strips. Cover and refrigerate until ready to cook.

Mix the flour, ground chile pepper, and a sprinkle of salt in a wide shallow bowl. Dredge the sweetbread slices through the mixture to coat, then shake off the excess.

Heat 2 inches of oil in a large, heavy-bottomed pot to 350°F. Working in batches, fry the sweetbread slices until they are golden brown, about 3 minutes. Using a slotted spoon, remove the sweetbreads from the oil and place them on a cooling rack to drain.

TO MAKE THE BÉARNAISE: Cook the butter in a small, heavy-bottomed saucepan over medium heat until it melts. Continue cooking while whisking constantly until it browns, about 3 minutes. Remove the pan from the heat and cover to keep it hot.

Combine the shallot, 1 tablespoon lemon juice, and 1 teaspoon Madeira in a blender or a tall cylindrical container if using an immersion blender. Blend for 30 seconds. Add the egg yolks and blend until smooth. With the machine running, slowly pour in the hot butter, blending until the mixture is thick and emulsified. Mix in the tarragon. Season to taste with salt. If a thinner consistency is desired, add more lemon juice or Madeira to thin the sauce to the desired consistency.

TO SERVE: Place a spoonful of the béarnaise sauce in the center of 4 plates and set the fried sweetbreads on top of the sauce. Garnish with the red-pepper flakes and sea salt and serve.

SERVES 4

Recipe courtesy of
BECKY REAMS

SKILL SET / How to Prepare Sweetbreads for Cooking

Sweetbreads are typically the thymus glands of lambs and calves.

They come from two different places: The "throat" sweetbread is the thymus gland, and the "stomach" sweetbread is actually the pancreas. Sweetbreads are only eaten from the young animals because the throat gland disappears as the calf ages. The stomach gland is considered by many chefs to be more flavorful, and it has a pleasing oval shape, rather than the more elongated throat gland. Lamb sweetbreads tend to be smaller than veal, and you will need two to three to make a serving.

Whatever sweetbread your market affords you, the classic preparation begins with soaking them in cold water for an hour or two to disgorge any impurities and sweeten the flavor (Christine Ha's recipe on page 55 soaks them in milk instead). Often, they are then blanched lightly to firm up the meat, but they should not be cooked through. To blanch, put the sweetbreads in a pot of cold water and add salt and a dash of lemon juice or vinegar, if you like—this helps to make the sweetbread whiter when cooked. Bring to a boil and simmer for 1 to 2 minutes, then instantly remove to cold water to stop the cooking. Many chefs cool them in a plastic bag in the water, to prevent them from becoming waterlogged.

Though some of the contestants strip the membrane immediately during the challenges, chefs typically wait until the sweetbreads are cool enough to handle, and then peel off and discard the thick, visible membrane on the exterior. Your hands are probably the best tool for the job, but you may need a knife to trim off any visible gristle or veins. (Whether you choose to blanch or not, the membrane must always be removed.) At this point, you can proceed with your recipe, but some chefs, like Ryan Umane, then go on to press the sweetbreads under a weight for several hours to firm and compress the meat (see his recipe on page 57).

GRILLED SWEETBREADS
WITH SALSA VERDE AND ROASTED ONIONS AND SHIITAKE MUSHROOMS

The roasted mushrooms and onions add a deeper, richer flavor to the quick-grilled sweetbreads in the third part of the Offal Trio. The entire dish is brightened by Becky Reams's salsa verde, which gets an herbal note from a wide variety of fresh herbs like tarragon and mint, a salty bite from capers, and a serious hit of red-pepper flakes—and is all brought together with the lemon zest. Even if you're not making the sweetbreads, make a dish of this salsa verde to spoon over roasted vegetables and grilled meats.

A well-seasoned grill pan is crucial here to cooking the sweetbreads properly. Be sure to warm the pan first over medium-high heat so that the sweetbreads need only sizzle for a couple of minutes once they hit the hot metal. They stay in the pan just long enough to heat through and take on some coloring, but not so long as to become overcooked and tough.

FOR THE SALSA VERDE

Small handful fresh chives

½ cup fresh flat-leaf parsley

¼ cup fresh mint

¼ cup fresh oregano

2 tablespoons tarragon

1 tablespoon drained capers

1 tablespoon red-pepper flakes

1 tablespoon fresh lemon juice and 1 teaspoon grated zest from the same lemon

2 cloves garlic, smashed

⅓ cup olive oil

Kosher salt

FOR THE ROASTED ONIONS AND MUSHROOMS

2 tablespoons olive oil

1 onion, thickly sliced

8 shiitake mushrooms, stemmed

¼ cup balsamic vinegar

Kosher salt

FOR THE SWEETBREADS

4 ounces pork fatback

1 pound sweetbreads, membranes removed

Kosher salt and freshly ground black pepper

TO MAKE THE SALSA VERDE: Combine the chives, parsley, mint, oregano, tarragon, capers, red-pepper flakes, lemon zest, lemon juice, and garlic in a food processor. Pulse a few times to mix the ingredients together. Continue pulsing while adding the oil to form a chunky consistency, but do not puree or emulsify. Season to taste with salt and transfer to a small bowl.

TO MAKE THE ROASTED ONIONS AND MUSHROOMS: Heat a medium, heavy-bottomed sauté pan over medium-high heat. Add the oil, then the onion and mushrooms, and sauté until softened and caramelized, about 8 minutes. Add the vinegar. Reduce the heat and simmer until most of the liquid evaporates, about 2 minutes. Remove the pan from the heat and season to taste with salt.

TO MAKE THE SWEETBREADS: Cook the fatback in a medium, heavy-bottomed sauté pan over medium heat until about ¼ cup of the fat is rendered, about 5 minutes. Remove the solid fatback from the pan and discard.

Preheat a heavy grill pan over medium-high heat. Brush the rendered fat over the sweetbreads to coat. Season the sweetbreads to taste with salt and pepper, and grill until grill marks form and the sweetbreads are heated through, 2 to 3 minutes per side. Remove from the pan and let rest for 2 minutes.

TO SERVE: Spoon the salsa verde onto 4 plates. Top with the sweetbreads. Garnish with the onions and mushrooms and serve immediately.

SERVES 4

Recipe courtesy of
BECKY REAMS

 / Plating Your "Offal Trio"

Becky Reams served the Chicken Liver Crostini and the

two sweetbread preparations as a trio on the show. She plated them up together for best effect. Here's how to do it:

- *Place a completed crostini on one end of 8 rectangular plates.*

- *Place a small spoonful of the salsa verde in the center of the plates, then place the grilled sweetbreads on top of the salsa. Garnish with the onions and mushrooms.*

- *Place a small spoonful of the béarnaise sauce on the other end of the plate. Set the fried sweetbreads on top of the béarnaise, and garnish with red-pepper flakes and sea salt.*

- *Serve at once.*

Plated together this way, the three recipes will make 8 starter-size servings.

SWEETBREADS NUGGETS
WITH BOK CHOY AND SOY-CHILE SAUCE

Christine Ha took her sweetbreads in a completely different direction from Becky Reams's elegant trio of offal dishes. The sweetbreads, cut into bite-size pieces, are marinated in milk and spices to sweeten them and permeate them with the pungent taste of garlic and Chinese five-spice powder. Then they're breaded with flaky, chili-spiked panko and deep-fried until each piece is crisp and golden. Add to that the addictively tasty soy-chile dipping sauce (which would also be excellent for dipping wontons or dumplings), and you might just find that this is the gateway dish that will make you start craving sweetbreads!

FOR THE SWEETBREADS

- 2 cups whole milk
- 1 small onion, sliced
- 3 cloves garlic, minced
- 1 small shallot, finely diced
- 4 fresh bay leaves
- ½ teaspoon Chinese five-spice powder
- 12 ounces sweetbreads, membranes removed, cut into 2-inch pieces
- 1 cup all-purpose flour
- ½ teaspoon garlic powder
- ½ teaspoon kosher salt
- ½ teaspoon freshly ground black pepper
- 6 large eggs
- 2½ cups panko (Japanese) bread crumbs
- ½ teaspoon red-pepper flakes
- Canola oil

FOR THE DIPPING SAUCE

- ½ cup soy sauce
- ¼ cup apple cider vinegar
- 2 tablespoons sugar
- 2 tablespoons peeled, minced fresh ginger
- 4 jalapeño chile peppers, thinly sliced into rounds (wear plastic gloves when handling)
- 2 teaspoons fresh lime juice

FOR THE BOK CHOY

- 4 bacon slices, diced
- 4 small bok choy, separated and cleaned

FOR THE GARNISH

- 1 jalapeño chile pepper, thinly sliced into rounds (wear plastic gloves when handling)
- 1 scallion, thinly sliced
- 4 sprigs cilantro

TO MAKE THE SWEETBREADS: Stir the milk, onion, garlic, shallot, bay leaves, and ¼ teaspoon of the five-spice powder in a large bowl. Add the sweetbreads and marinate for 20 minutes.

Whisk the flour, garlic powder, salt, pepper, and the remaining ¼ teaspoon five-spice powder in a large bowl to blend. Whisk the eggs in a wide shallow bowl to blend, then season to taste with salt and pepper and set aside. Mix the panko and red-pepper flakes in another wide shallow bowl and set aside.

Remove the sweetbreads from the marinade and pat dry. Roll the sweetbreads in the flour mixture to coat, then submerge in the egg

SWEETBREADS NUGGETS
(continued)

mixture to coat. Lift the sweetbreads from the egg mixture, allowing the excess egg to drip back into the bowl. Coat the sweetbreads in the panko mixture. Set the sweetbreads aside for 5 minutes.

Heat 3 inches of oil in a large wok or pot over medium-high heat to 375°F. Toss the sweetbreads in the panko to coat again. Working in batches, fry the sweetbreads until they are browned on all sides, about 3 minutes. Using a slotted spoon, remove the sweetbreads from the wok and drain on paper towels.

TO MAKE THE DIPPING SAUCE: Whisk the soy sauce, vinegar, sugar, ginger, jalapeños, and lime juice in a small bowl to blend. Season to taste with salt.

TO MAKE THE BOK CHOY: Meanwhile, heat a large sauté pan over medium-high heat. Add the bacon and sauté until some of the fat is rendered, about 3 minutes. Using a slotted spoon, remove the bacon pieces from the pan and discard. Add the bok choy to the pan and sauté until crisp-tender, about 2 minutes.

TO SERVE: Lay the bok choy on 4 long rectangular plates. Place the sweetbreads on top of the bok choy, across the whole length of the plate. Fill 4 small ramekins or bowls with the dipping sauce and place them at one end of the plates. Garnish with the jalapeño slices, scallion, and cilantro if desired.

SERVES 4

Recipe courtesy of
CHRISTINE HA

PAN-FRIED SWEETBREADS AND WATERCRESS SALAD,
ROASTED VEGETABLES, AND CRISPY PORK BELLY

Following the basic principle that everything tastes better with bacon (or some kind of pork fat), Ryan Umane cooks cubes of pork belly until they're crisp and have rendered most of their fat into the pan. Then he fries blanched and compressed sweetbreads in the pork fat until they have browned, basting them with a little butter for good measure. Plated with roasted carrots and potatoes and topped with fragrant curry oil, this is a warm and filling dish that really plays up the creamy texture of the sweetbreads. The watercress and frisée salad adds just the right edge of bitterness to play off all that richness.

FOR THE SWEETBREADS

- 8 cups beef stock
- 1 shallot, minced
- 2 cloves garlic, peeled
- 1 sprig fresh flat-leaf parsley
- 3 sprigs fresh thyme, 1 whole and 2 with leaves removed and chopped
- 2 tablespoons strained fresh lemon juice
- 2 sweetbreads, membranes removed
- 8 ounces pork belly, diced
- 2 cups all-purpose flour

  Kosher salt and freshly ground black pepper
- 2 tablespoons unsalted butter

FOR THE VEGETABLES

- 12 baby carrots, trimmed and peeled
- 2 teaspoons plus 1½ tablespoons olive oil

  Kosher salt and freshly ground black pepper
- 2 fresh sage leaves, chopped
- 6 red-skinned potatoes, cut into ⅛-inch-thick rounds

  Pinch of garlic powder

FOR THE CURRY OIL

- 1 teaspoon plus ½ cup canola oil
- 1 shallot, minced
- 1 tablespoon garam masala
- ½ teaspoon ground cinnamon

FOR THE SALAD

- 1 cup watercress
- 1 cup frisée
- ¼ cup Champagne vinegar
- 1 tablespoon fresh lemon juice
- 2 teaspoons Dijon mustard
- 1 clove garlic, minced
- ½ cup canola oil

  Kosher salt and freshly ground black pepper

  About 3 tablespoons Curry Oil

PAN-FRIED SWEETBREADS AND WATERCRESS SALAD

(continued)

TO MAKE THE SWEETBREADS: Bring the beef stock to a boil in a large, heavy-bottomed pot over high heat. Add the shallot, garlic, parsley, the whole thyme sprig, and lemon juice. Add the sweetbreads and simmer for 90 seconds. Remove the sweetbreads from the liquid and place them in a large resealable plastic bag, but do not seal the bag.

Place the bag in a large bowl of ice water and submerge just enough to keep the sweetbreads below the surface, being careful not to allow water to enter through the top. Set aside until the sweetbreads are completely cooled, about 10 minutes. Remove the sweetbreads from the bag and pat them dry with a towel. Place them in a colander and place a bowl on top. Place a can (a large can of tomatoes works well) in the bowl to weight down the sweetbreads. Set aside for 45 minutes to drain the excess liquid from the sweetbreads.

Place the pork belly in a large, heavy-bottomed sauté pan, then set the pan over medium-high heat. Cook, stirring occasionally, until the pork belly begins to crisp and most of its fat has rendered out, about 5 minutes. Using a slotted spoon, remove the pork belly from the pan and set aside.

Set the pan of rendered fat over medium-high heat and put the flour in a shallow dish. Season the drained sweetbreads to taste with salt and pepper, then dredge them in the flour to coat lightly. Fry the sweetbreads in the fat until they are browned all over, about 2 minutes per side. Reduce the heat to medium and add the butter and chopped thyme. Baste the sweetbreads with the melted butter for 1 minute, turning once or twice to cook evenly. Transfer the sweetbreads to a plate lined with paper towels to drain the excess butter.

TO MAKE THE VEGETABLES: Preheat the oven to 350°F. Toss the carrots with 2 teaspoons of the oil in a large bowl to coat. Season to taste with salt and pepper. Lay the carrots in a single layer on a baking sheet. Scatter the sage over the carrots and roast until the carrots are crisp-tender, about 10 minutes.

Meanwhile, toss the potatoes with the remaining 1½ tablespoons oil in the same bowl to coat. Season to taste with salt and pepper. Lay the potato slices in a single layer on a large heavy baking sheet and lightly dust with garlic powder. Bake until tender, about 10 minutes.

TO MAKE THE CURRY OIL: Heat 1 teaspoon of the oil in a medium, heavy-bottomed saucepan over medium heat. Add the shallot and sauté until translucent, about 2 minutes. Add the garam masala, cinnamon, and the remaining ½ cup oil. Heat until the oil is hot, then set the pan aside until the oil is completely cooled. Store in a sealed jar at room temperature.

TO MAKE THE SALAD: Soak the watercress and frisée briefly in cold water to remove any excess dirt. Drain well and pat dry, then trim to the desired size. Cover and refrigerate until ready to use.

Combine the vinegar, lemon juice, Dijon mustard, and garlic in a blender and blend on medium-low speed. With the machine running, gradually add the oil, blending until the mixture is emulsified. Season to taste with salt. Transfer the vinaigrette to a jar, seal, and refrigerate until ready to use.

TO SERVE: Toss the watercress and frisée with the vinaigrette in a large bowl to coat. Season the salad to taste with salt and pepper. Mound the salad in the center of 4 plates and arrange 4 to 5 potato slices around the salad on each plate. Arrange the carrots on the salad and set the sweetbreads on top of the carrots and salad. Drizzle with some of the curry oil and garnish with the reserved crisp pork belly pieces. Serve immediately.

SERVES 4

Recipe courtesy of
RYAN UMANE

SWEET CORN BISQUE
WITH CILANTRO MARSHMALLOW

MasterChef judges give their opinions with such force that sometimes it's hard to remember that they're only human—and cooks, too! If Graham Elliot were a contestant, what would a four-star chef bring to the table? Some pretty tough competition, if his Sweet Corn Bisque is anything to go by, especially as Graham serves it, with a red pepper jam and lime crema.

Think you have the chops to work in a high-end professional kitchen? You'll see here what a trained line cook might be handed upon entering Graham's kitchen: metric measurements, industry shorthand, and nonstandard ingredients you won't always find in the supermarket. Unquestionably, it's fascinating reading; attempt it if you dare!

This is one of several dishes that Graham presented to Joshua Marks, who then chose one for his fellow contestants to attempt.

SWEET CORN BISQUE

- 20 ears corn, freshly shucked
- 1 bulb garlic, separated into cloves
- 10 coriander seeds
- 5 sprigs Mexican oregano
- 5 black peppercorns
- 1 bunch cilantro
- 3 quarts water

- 1 jalapeño chile pepper, split in half, seeds and ribs removed (wear plastic gloves when handling)
- 2 medium onions, diced
- 1 carrot, peeled and diced
- 2 g saffron threads
- 5 ml grapeseed oil
- 2 limes
- Salt

CILANTRO MARSHMALLOW

- 4 sheets gelatin
- 200 g sugar
- 50 g water
- 25 g glucose
- 250 g cilantro, roughly chopped
- 1 egg white
- 200 g 10x sugar for dusting tray and tops of marshmallow

SWEET CORN BISQUE

Using a sharp knife, cut the kernels off the cob. Reserve the cobs.

Gather the garlic, coriander, oregano, peppercorns, and cilantro together into a sachet.

Fill a large stockpot with the water and add the chile pepper, onions, carrot, saffron, corn cobs, and the sachet. Simmer the stock until it is a bright vibrant yellow, 30 minutes.

In a separate large pot, heat the oil and gently roast the corn kernels over medium-high heat. Using a colander, strain the cooked stock into the pot directly over the roasted corn. Simmer for 20 minutes.

Puree the soup until smooth and homogenized in a blender and strain with a chinois. Season with freshly squeezed lime juice and salt.

CILANTRO MARSHMALLOW

Bloom the gelatin in ice water.

Combine the sugar, water, and glucose in a saucepan and heat to 238 degrees. Add the cilantro to the syrup and steep for 5 minutes. Strain out the cilantro.

Remove the gelatin from the ice water and carefully melt over low heat.

In a standing mixer, whip the egg white to stiff peaks and slowly add the syrup. Once all the syrup is incorporated and the meringue is fluffy, add the melted gelatin.

Dust a parchment paper–lined ¼ sheet tray with 50 grams of 10x sugar and pour the meringue onto the pan, gently tapping it to release any air bubbles. Allow to cool and cut with ring cutters or any other desired shape.

YIELDS 1 GALLON

Chapter 3 / Pastas and Rice Dishes

STIR-FRY NOODLES
WITH SEARED SCALLOPS

O vercooking rice vermicelli ruins it. The threadlike strands go from pliable noodles to soggy mush in a matter of seconds. Christine Ha dips hers in boiling water for literally 10 seconds before instantly shocking them in ice water to stop the cooking. Because the rice vermicelli is meant to be stir-fried, you're not trying to cook it long enough to make it tender and toothsome, only long enough to soften it. In a little hot oil in the wok, the noodles will become tender and perfect in about 30 seconds.

Like a lot of Asian dishes, this one is all about prep. The actual cooking takes a matter of moments, but that's only once everything is completely ready to go and lined up next to the wok. It's also crucial not to overcook the scallops. Heat the sauté pan to blazing hot—don't be afraid to turn up the heat to high. If you're timid, the scallops will steam and not brown.

FOR THE NOODLES

- 3 tablespoons fish sauce
- 3 tablespoons soy sauce
- 2 tablespoons chicken stock
- 1 tablespoon fresh lime juice
- 1 tablespoon mirin
- 1½ teaspoons rice vinegar
- 1½ tablespoons sugar
- 8 ounces dried rice vermicelli, soaked in cold water for 30 minutes

- 2 tablespoons canola oil
- 3 shallots, diced
- 1 tablespoon finely chopped garlic
- 1 tablespoon peeled, finely chopped fresh ginger
- 1 pound oyster mushrooms, halved if large
- 2 carrots, peeled and julienned
- 2 scallions, thinly sliced

FOR THE SCALLOPS

- 16 large sea scallops
  - Kosher salt
- 2 tablespoons canola oil
- 2 tablespoons chili oil
  - Sprigs fresh cilantro

STIR-FRY NOODLES

(continued)

TO MAKE THE NOODLES: Whisk the fish sauce, soy sauce, chicken stock, lime juice, mirin, vinegar, and sugar in a small bowl until the sugar dissolves. Set aside.

Bring a large pot of salted water to a boil over high heat. Prepare a large bowl of ice water. Drain the soaking water from the vermicelli. Add the vermicelli to the boiling water and cook for just 10 seconds. Quickly drain the noodles, then place them in the ice water to cool completely. Drain well.

Heat a large heavy wok over medium-high heat. Add the canola oil, then stir in the shallots, garlic, and ginger. Cook until fragrant and the shallots begin to soften, about 1 minute. Add the mushrooms and carrots and stir-fry until they soften slightly, about 5 minutes. Stir in the vermicelli and the reserved sauce and stir-fry to coat, about 30 seconds. Stir in the scallions.

TO MAKE THE SCALLOPS: Season the scallops with salt. Heat a large heavy sauté pan over high heat. Add the canola and chili oils and swirl to coat the pan, then add the scallops and cook until dark brown, about 2 minutes per side.

To serve, divide the vermicelli among 4 wide bowls. Top with the scallops, garnish with the cilantro, and serve immediately.

SERVES 4

Recipe courtesy of
CHRISTINE HA

HOMEMADE TORTELLINI IN CHICKEN BROTH

I f you've only ever had store-bought tortellini—those dry, hard little rings with fillings like "cheese" or "spinach"—you're missing out. The dry kind never cooks up as tender and toothsome as homemade tortellini. The most complicated part here is running the dough through a pasta maker to stretch and smooth it. If you have a pasta maker, you know it's not hard, but if you're just starting out, it helps to handle the dough boldly! It is most likely not going to tear, but if it does, the next pass through the pasta maker will repair and smooth it.

Monti Carlo's filling for the pasta is a real highlight: ricotta cheese mixed with an equal amount of diced prosciutto and a little mortadella, making it creamy, salty, sweet, and tangy. Each little pillow of pasta floating in the savory broth packs a real punch of flavor.

FOR THE PASTA DOUGH

- 1½ cups all-purpose flour plus more for dusting
- 2 large eggs
- 2 large egg yolks

FOR THE TORTELLINI

- 6 tablespoons ricotta cheese
- 3 tablespoons finely chopped fresh flat-leaf parsley
- 6 tablespoons minced prosciutto
- 3 tablespoons minced mortadella

  Pinch of freshly grated nutmeg

- 1 large egg, beaten to blend

FOR THE SOUP

- 6 cups reduced-sodium chicken broth

  Kosher salt and freshly ground black pepper

- 4 teaspoons extra-virgin olive oil
- 12 small fresh flat-leaf parsley leaves

HOMEMADE TORTELLINI IN CHICKEN BROTH

(continued)

TO MAKE THE PASTA DOUGH: Mound the flour on a work surface and form a well in the center. Crack the whole eggs and egg yolks into the center of the well. Using a fork, whisk the eggs to blend. Gradually whisk the flour into the egg mixture until a thick batter forms. Using your hands, gradually mix in enough of the remaining flour to form a shaggy dough. Transfer the dough to a floured work surface and knead until the dough is smooth and semisoft. Do not incorporate any hardened bits of flour into the dough. Divide the dough into 4 equal pieces, then wrap each separately in plastic and refrigerate for 1 hour.

TO MAKE THE TORTELLINI: Spread the ricotta and parsley over paper towels and set aside for 10 minutes to drain their excess moisture. Transfer them to a medium bowl and stir in the prosciutto, mortadella, and nutmeg.

Unwrap 1 dough piece, then dust it with flour and flatten it with your hand into a rectangle. Run the dough through the widest setting of the pasta maker. Fold into thirds and repeat rolling and folding the dough about three times, dusting the folded dough piece with flour as needed before running it through the machine each time (this helps knead the dough and make it more elastic). Reduce the space between the rollers one setting at a time until the dough is about $\frac{1}{16}$ inch thick. Dust the work surface with flour and lay the pasta sheet on the work surface Using a 2½-inch round cookie cutter, cut the pasta sheet into rounds. Place ½ teaspoon of the ricotta mixture in the center of each round. Brush the egg on the bottom half of the round and fold over to seal. Fold the ends back around your finger and turn down the top edge to form a tortellini. Repeat, rolling out the remaining pieces of pasta dough and using the remaining ricotta mixture to form about 52 tortellini total.

TO MAKE THE SOUP: Bring the broth to a boil in a large, heavy-bottomed saucepan over high heat. Add a pinch of salt and pepper, then add the tortellini and boil until the tortellini float to the surface and the pasta is tender, about 5 minutes. Using a slotted spoon, divide the tortellini among 4 wide shallow soup bowls.

Return the broth to a boil and season it to taste with salt and pepper. Ladle the broth over the tortellini. Drizzle a teaspoon of olive oil over each serving and garnish with the parsley leaves. Serve immediately.

SERVES 4

Recipe courtesy of
MONTI CARLO

Whitney Miller

As a senior in college, Whitney Miller

was the youngest contestant of them all when she won the first season of *MasterChef*. Well before she won, Whitney was told she was too young to be competing and that she should finish school and try again someday. But that only steeled her resolve. Whitney says, "In my senior year of college, I took a risk to follow my dream of cooking by auditioning for *MasterChef*. I had no idea what chain of events would follow and how my life would change. As the youngest contestant at age 22, I gained the title of America's first MasterChef.

"Following the win, I had the awesome opportunity to participate in the 2011 Chicago Housewares Show cooking demonstrations with a lineup of celebrity chefs such as Curtis Stone, Guy Fieri, and Paula Deen. However, the culmination of my dream came when my first cookbook was completed and launched in July 2011 with a multistate cookbook tour. I was delighted when *People* magazine featured my Cauliflower Mac 'n' Cheese recipe shortly afterward. *Women's Health* magazine's "Are You Game?" events provided me with fun opportunities to introduce lighter takes on Southern recipes to residents of Chicago and New York.

"Cooking for charity has a big place in my heart, and I have enjoyed cooking with Emeril Lagasse at the Viking Classic in Mississippi and working with the Tim Tebow Foundation in Florida. This year has resulted in the fulfillment of another dream: international travel. International trips have included a speaking engagement at a food leader summit at the Gulf Food Show in Dubai; and a promotional cooking engagement to publicize my book and Southern cuisine at the St. Regis hotel in Shenzhen, China. When not traveling, I love spending time in the kitchen at my home in Poplarville, Mississippi [pop. 3,008], creatively cooking for my family and experimenting with recipes for my upcoming second cookbook."

Recipe courtesy of
Whitney Miller

WHITNEY'S CAULIFLOWER MAC 'N' CHEESE

Whitney Miller writes, "Who doesn't love a side of mac 'n' cheese with their fried chicken? My version of this indulgent side dish swaps pasta for cauliflower. Roasting the cauliflower adds a nutty flavor and hearty texture to the dish. You'll never miss the pasta in this mac 'n' cheese." Whitney Miller, Modern Hospitality: Simple Recipes with Southern Charm (Rodale Books, 2011)

- 8 **cups cauliflower florets (about 1 head)**
- 2 **tablespoons extra-virgin olive oil**
- ½ **teaspoon kosher salt**
- ½ **teaspoon freshly ground black pepper**
- 2 **tablespoons unsalted butter**
- 2 **tablespoons all-purpose flour**
- 1½ **cups fat-free milk**
- ½ **cup heavy cream**
- ½ **teaspoon salt**
- 1 **cup grated sharp cheddar cheese (4 ounces)**

Preheat the oven at 400°F.

Toss the cauliflower florets in the oil on a baking sheet. Sprinkle with the kosher salt and ¼ teaspoon of the pepper. Roast until fork-tender and lightly browned in spots, 25 to 30 minutes. Remove from the oven but leave the oven on and reduce the temperature to 350°F.

Meanwhile, melt the butter in a medium skillet over medium heat. Add the flour and cook, stirring, for 1 minute. Gradually whisk in the milk. Simmer over medium heat, stirring frequently, until thickened, 2 to 4 minutes. Whisk in the cream and cook for 5 minutes. Reduce the heat to low and stir in the table salt, all but 2 tablespoons of the cheese, and the remaining ¼ teaspoon pepper. Stir until the cheese melts, then cook, stirring often, until thickened, 8 to 10 minutes.

Place the cauliflower florets in an 8 x 8-inch glass baking dish or four 10-ounce ramekins. Pour the cheese sauce on top. Sprinkle the top of the cauliflower with the remaining 2 tablespoons cheese.

Bake until the cheese is bubbling, 20 to 25 minutes. Serve warm.

SERVES 4

WINE PAIRING

This simple but delicious dish from the Season 1 winner calls for an easy-drinking and not overly complex white wine. Because the dish is creamy, and heavy in starch and fat, it calls for something to cut through that density and cleanse the palate. Rather than a wine to harmonize or contrast the flavors, pick up a basic but well-made Pinot Grigio, fresh and brisk enough to do the job nicely.

HOMEMADE ORECCHIETTE
WITH RUSTIC TOMATO-BEEF SAUCE

Orecchiette means "little ears," and it's a pasta shape particularly suited to a heavy, meaty sauce. The little indentations made with a thumbprint in each oval of pasta act as a sort of "scoop," catching and holding the sauce and ensuring that each bite is fully rounded.

Scott Little, an interactive producer from Anandale, Virginia, could not have chosen a better shape for his sauce when faced with a Ground Beef challenge. With only 5 plum tomatoes and a few tablespoons of tomato paste to ¾ pound of ground beef, it's definitely more meaty than tomatoey, and is strongly flavored with rough red wine and fresh rosemary. A hint of warm spices—allspice and cinnamon—brings out the sweetness of the tomatoes. Paired with plump and tender orecchiette, a little sauce goes a long way. When serving, don't forget to shave on fresh Parmesan with a generous hand.

FOR THE SAUCE

1 tablespoon olive oil

12 ounces ground beef

1 medium onion, finely chopped

4 cloves garlic, finely chopped

⅔ cup beef stock

5 plum tomatoes

½ cup dry red wine

2 tablespoons tomato paste

½ teaspoon fresh rosemary, chopped

¼ teaspoon ground allspice

¼ teaspoon ground cinnamon

Kosher salt

Shaved Parmesan cheese

FOR THE PASTA

1½ cups unbleached all-purpose flour

Pinch of kosher salt

2 large eggs

1½ teaspoons olive oil

Fresh rosemary sprigs for garnish, if desired

TO MAKE THE SAUCE: Heat the oil in a large, heavy-bottomed saucepan over medium heat. Add the ground beef and cook until browned, breaking the beef into small pieces with the back of a spoon, about 10 minutes. Stir in the onion and garlic. Add the beef stock and simmer until the onion is tender and the stock is reduced by half, about 5 minutes.

Squeeze the tomatoes to coarsely crush them and add to the ground beef mixture. Stir in the wine, tomato paste, rosemary, and allspice. Cover and simmer over medium-low heat until the sauce thickens slightly and the flavors blend, stirring occasionally, about 1 hour. Stir in the cinnamon. Season to taste with salt.

TO MAKE THE PASTA: Meanwhile, mix the flour and salt on a work surface and form a well in the center. Add the eggs and oil to the well. Using a fork, whisk the eggs and oil to blend. Gradually whisk the flour into the egg mixture until a thick batter forms. Using your hands, gradually mix in enough of the remaining flour to form a moist dough. Knead the dough, adding more flour as needed, to form a smooth and semi-soft dough. Do not incorporate any hardened bits of flour into the dough. Wrap the dough in plastic and refrigerate for 1 hour.

Dust 2 baking sheets with flour. Flatten and cut the dough into 1-inch-wide strips. Keeping the remaining strips covered, roll one strip into a ½-inch-wide rope. Cut the rope into ¼-inch pieces. Dust your thumb with some flour and press down on each piece of dough, pushing away from you and twisting your thumb slightly to form an indented ear-shaped pasta shell. As you work, transfer the formed pasta to the baking sheets.

Bring a large pot of salted water to a boil over high heat. Add the pasta and cook until al dente, stirring gently and often, about 4 minutes. Drain and divide the pasta among 4 wide shallow pasta bowls. Toss the pasta with the sauce. Garnish with Parmesan cheese and rosemary sprigs as desired and serve immediately.

SERVES 4

HOMEMADE ORECCHIETTE
(continued)

Recipe courtesy of
SCOTT LITTLE

UNI TAGLIARINI

When the contestants opened one of their Mystery Boxes, they all found a single live sea urchin literally moving around in the bottom of the box. More than one contestant felt a little intimidated trying to figure out how to clean the uni before they could even begin to figure out a dish. Joshua Marks made a particularly elegant dish out of his uni, smoothing the strong briny essence of the roe fillets with an extremely light-flavored cream sauce that held a hint of bacon. It perfectly suited the delicate, tender texture of his homemade pasta. He bolstered the dish with a judicious amount of rock shrimp to increase the seafood flavor—a creation that could easily serve as an appetizer or a main course.

FOR THE PASTA

- 1½ cups all-purpose flour plus more for dusting
- 2 large eggs
- 1 large egg yolk
- Pinch of salt

FOR THE SAUCE

- 2 bacon slices, cut into thin strips
- 12 pearl onions (about 5 ounces), thinly sliced
- ½ cup dry white wine
- 2¾ cups heavy cream
- 16 uni fillets (sea urchin roe)
- Kosher salt and freshly ground black pepper
- 2 tablespoons olive oil
- 10 ounces rock shrimp, peeled and deveined
- ¼ cup fresh basil chiffonade

TO MAKE THE PASTA: Mound the flour on a work surface and form a well in the center. Place the whole eggs, egg yolks, and salt in the center of the well. Using a fork, whisk the eggs to blend. Gradually whisk the flour into the egg mixture until a thick batter forms. Using your hands, gradually mix in enough of the remaining flour to form a moist dough. Knead the dough, adding more flour as needed, to form a smooth and semisoft dough. Do not incorporate any hardened bits of flour into the dough. Divide the dough into 4 equal pieces, then wrap each separately in plastic and refrigerate for 1 hour.

Dust a baking sheet generously with flour. Unwrap 1 dough piece, then dust it with flour and flatten it with your hand into a rectangle. Run the dough through the widest setting of the pasta maker. Fold into thirds and repeat rolling and folding the dough about six times, dusting the folded dough piece with flour as needed before running it through the machine each time (this helps knead the dough and make it more elastic). Reduce the space between the rollers one setting at a time until the pasta is ⅛ inch thick. Cut the pasta sheet into tagliarini (⅛-inch-wide ribbons). Dust generously with flour and lay them on the baking sheet. Set aside for 30 minutes to dry slightly.

In a large pot of boiling salted water, cook the pasta until al dente, stirring often, about 3 minutes.

TO MAKE THE SAUCE: Meanwhile, set a medium, heavy-bottomed saucepan over medium heat. Add the bacon and sauté until crisp, about 5 minutes. Using a slotted spoon, transfer the bacon to a plate lined with paper towels and set it aside.

Add the onions to the bacon drippings in the pan and sauté until tender, about 3 minutes. Add the wine and simmer until it is reduced by half, about 2 minutes. Add the heavy cream and bring to a simmer. Reduce the heat to low and simmer until the sauce thickens slightly, about 8 minutes. Do not allow the sauce to thicken too much since it will continue to thicken once it coats the pasta. Stir in 12 of the uni fillets. Using an immersion blender, puree the sauce until smooth. Season to taste with salt and pepper.

Heat the oil in a large, heavy-bottomed sauté pan over high heat. Add the shrimp and sauté until just cooked through, about 2 minutes.

Using a pasta fork, remove the pasta from the water and add it to the shrimp in the sauté pan. Spoon 2 cups of the sauce over the pasta and shrimp, and gently toss to coat, adding some of the pasta cooking water to thin the sauce, if necessary.

Mound the pasta in 4 wide shallow pasta bowls. Spoon some of the remaining sauce over and around the pasta. Top with the remaining uni, the reserved bacon, and the basil. Serve immediately.

SERVES 4

Recipe courtesy of
JOSHUA MARKS

Wearing work gloves or kitchen rubber gloves to protect your hands from the spikes, flip the live sea urchin over, where the mouth is visible. Using kitchen shears, make an incision in the base of the urchin and cut a wide circle around the mouth. There is a sort of outer rim for the scissors to follow, where there are either no spikes or really short spikes. The long ones are all on the top.

Once you've exposed the interior, you will see that the shell is filled with the urchin's viscera, a sort of viscous fluid. Tip it upside down to discard this. Now you can see, in the bottom of the shell, the star-shaped roe, or uni. Use a spoon to very gently scoop out the uni, which will easily come out in five pieces—each arm of the star is one piece, or fillet.

If necessary, rinse the fillets of uni very gently and lightly in cold water.

Because she was unable to see the uni in order to cut around the mouth, Christine Ha's method was to make an incision near the mouth and then, feeling inside with her bare hands, she ripped the shell wide open to expose the viscera and felt her way to the uni inside.

UNI RISOTTO

East definitely meets West in the risotto that Felix Fang created for the Uni Mystery Box challenge. She jam-packed her risotto with Japanese flavors such as tangy *yuzu* juice, grated ginger, sake instead of the usual white wine, and *shiso* leaves. Then, in a nod to the dish's Italian roots, she smoothed and melded the flavors with a little butter and cream, added fresh green peas for color, and complemented it all with the briny essence of the uni. It was a daring take on a classic that summed up her tastes in food and wowed the judges.

FOR THE UNI CREAM

- 8 uni fillets (sea urchin roe)
- 2 tablespoons unsalted butter, at room temperature
- ½ cup heavy cream
- 1 teaspoon yuzu juice or Meyer lemon juice

  Kosher salt

FOR THE RISOTTO

- 3½ cups fish stock
- ½ cup shucked fresh English peas (from about 12 ounces of pods)
- 2 tablespoons unsalted butter
- ½ cup finely chopped pearl onions
- 1½ teaspoons peeled, grated fresh ginger
- 1 cup Arborio rice
- ½ cup sake

  Kosher salt

- 2 purple shiso, very thinly sliced
- 2 teaspoons grated Meyer lemon zest

TO MAKE THE UNI CREAM: Blend the uni fillets and butter in a small food processor until smooth. Bring the cream to a simmer in a small, heavy-bottomed saucepan over medium heat. Whisk the uni butter into the cream. Whisk in the yuzu juice and season to taste with salt. Set the cream aside.

TO MAKE THE RISOTTO: Place the fish stock in a medium, heavy-bottomed saucepan over high heat. Cover and bring to a simmer. Cook the peas in the stock until bright green and crisp-tender, about 2 minutes. Using a slotted spoon, remove the peas from the stock and set them aside. Cover the stock and keep warm over low heat.

Melt the butter in a large, heavy-bottomed saucepan over medium heat. Add the onions and ginger and sauté until the onions are tender, about 3 minutes. Add the rice and stir until shiny and slightly translucent, about 4 minutes. Add the sake and simmer until absorbed, stirring constantly, about 2 minutes. Add 1 cup of the fish stock. Simmer until the rice is just tender and the mixture is creamy, adding the remaining stock ¼ cup at a time as needed and stirring often, about 18 minutes.

Stir in the peas and cook until they are heated through, about 1 minute. Fold in the uni cream. Season the risotto to taste with salt.

Divide the risotto among 4 shallow bowls. Garnish with the sliced shiso leaves and lemon zest, and serve immediately.

SERVES 4

Recipe courtesy of
FELIX FANG

POBLANO AND SCALLOP RISOTTO

When he created this risotto, David Martinez, an educational administrator from Glencoe, Illinois, threw away the rulebook. From the tequila in the risotto to the mild chile flavor of the poblano sauce, there's nothing ordinary about this dish. Each serving gets a seared scallop on top before it's napped with the bright green sauce, scattered with diced poblanos, and garnished with Parmesan shavings. The judges felt that this was the best dish that he had made during his entire time as a contestant.

To make the sauce, you'll need cape gooseberries, also called ground cherries or physallis. They're a member of the nightshade family, usually orange-yellow in color and about the size of a cherry. Each fruit has a distinctive husk, or "cape," that's like the papery husk on a tomatillo, a relative. It has a firm texture, edible small seeds, gentle sweetness, and a pleasant acidity. Look for cape gooseberries in gourmet grocery stores, particularly in the spring, and store in the refrigerator until you're ready to use them.

FOR THE POBLANO SAUCE

- 2 poblano chile peppers (wear plastic gloves when handling)
- 12 cape gooseberries, husks removed
- ¾ cup loosely packed fresh cilantro
- 1 cup (or more) chicken stock

  Kosher salt

FOR THE RISOTTO

- 4 cups veal stock
- 3 tablespoons canola oil
- 2 tablespoons minced garlic
- 2 tablespoons minced shallots
- 8 ounces Arborio rice
- 1 cup dry white wine
- ⅔ cup tequila
- 2 tablespoons unsalted butter, diced
- 3 tablespoons (about 1 ounce) grated Pecorino Romano cheese

  Kosher salt and freshly ground black pepper
- 4 large sea scallops
- 3 tablespoons (about 1 ounce) shaved Parmigiano-Reggiano cheese

TO MAKE THE POBLANO SAUCE: Roast the chile peppers over a gas flame or in the broiler until the skin is charred evenly. Place them in a medium bowl and cover with a tight-fitting lid or plastic wrap, and let the chiles steam for about 10 minutes. When they are cool enough to handle, peel the charred skin. Cut them in half, clean out the seeds, and cut into medium dice.

Combine the gooseberries, cilantro, and half of the poblanos in a blender and blend well. Slowly add 1 cup chicken stock and blend, adding more stock if needed to reach desired consistency. Season to taste with salt. Set aside the remaining diced poblanos and the sauce.

TO MAKE THE RISOTTO: Bring the veal stock to a simmer in a medium, heavy-bottomed saucepan over high heat. Cover and keep warm over low heat.

Heat 1 tablespoon of the oil in a large, heavy-bottomed saucepan over medium-low heat. Add the garlic and shallots and sauté until translucent, about 2 minutes. Add the rice and stir until it is slightly translucent, about 4 minutes. Add the wine and tequila and cook until most of the liquid is absorbed, about 5 minutes.

Add 1 cup of the warm veal stock and stir until almost all of the liquid is absorbed, about 3 minutes. Continue adding the stock ¼ cup at a time until the rice is just tender but still firm to the bite and the mixture is creamy, stirring almost constantly, about 18 minutes. Remove the pan from the heat and add the butter. Fold continuously until the butter is completely melted and incorporated. Fold in the Pecorino Romano cheese. Season the risotto to taste with salt.

Meanwhile, season the scallops with salt and pepper. Heat a large, heavy-bottomed sauté pan over high heat. Add the remaining 2 tablespoons oil to the hot pan and swirl to coat. Lay the scallops in the pan and cook until golden brown, about 2 minutes per side.

TO SERVE: Divide the risotto among 4 plates, allowing it to spread slightly. Place 1 scallop in the center of each dish. Garnish with the poblano sauce, diced poblanos, and Parmigiano-Reggiano. Serve immediately.

SERVES 4

Recipe courtesy of
DAVID MARTINEZ

ARTICHOKE RISOTTO
WITH CLAMS AND BLOOD ORANGES

This risotto is so packed with good things that it's almost more like a dense rice stew. Frank Mirando, a stockbroker from Holtsville, New York, started by toasting fennel seeds and grinding them with fruity guajillo chiles, a dried chile with a mild heat and an almost berrylike taste. At the end of cooking, he used this mixture to season the risotto.

Even more unusual, he beat butter and the juice of blood oranges into the risotto, making a sort of creamy citrus emulsion that both colors and flavors the dish. Blood oranges, with their almost startlingly crimson juice, taste intensely orange but with a hint of berry. Once the artichoke pieces, the crisp cubes of pancetta, the clams, and sliced scallions are folded in, this risotto becomes a whole meal in a bowl.

2	teaspoons fennel seeds
2	teaspoons crushed dried guajillo chile peppers
24	littleneck clams, scrubbed
1	cup water
8	cups vegetable stock
2	large fresh artichoke hearts, chokes removed
6	slices (⅛ inch thick) pancetta, roughly diced
1	onion, finely diced
4	cloves garlic, minced
1½	cups Arborio rice
	About 6 small blood oranges
1	cup dry white wine
4	tablespoons (½ stick) unsalted butter, diced
2	scallions, thinly sliced on a bias
	Kosher salt
¼	cup fresh basil chiffonade

In a small, heavy-bottomed sauté pan over medium heat, stir the fennel seeds until fragrant and toasted, about 3 minutes. Cool the fennel seeds, then grind them with the chile pepper in a spice grinder. Set the spice mixture aside.

Heat a large, heavy-bottomed pot over medium-high heat. Add the clams and water, then immediately cover and steam the clams until they open, about 3 minutes. Strain the clams, reserving the cooking liquid. Remove the meat from the shells and set aside. Discard the shells.

Combine the vegetable stock and the clam cooking liquid in a large, heavy-bottomed saucepan and bring to a boil over high heat. Add the artichoke hearts and cook until crisp-tender, about 3 minutes. Remove the artichokes from the stock, cut them into ½-inch pieces, and set aside. Remove the stock from the heat, cover, and keep it hot.

Place the pancetta in a large, heavy-bottomed sauté pan. Set the pan over medium heat and cook until the fat is rendered and the pancetta is crisp, about 5 minutes. Using a slotted spoon, transfer the pancetta to a plate lined with paper towels to drain.

Return the pan to medium-low heat. Add the onion and garlic and cook until the onion is tender, about 5 minutes. Add the rice and stir until it is slightly toasted, about 2 minutes. Using a Microplane, grate the peel from 2 of the oranges into the rice. Add the wine, increase the heat to

ARTICHOKE RISOTTO
(continued)

medium, and bring to a simmer. Simmer, stirring until most of the liquid is absorbed, about 5 minutes. Add 1 cup of the hot vegetable-clam stock and stir constantly until the liquid is absorbed. Continue adding the stock 1 cup at a time, allowing the liquid to be absorbed and checking for doneness before each addition, until the rice is al dente and the mixture is creamy, about 18 minutes.

Squeeze ¾ cup juice from the blood oranges. Remove the risotto from the heat and add the butter and orange juice. Fold constantly until the butter is completely melted and incorporated. Fold in the scallions and the reserved clams, artichokes, and pancetta. Season the risotto to taste with the reserved spice mixture and salt.

To serve, divide the risotto among 4 flat plates, spreading slightly. Top with the basil and serve immediately.

SERVES 4

Recipe courtesy of
FRANK MIRANDO

PASTA ALLA NORMA

In his restaurants and food ventures such as Del Posto and Eataly, restaurateur Joe Bastianich, author of *New York Times* bestseller *Restaurant Man*, is known for his Italian sensibility—using high-quality, local ingredients prepared as simply as possible. This is a primo example: a dish with its roots in Sicily, from whence hailed composer Vincenzo Bellini. His 1831 opera *La Norma* has long been believed to be the source of the time-honored name of this homey pasta dish, honoring both the opera and the typical dish of its composer's birthplace.

Noted Italian food writer Giuliano Bugialli, however, whose opinion is usually well worth hearing, feels this is nonsense, that the name simply means "pasta in the usual manner," a nod to its everyday status in Sicily. That's a far less romantic story, but whichever one you prefer, there's no denying the homey, hearty appeal of a plate of tender pasta, fried eggplant cubes, tomato sauce, and cheese.

In Sicily, the usual finish is a sprinkle of salty, dry ricotta salata, but that can be difficult to find in the States. Bastianich embellishes his version with onions for extra flavor and finishes it with a dollop of creamy ricotta. Even Bellini would have to be pleased with that.

Pomodoro sauce is the simplest tomato sauce, just garlic sautéed in olive oil and then simmered with crushed tomatoes. In Italian kitchens, it's considered so simple and basic that no recipe is used. If you're not Italian, sauté 2 crushed cloves of garlic in a couple tablespoons olive oil, then add a 28-ounce can crushed tomatoes and simmer gently over medium-low heat while you prepare the rest of the dish.

PASTA ALLA NORMA

Pomodoro sauce

1 medium eggplant

Kosher salt

All-purpose flour

Olive oil

2 cloves garlic

1 medium onion, thinly sliced

Freshly ground black pepper

1 pound rigatoni or other dried pasta

¼ cup ricotta cheese

Heat the pomodoro sauce in a saucepan on low heat. Meanwhile, remove the skin from the eggplant and cut the eggplant into 1-inch cubes. Sprinkle them with salt and place them on paper towels to allow some of the bitter liquid to drain out. Dust the eggplant cubes with the flour.

Heat ¼ inch of olive oil in a saucepan. Crush the garlic cloves with the heel of your hand and add them to the pan. Cook, stirring frequently, until golden brown. Add the eggplant cubes. Cook over medium heat, turning frequently to brown on all sides, and adding a little more oil if needed. The eggplant should be crisp and browned on the outside and tender on the inside. Remove and place on paper towels to allow the oil to drain.

In the same pan, cook the onion in the oil, stirring frequently, until tender. Add it to the pomodoro sauce. Season the sauce to taste with salt and pepper.

Cook the pasta in boiling salted water according to package directions. While it cooks, add the eggplant cubes to the pomodoro sauce and heat. Two minutes before the pasta is done, remove the pasta from the water and add it to the pomodoro sauce. Add a little pasta water, if necessary, to keep the sauce liquid. Cook until the pasta is tender. Serve with a dollop of ricotta cheese.

SERVES 4

WINE PAIRING

"If it grows together, it goes together!" Italians have long known that a wine is at its best when served with food from the same soil. The perfect regional pairing, this classic Sicilian dish should be paired with wine from the great Sicilian grape Nero d'Avola. Not too tannic, and a fruity, spicy, full-bodied red, it's a great match for the beautiful ripe San Marzano tomatoes that are the base of the pomodoro sauce.

SAVORY BREAD PUDDING
WITH TOMATO SAUCE AND SAUTÉED BEET TOPS

A contract specialist for the US Army, Joshua Marks seemed to be showing his lack of chef credentials when this dish was served up—the judges all thought it looked awful! Plated up, the dish seemed to be a disorganized mess: a ring of bread pudding sitting on a pool of tomato sauce, with beet greens haphazardly strewn around it and onion rings incongruously scattered over the top.

Then they tasted it, and all the judges were caught off guard. It was outstanding. The chewy baguette soaks up the egg and milk and puffs to a delicate custard, plumped with chunks of sweet Italian sausage and melting cubes of fresh mozzarella. The intense flavor of the wine-rich tomato sauce is complemented by the sweetness of tender beet greens. And the crispy onion rings on top? That's just a bonus, but what a treat—don't skip it.

FOR THE BREAD PUDDING

- 6 ounces baguette, cut into ½-inch cubes
- 6 large eggs
- 4 large egg yolks
- ½ cup whole milk
- 2 teaspoons kosher salt
- 2 teaspoons fennel seeds
- 1 teaspoon sweet paprika
- ½ teaspoon cayenne

  Pinch of ground cinnamon

- 3 tablespoons extra-virgin olive oil
- 1 pound Italian sausages, casings removed
- 4 ounces fresh mozzarella cheese, drained and diced

FRIED ONION RINGS

  Canola oil

- 1 large egg
- 1 tablespoon whole milk
- 1 cup all-purpose flour
- 1 teaspoon kosher salt plus more for seasoning
- 1 small onion, very thinly sliced (⅛-inch-thick)

FOR THE TOMATO SAUCE

- 2 tablespoons olive oil
- 4 large scallions (dark green parts only), finely chopped
- 1 Fresno chile pepper, chopped (wear plastic gloves when handling)

- 2 cloves garlic, chopped
- 1 pound heirloom grape tomatoes, halved
- 1¼ cups Merlot or other dry red wine

  Kosher salt

FOR THE BEET GREENS

- 1½ tablespoons olive oil
- 4 large scallions (white and pale green parts only), finely chopped
- 2 cloves garlic, chopped
- 32 beet green leaves

TO MAKE THE BREAD PUDDING: Preheat the oven to 400°F. Lightly coat a 2-quart baking dish with oil.

Spread the bread on a large rimmed baking sheet. Bake until just dry, stirring occasionally, about 8 minutes. Whisk the whole eggs, egg yolks,

SAVORY BREAD PUDDING

(continued)

milk, salt, fennel seeds, paprika, cayenne, and cinnamon in a large bowl to blend. Fold in the bread cubes and set aside until the bread is completely saturated, stirring occasionally, about 1 hour.

Heat the oil in a large, heavy-bottomed sauté pan over medium-high heat. Add the sausages and cook until browned, breaking them up into pieces with the back of a wooden spoon, about 12 minutes. Stir the cooked sausages and pan drippings into the bread mixture. Spoon the bread mixture into the prepared loaf pan and bake for 15 minutes. Scatter the cheese over the top of the bread pudding and continue baking until the cheese has melted and begins to brown in spots, about 15 minutes longer. Set aside to cool for 10 minutes.

TO MAKE THE ONION RINGS: Heat 2 inches of oil in a large, heavy-bottomed saucepan over medium heat to 375°F. Whisk the egg and milk in a shallow dish to blend. Mix the flour and 1 teaspoon of salt in another shallow dish.

Dredge the onion rings in the egg mixture, then in the flour to coat, then fry the onions until they are crisp and golden brown, about 3 minutes per batch. Using a slotted spoon, transfer the fried onions to paper towels to drain the excess oil. Season the hot fried onions with salt.

TO MAKE THE SAUCE: Heat the oil in a small, heavy-bottomed saucepan over medium heat. Add the scallion greens and sauté until tender, about 1 minute. Add the chile and garlic and sauté until fragrant, about 30 seconds. Add the tomatoes and cook until they begin to release their juice, about 5 minutes. Add the Merlot and bring to a simmer. Reduce the heat to medium-low and simmer gently until the tomatoes are very tender and falling apart and the wine has reduced slightly, occasionally smashing the tomatoes with a spoon as they soften, about 35 minutes. Transfer to a food processor and blend until nearly smooth. Season the sauce to taste with salt. Return the sauce to the saucepan and simmer until thickened slightly, about 10 minutes.

TO MAKE THE GREENS: Heat the oil in a large, heavy-bottomed saucepan over medium heat. Add the scallions and garlic and sauté until tender, about 1 minute. Add the beet greens and sauté until they wilt, about 4 minutes. The greens will fill the pan when first added, but they will cook down considerably when they wilt.

Spoon the tomato sauce in the centers of 4 plates. Cut the bread pudding and place a piece on top of the sauce on each plate. Arrange the greens around the pudding. Garnish with the onion rings and serve immediately.

Recipe courtesy of
JOSHUA MARKS

SERVES 4

ROASTED BEET SALAD WITH BEET GREENS, GOAT CHEESE, AND CABERNET VINAIGRETTE

Christine Ha created this recipe to accompany a roast chicken dish. The creamy mushroom sauce and earthy sautéed mushrooms of her chicken dish needed something sharp to accompany them, and the tangy goat cheese in this salad—not to mention the Cabernet vinaigrette—did the trick perfectly. In addition, chicken and mushrooms can make quite a brown plate, and the rich crimson of the roasted beets was a beautiful complement. This salad is both pretty enough and delicious enough to stand on its own as an appetizer or to accompany any roast meat.

6　medium beets with fresh green tops

1　tablespoon plus ¼ cup olive oil

　Kosher salt and freshly ground black pepper

3　tablespoons Cabernet Sauvignon or other dry red wine

3　tablespoons white balsamic vinegar

3　tablespoons finely diced shallots

1　teaspoon minced garlic

2　ounces soft fresh goat cheese

Recipe courtesy of
CHRISTINE HA

Preheat the oven to 400°F. Line a heavy baking sheet with foil.

Cut the green leaves off the beets. Wash and reserve 12 small tender greens. Cover and keep the tender greens refrigerated.

Scrub the beets, then toss them with 1 tablespoon of the oil on the baking sheet to coat. Season with salt and pepper. Cover and roast until a skewer can glide through the beets with a little resistance, turning them over occasionally to ensure they cook evenly, about 45 minutes. Set aside to cool.

When the beets are cool enough to handle, peel and cut them into ¼-inch-thick round slices. Cover and refrigerate the beet slices until they're cold.

Whisk the wine, vinegar, shallots, and garlic in a medium bowl to blend. Whisk in the remaining ¼ cup oil. Season the vinaigrette to taste with salt and pepper.

Lay the beet leaves on 4 plates. Gently toss the beet slices in a large bowl with enough vinaigrette to coat. Season to taste with salt and pepper. Place the beets over the beet leaves and spoon some vinaigrette over the beets and leaves. Crumble the goat cheese over the beets and serve.

SERVES 4

WINE PAIRING

Most Sauvignon Blancs have an edge of grassiness, citrus, or both—and either flavor profile would be a fantastic complement to a roasted beet salad. Sauvignon Blanc is also a perfect partner for goat cheese, cutting through the creamy texture, while harmonizing with the slight tartness the citrus notes impart to the wine. Choose a medium-bodied bottle with enough weight to stand up to the strong flavor of the beets.

COLESLAW

You know ordinary coleslaw, made primarily of cabbage and mayonnaise? Well, if that's what you prefer, look away, because this slaw is an absolute riot of color. Yellow corn, red cabbage, red onion, orange carrots, and fresh green herbs. The dressing is like the perfect mashup between the mayonnaise variety and a vinaigrette, fresh lemon juice and olive oil made creamy with a little mayo. It's satisfyingly savory with fresh basil and oregano as well as a hint of dried Italian seasoning to amp up the herbal taste. It's the best of both worlds, and the resulting slaw is pretty enough to stand alone as a side dish and flavorful enough to make it a fantastic topper for sandwiches.

1   ear yellow corn

1   head red cabbage, shredded

1   red onion, very thinly sliced

1   carrot, peeled and julienned

Juice of 2 lemons

¼   cup mayonnaise

2   tablespoons chopped fresh basil

2   tablespoons chopped fresh oregano

1   tablespoon dried Italian seasoning

½   cup olive oil

Kosher salt

Cook the corn in a large pot of boiling salted water just until it turns bright yellow, about 2 minutes. Drain and cool. Cut the kernels off the cob and transfer to a large bowl.

Add the cabbage, onion, and carrot to the corn kernels and toss to blend. Whisk the lemon juice, mayonnaise, basil, oregano, and Italian seasoning in a medium bowl to blend. Gradually whisk in the oil to blend. Pour the dressing over the corn mixture and toss to coat. Season to taste with salt and serve.

SERVES 4

Recipe courtesy of
THE RED TEAM
(Frank Mirando, Christine Ha, David Martinez, Stacey Amagrande)

MASHED SWEET POTATOES

Sweet potatoes so often get an overly sweet treatment, but the Red Team allowed the natural sugars to shine through in an otherwise savory and simple treatment with butter, salt, and a little nutmeg. The result is like fluffy mashed potatoes with a little more texture, a pale orange color, and a lot more style than regular mash. The Red Team served these with the Ribeye Steaks with Whiskey-Chile Butter (page 196).

- 2 orange-fleshed sweet potatoes (about 1½ pounds total), peeled and cut crosswise into 1-inch-wide pieces

- 3 tablespoons unsalted butter

- 1 teaspoon kosher salt

- ¼ teaspoon grated nutmeg

Cook the sweet potatoes in a large saucepan of boiling salted water until tender, about 18 minutes. Drain well. Transfer the sweet potato chunks to a food processor and puree until smooth or mash with a potato masher. Mix in the butter, salt, and nutmeg. Transfer the puree to a small, heavy-bottomed saucepan and rewarm over medium heat before serving.

SERVES 4

Recipe courtesy of
THE RED TEAM
(Frank Mirando, Christine Ha, David Martinez, Stacey Amagrande)

SAUTÉED GREEN BEANS
WITH HAM

These green beans are hearty and meaty. They have a layered pork flavor, redolent of smoky ham that is fried in the fat rendered from salt pork. Onion adds more depth, but it's the pepper flakes that make these beans more of a star than a mere side dish. These meaty beans are an excellent way to get the meat-lovers in your family to eat more vegetables. They're also an ideal accompaniment to the Ribeye Steaks with Whiskey-Chile Butter on page 196.

1   pound green beans, trimmed

3   ounces diced salt pork

4   ounces finely diced ham

½   cup finely diced red onion

¼   teaspoon red-pepper flakes

Kosher salt and freshly ground black pepper

Cook the green beans in a large saucepan of boiling salted water until crisp-tender, about 2 minutes. Drain, then submerge the beans in a bowl of ice water to cool completely. Drain well.

Cook the salt pork in a large sauté pan over medium-low heat until the fat is rendered, about 20 minutes. Discard the salt pork. Add the ham to the pork drippings and sauté until warm, about 2 minutes. Add the onions and red-pepper flakes and sauté until tender, about 2 minutes. Add the beans and sauté until they are heated through, about 5 minutes. Season to taste with salt and black pepper.

SERVES 4

Recipe courtesy of
THE RED TEAM
(Frank Mirando, Christine Ha, David Martinez, Stacey Amagrande)

Derrick Prince really stood out on Season 2, not least because of his flowing dark hair and his lip piercing. He plays in a heavy metal band, and he's always been a serious cook, but since *MasterChef*, he's been able to pursue his passion for food more intensely. Derrick says, "As a result of the show, I developed a healthy, interactive Web following. I run a recipe Website and food blog at www.borntobraisehell.com, which gives me the chance to develop recipes and share them with everyone.

"The most rewarding things that have happened all revolve around professional food service. I was able to spend a week and a half in judge Graham Elliot's Michelin-starred kitchen. I worked very long shifts and loved every minute of it. I learned more than I can express and met some amazing people. That little bit of time there was so intense, it prepared me for my own pop-up restaurants or kitchen takeovers where I commandeer an existing restaurant's kitchen for a single night's service of a five-course meal. These takeovers, although ridiculously work intensive (at least two days of prep prior to the night) give me the opportunity to be a chef for a day, cook my food, and run a kitchen. Building off all of that experience, I now find myself as an on-call line cook as well.

"I'm still learning more and more about cooking every day, and I consider myself a cook and not a chef, but *MasterChef* has opened some amazing doors for me. I have found myself giving cooking demonstrations at high-end retail stores (which is very impressive, considering my look) and public libraries, product demonstrations, and even private cooking lessons in people's home kitchens. It's been a great ride, and so far it doesn't look like it's going to stop any time soon."

ASIAN AVOCADO, KALE, AND MUSTARD GREEN SALAD

Sturdy kale and mustard greens aren't usually eaten raw, but this potent Asian dressing on the thinly sliced greens makes for a most unusual and refreshing salad. For best results, let the dressed salad sit for 10 minutes to soften up the greens a bit before garnishing with the crumbled tortilla chips. Serve it right after adding the chips so they retain their crunch.

½   bunch kale

½   bunch mustard greens

4   teaspoons toasted sesame oil

1   tablespoon rice vinegar

1   tablespoon soy sauce

2   teaspoons fresh lemon juice

1   shallot, finely chopped

1   clove garlic, finely chopped

¼   teaspoon red-pepper flakes

2   avocados, peeled, pitted, and cubed

Tortilla chips, coarsely crushed, for garnish

Cut out the thick stem and rib that run down the length of the kale and mustard green leaves. Stack the leaves and cut them into ¼-inch-wide ribbons to get 2 cups of each.

Whisk the sesame oil, vinegar, soy sauce, and lemon juice in a large serving bowl to blend. Whisk in the shallot, garlic, and red-pepper flakes. Add the mustard greens and kale and toss to coat. Add the avocados and gently toss to coat.

Divide the salad among 4 plates, garnish with the tortilla chips, and serve immediately.

SERVES 4

SPICY EGG CURRY AND PILAF
WITH PEAS AND POMEGRANATE RAITA

Vegetarian dishes typically don't play a big part in the *MasterChef* kitchen, where facility with a wide variety of meats (sweetbreads, anyone?) is often an excellent test of a contestant's range. But Nandini Anant, a homemaker from West Orange, New Jersey, arrested the judges' attention with this unusual and colorful egg curry. The complexity of flavors that arises from the layering of so many spices raises it from the realm of the ordinary, as does her innovative pomegranate raita, a yogurt-based relish that's spooned on just before serving. The easy rice pilaf results in an aromatic finish that belies its simple ingredients and could easily be used as part of a different meal, to accompany roast chicken, for example.

If you can't find fresh curry leaves, you can still get an excellent result without them, but they are often available fresh (and sometimes frozen) at specialty gourmet stores.

FOR THE CURRY

- 6   large organic eggs
- 5   tablespoons canola oil
- 3   large white onions, chopped
- 3   cloves garlic, minced
- 2   tablespoons peeled, minced fresh ginger
- 3   teaspoons fenugreek
- 2   teaspoons ground coriander
- 2   teaspoons ground cumin
- 2   teaspoons kosher salt plus more to taste
- 2   teaspoons lemon pepper
- 1   teaspoon turmeric
- 6   tomatoes, chopped
- 2   teaspoons garam masala
- 3   to 4 green chile peppers (such as Anaheim), seeded and diced (wear plastic gloves when handling)

- 1   teaspoon cumin seeds
- 1   teaspoon mustard seeds
- 5   to 6 fresh curry leaves, chopped
- 1   teaspoon chili powder
- 1   teaspoon paprika
- 1   cup heavy cream

FOR THE PILAF

- 4   tablespoons (½ stick) unsalted butter
- 1   teaspoon cumin seeds
- 1   cinnamon stick
- ¼   teaspoon ground cloves
- 1   cup basmati rice
- 2   cups water
- 1   cup fresh or thawed frozen peas

    Kosher salt

FOR THE POMEGRANATE RAITA

- 1   pomegranate
- 2½ cups plain yogurt
- 1   teaspoon cumin seeds
- ¼   teaspoon freshly ground black pepper

    Kosher salt

    Fresh cilantro leaves, for garnish

SPICY EGG CURRY AND PILAF

(continued)

TO MAKE THE CURRY: Place the eggs in a large pot of cold water and bring to a boil over high heat. Once the water comes to a boil, immediately turn off the heat, cover the pot, and let sit for 10 minutes. Transfer the eggs to a bowl of cold water and set aside.

Meanwhile, heat a large sauté pan or heavy pot over medium-high heat. Add 3 tablespoons of the oil, then add the onions, garlic, and ginger and sauté until the onions are tender and translucent, about 10 minutes. Add the fenugreek, coriander, cumin, salt, lemon pepper, and turmeric. Sauté for 5 minutes. Add the tomatoes and 1 teaspoon of the garam masala. Cover and cook until the tomatoes are very tender, about 8 minutes. Set the mixture aside to cool slightly, then transfer to a blender and puree until smooth. Season the sauce to taste with salt. Set the sauce aside.

Peel the boiled eggs and cut them in half.

Heat the remaining 2 tablespoons oil in a large, heavy-bottomed sauté pan over medium heat. Add the chiles, cumin seeds, mustard seeds, and curry leaves. Lay the halved eggs in the pan and sprinkle with the chili powder, paprika, and remaining 1 teaspoon garam masala. Cook for 5 minutes. Add the sauce and cream and cook for 2 minutes.

TO MAKE THE PILAF: Melt the butter in a large, heavy-bottomed saucepan over medium-low heat. Add the cumin seeds, cinnamon stick, and cloves and sauté until fragrant, about 2 minutes. Add the rice and sauté for 2 minutes. Add the water and bring to a boil. Reduce the heat to low, cover, and simmer until the rice is tender and the water is absorbed, about 15 minutes. Remove the saucepan from the heat, add the peas, then cover and steam until the peas are hot, about 5 minutes. Season to taste with salt and fluff the rice with a fork.

TO MAKE THE POMEGRANATE RAITA: Remove the seeds from the pomegranate and place them in a medium bowl. Fold in the yogurt, cumin seeds, and black pepper. Season to taste with salt. Cover and refrigerate until ready to serve.

TO SERVE: Mound the pilaf on 4 plates. Spoon the eggs and curry sauce alongside the rice on the plates. Place the raita in serving bowls. Sprinkle the cilantro leaves over the curry, rice, and raita. Serve immediately.

Recipe courtesy of
NANDINI ANANT

SERVES 4

A vegetable peeler takes off too much of the juicy ginger

under the papery skin, and a paring knife presents the same difficulties. How to practically peel a knobby, twisting root of ginger without taking off a finger or too much of the root? The answer is a simple teaspoon.

Holding the bowl of the spoon away from you, scrape the edge of the teaspoon against the papery skin. You don't even need a spoon with a sharp edge. You'll be astonished to find how readily it peels off the skin, and only the skin, leaving a beautifully denuded knob of ginger with no waste, no fuss, ready to be chopped or grated as the recipe requires. The best part of using a spoon is that it easily curves over the turns and crevices of the rhizome, pulling the skin out without wasting any of the ginger beneath.

GRILLED CORN ON THE COB

This sweet and tangy grilled corn was part of the Cowboy Challenge, where the teams went to a dude ranch to cook for all the novice cowboys. The grilled corn covered in a spicy sauce was served with the Grilled NY Strip Steak on page 206. It's a delight for anyone who's looking for something to dress corn with besides the usual butter. Everything didn't work out quite perfectly in the challenge rendition, however: The team forgot to soak their corn in its husks before they put it on the grill, and they set Christine Ha to grilling it. And of course the husks dried right out and caught fire. One of the judges ran over to her and said, "Christine, do you know your entire grill is on fire?" Christine said, a little disconcerted, "What?!" and then she turned to her team and reminded them, accusingly, "Guys! I'm blind!"

In this version, you'll husk the corn first, which may help you avoid a similar flame-up, but if you prefer to grill it in the husk, which makes it a bit more tender, pull them back just to loosen, then pull the husks back up around the corn and soak the whole ears in cold water for 30 minutes before grilling.

½   **red onion, coarsely chopped**

¾   **cup (1½ sticks) unsalted butter, at room temperature**

1½   **teaspoons sweet paprika**

2   **tablespoons fresh lime juice**

2   **tablespoons sour cream**

    Kosher salt and freshly ground black pepper

6   **ears corn, shucked**

Blend the onion in a food processor until pureed. Transfer the onion puree to a large, heavy-bottomed sauté pan. Add the butter and paprika and cook over medium heat until the butter melts. Whisk in the lime juice and sour cream. Season the sauce to taste with salt and pepper.

Meanwhile, prepare a barbecue grill for high heat. Place the corn on the grill, close the grill hood, and cook, turning a couple times, until the corn is hot and juicy and slightly charred all over, about 12 minutes.

Transfer the corn to the butter sauce and turn to coat. Serve immediately.

SERVES 6

Recipe courtesy of
THE BLUE TEAM
(Frank Mirando, Christine Ha, David Martinez, Stacey Amagrande)

WINE PAIRING

An American classic for an American classic! A buttery California Chardonnay would provide great complementary flavors to succulent grilled corn on the cob. Most Chardonnays are weighty wines with strong flavors that won't disappear against the sweet corn and salty melted butter. Choose one that has been aged in oak. Since it's one of the most popular wines in the world, you won't have trouble finding a nice bottle that suits your budget.

GARLIC MASHED POTATOES

Cowboys work hard on a dude ranch—well, some of them do—and the Blue Team wanted to be sure they served up a hearty meal. Along with the Grilled NY Strip Steak on page 206, they made these unabashedly creamy and garlicky mashed potatoes, more like something from a high-end restaurant kitchen than a chuck wagon. Loaded with butter and sour cream, they're gorgeously rich. A little goes a long way.

½ cup (1 stick) unsalted butter

4 cloves garlic, minced

3 pounds Yukon Gold potatoes, peeled and quartered

2 cups sour cream

Kosher salt

Melt the butter in a small, heavy-bottomed saucepan over low heat. Add the garlic and sauté until tender, about 8 minutes.

Meanwhile, place the potatoes in a large, heavy-bottomed pot of salted cold water and bring the water to a boil. Cook until the potatoes are very tender, about 15 minutes. Drain and return the potatoes to the pot.

Add the sour cream and garlic butter to the potatoes and mash together until smooth but not pureed. Season to taste with salt.

SERVES 6

Recipe courtesy of
THE BLUE TEAM
(Frank Mirando, Christine Ha, David Martinez, Stacey Amagrande)

PAN-FRIED POTATOES
WITH CHEESE AND BACON

Sometimes the beauty of a dish is in its simplicity...and in the bacon. Think of this rich side dish as a modern take on the hash brown. It's great alongside a pile of scrambled eggs, but just as delectable as a side dish for hamburgers, chicken, or even a steak. The Red Team served these potatoes with the Barbecue Pork Chops on page 214.

As with the simplest dishes, it's all about the technique: Parboil the potato cubes until they're nearly done but not quite cooked through. A knife should pierce the exterior with ease but should not readily reach the center. Quickly toss them in hot oil until they're golden and crisp, and then the potatoes are ready to be covered with shredded cheese and crisp bacon. Be sure to serve them hot.

6   red-skinned potatoes, cut into 1-inch cubes

3   tablespoons olive oil

    Kosher salt

6   ounces cheddar cheese, shredded

8   bacon slices

Place the potatoes in a large pot of heavily salted boiling water, and cook until they are easily pierced with a fork but still holding their shape, about 8 minutes. Drain well.

Preheat the oven to 400°F. Heat the oil in a large, heavy-bottomed sauté pan over high heat. Add the hot potatoes and sprinkle them with salt. Cook the potatoes until they are crisp and golden, about 10 minutes.

Meanwhile, cook the bacon in a large skillet over medium-high heat until crisp, about 7 minutes. Transfer the bacon to a plate lined with paper towels to drain the excess oil.

Sprinkle the cheese over the potatoes in the pan and put the pan in the oven for 5 minutes, just to melt the cheese. Crumble the bacon over the potatoes and serve.

SERVES 4

Recipe courtesy of
THE RED TEAM
(Stacey Amagrande, Monti Carlo, Helene Leeds, Mike Hill,
Anna Rossi, Joshua Marks, Ryan Umane, David Martinez)

MIXED TEMPURA

When Felix Fang, a food runner from Hollywood, met Monti Carlo, a homemaker from Los Angeles, the competition was rife. Their rivalry was so apparent that the curious producers paired them up to work together on the Sushi challenge, expecting the resulting conflict to make some exciting sparks fly. Working on the same team, however, they soon discovered that they had a deep meeting of the minds when it came to food. Not only were their joint creations real winners, but they actually ended up becoming great friends!

This simple but impeccable dish is a prime example of Felix and Monti's working relationship. It takes attention to detail and a light touch: Be sure to use ice water in the tempura batter, and don't overstir it, or it won't be as brittle and delicate when fried.

Canola oil

1 cup ice-cold water

1 large egg

1 cup all-purpose flour

12 broccoli florets

3 medium carrots, peeled and cut into 3 x 1 x ⅓-inch slices

2 Japanese eggplants, cut on bias into ⅓-inch-thick slices

12 asparagus spears, trimmed

Heat 3 inches of oil in a large, heavy-bottomed pot or wok over medium-high heat to 375°F.

Whisk the ice water and egg in a large bowl to blend. Add the flour and stir with chopsticks just until a thin batter forms and some small lumps remain. The colder the water and the less the batter is mixed, the crispier the coating will be when fried.

Working in batches, coat the vegetables in the batter and place them into the hot oil to fry until the coating is crisp and the vegetables are crisp-tender, about 2 minutes for the broccoli, carrots, and eggplant and 1 minute for the asparagus. Using a slotted spoon, transfer the vegetables to a baking sheet lined with paper towels to drain the excess oil.

Place the tempura on a serving dish and serve immediately.

SERVES 4

Recipe courtesy of
FELIX FANG AND MONTI CARLO

CORN FREGOLA SALAD

Fregola is a Sardinian pasta that's shaped into little spheres, somewhat similar in looks to the large pearls of Israeli couscous, but a completely different product on the plate. Fregola is made of a coarse semolina. The little pearls are toasted in large batches, so when you open a package of fregola, the colors vary widely even within the same package. Some are pale, some very dark brown, others a light tan. The differences in the roast give fregola a particularly nutty, addictive flavor that helps it stand up well in fish soups, as it's frequently used in Sardinia. But it's also dressed with light sauces, such as oils and herbs.

In this effortlessly good side dish, Joe Bastianich underscores fregola's unusual shape by mixing it with blanched corn sliced off the cob. The little nubs of pasta are roughly the same size and shape as the corn kernels, but the sweet chewiness of the corn plays beautifully off the nutty pasta, especially when dressed so simply. If you've never tried fregola, this dish will win it a place in your kitchen.

---

2 **cups corn (about 4 ears' worth)**

8 **ounces fregola**

½ **cup olive oil**

Kosher salt and freshly ground black pepper

Chopped scallions

Cook the corn in a 2- to 2½-quart saucepan of boiling water, blanching it for 1 minute. Drain it, then rinse under cold running water until it is thoroughly cool and the cooking process has stopped. Place the corn in a large bowl.

Cook the fregola in 4 quarts of boiling salted water until al dente. Drain, then add it to the corn. Stir in the olive oil and salt and pepper to taste, tossing gently.

Serve in small bowls or on plates, and top each with 1 tablespoon of chopped scallions.

SERVES 4

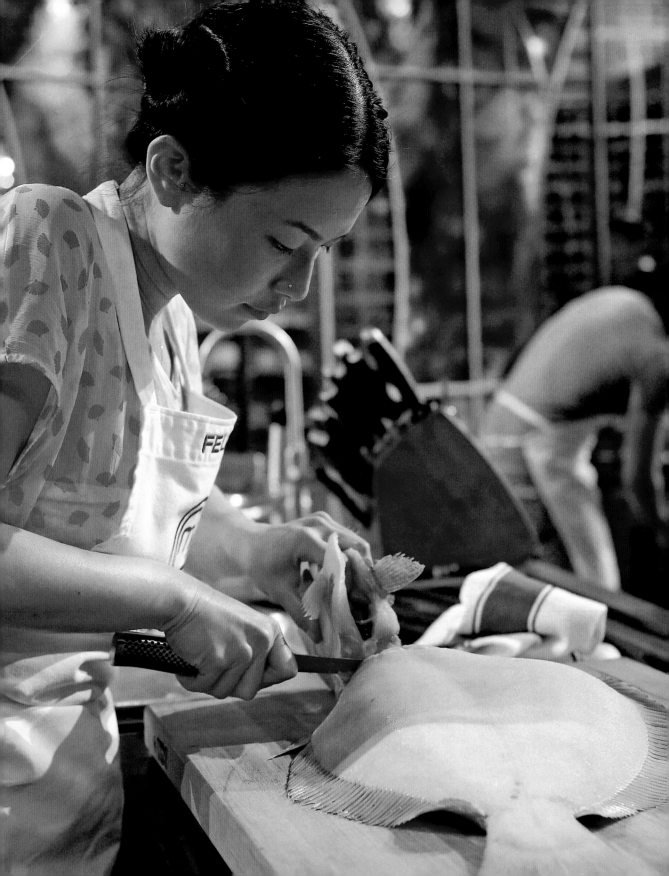

THAI SEAFOOD SOUP
WITH TABLESIDE BROTH

Working together as the Girls Team for the Michelin Star challenge, Christine Ha and Becky Reams created this elegant soup so full of good things. Unlike other soups, this one is served by first placing four types of perfectly prepared seafood, including 3 thin slices of halibut, as well as a scattering of micro-greens and flowers into the bowl. Then a teapot full of steaming, fragrant broth is poured over the edible still life. Every detail has been considered, down to the fleur de sel, with its crisp flakes sprinkled over the sliced fish in the bowl before the broth is added. It's a delicate, almost feminine dish—except that the flavors are so intense.

To make it that way, you do need certain specialty ingredients. Some recipes will tell you to substitute ginger for galangal if you can't find it; the rhizomes are in the same family and closely resemble one another, but the tastes are decidedly different, with galangal much stronger and more noticeable in the finished dish. If you can find a specialty or ethnic Asian market that stocks galangal, it will also have kaffir lime leaves and lemongrass.

Tomato powder is the result of tomatoes being ground to a slurry that is sprayed and dried; the resulting dull-red powder has an intense tomato taste. It adds flavor and tomato acidity to a dish without diluting it with liquid, making all the other flavors leap into sharp relief. Deep red tomato granules, on the other hand, are dried tomato flakes. They add flavor but also color and a bit of texture to the final dish.

FOR THE BROTH

- 6 cups fish stock
- 3 kaffir lime leaves
- 3 lemongrass stalks, thinly sliced
- 1 (2-inch) piece fresh ginger, peeled and thinly sliced
- 1 (2-inch) piece galangal, thinly sliced
- 3 tablespoons fresh lime juice
- 2 tablespoons fish sauce

FOR THE SEAFOOD

- 4 mussels, scrubbed and debearded
- 4 manila clams, scrubbed
- 1 (8-ounce) piece boneless, skinless halibut, cut into 12 thin slices
- 4 live spot prawns, peeled, deveined, and halved lengthwise
- 4 thin slices peeled fresh ginger, cut into diamond-shaped pieces
- 1 teaspoon tomato powder
- ½ teaspoon tomato granules

  Fleur de sel
- 2 tablespoons micro Thai basil
- 2 tablespoons micro daikon radish greens
- 2 tablespoons micro tatsoi or small edible flowers
- 1 scallion, very thinly sliced diagonally

THAI SEAFOOD SOUP

(continued)

TO MAKE THE BROTH: Combine the fish stock, lime leaves, lemongrass, ginger, and galangal in a medium, heavy-bottomed saucepan. Cover and bring to a simmer over medium-high heat. Remove from the heat and steep for 30 minutes. Strain the broth through a fine-mesh sieve into another medium saucepan, then cover and return to a boil before serving.

TO MAKE THE SEAFOOD: Place the mussels and clams in ¼ inch of water in a large, heavy-bottomed saucepan over high heat. Cover and steam until they open, about 5 minutes.

Fan 3 slices of halibut in the bottom of each of 4 wide shallow bowls. Set 1 clam, 1 mussel, 2 shrimp halves, and 1 ginger slice in each bowl. Sprinkle the tomato powder in a thin line across each bowl, then sprinkle some tomato granules over the tomato powder. Sprinkle fleur de sel over the fish. Garnish with the basil, radish greens, tatsoi, and scallion.

TO SERVE: Remove the boiling broth from the heat and add the lime juice and fish sauce to the broth. Carefully pour the hot broth into a teapot. Serve the bowls of seafood and immediately pour the hot broth from the teapot over the fish at the table.

SERVES 4

Recipe courtesy of
CHRISTINE HA AND BECKY REAMS

CALIFORNIA ROLLS

Monti Carlo and Felix Fang found that their rivalry contained the seeds of a great friendship during this Sushi challenge, and these California Rolls are a great example of their working relationship. They took an ordinary sushi variation and made it special in two ways: by including a layer of smelt roe, known as *masago* in Japan, which added salt and the subtly delicious texture of firm eggs that "pop" in the mouth; and, a clever twist, by using real crab.

This is noteworthy because California rolls nearly always contain surimi, an imitation crabmeat made from some sort of whitefish, often pollock. Surimi is not intended to be a "fake" food; it has been part of many Asian cultures for centuries, and it appears in many forms besides crab, such as "fish balls" or imitation lobster. But while its texture is decidedly crablike, the flavor of a fish puree (*surimi* is a Japanese word meaning "fish slurry") can never match the fresh sweetness of real crab. Only one large leg from an Alaskan king crab is needed for this recipe, but it makes all the difference.

---

1   **large cooked Alaskan king crab leg**

4   **(8 x 7-inch) toasted dried nori sheets**

Sushi Rice (recipe follows)

1   **small Japanese cucumber, peeled, seeded, and cut lengthwise into thin strips**

1   **firm but ripe avocado, pitted, peeled, and thinly sliced**

½   **cup smelt roe**

Pickled ginger

Soy sauce

Wasabi paste

Recipe courtesy of
**FELIX FANG
AND MONTI CARLO**

Cut open the crab shell with kitchen shears and extract the meat. Gently squeeze the crabmeat to remove any excess liquid, then coarsely tear the meat into large pieces. You should have about 6 ounces of crabmeat.

Place 1 nori sheet, shiny side down, on the work surface with one long side positioned closest to you. Using moistened hands, spread about 1 cup of the rice in an even layer over the nori sheet, leaving a ½-inch border on the top long side.

Turn the rice-covered nori sheet over onto a sheet of plastic wrap with the same long side positioned closest to you. Arrange one-fourth of the cucumber horizontally over the middle of the nori. Place one-fourth of the avocado slices and crabmeat over the cucumber. Lift the edge of the plastic wrap closest to you and roll the rice-covered nori away from you to enclose the filling, pressing gently on the plastic to form a tight roll. Place a bamboo sushi mat over the roll and plastic wrap, hold the mat in position, and press to make the roll firm.

Remove the mat and plastic wrap. Spoon the smelt roe over the sushi roll. Cover the sushi roll with plastic wrap again and pat the smelt eggs so they adhere to the top of the roll. Repeat to make 4 rolls total.

Dip a large, very sharp knife in water to moisten the blade. Cut each roll crosswise into 6 to 8 slices, cutting gently so they retain their shape, moistening the knife as needed before each slice.

Serve the rolls immediately with the pickled ginger, soy sauce, and wasabi.

SERVES 4

SUSHI RICE

1½ **cups short-grain white rice**

3 **tablespoons rice vinegar**

1½ **tablespoons sugar**

¼ **teaspoon salt**

1⅔ **cups water**

Put the rice in a large bowl and fill the bowl with cold water. Mix the rice gently with your hand until the water is cloudy. Drain in a sieve and repeat 3 times or until the water is nearly clear. This will help remove the starch from the rice.

Set the bowl of rice under cold running water for 1 minute. Drain well in a sieve for 15 to 30 minutes.

Meanwhile, stir the vinegar, sugar, and salt in a small bowl until the sugar dissolves. The mixture can be gently heated in a small saucepan over low heat to dissolve the sugar and make the vinegar slightly milder. Set the vinegar mixture aside.

Combine the rice and water in a medium, heavy-bottomed saucepan and bring the water to a boil over high heat. Reduce the heat to medium-low. Cover and simmer gently until all the water is absorbed and the rice is tender, about 12 minutes. Remove from the heat and let stand with the lid on for 10 to 15 minutes to complete the cooking process.

Spread the rice over a large, flat-bottomed wooden bowl or a baking sheet. Using a rice paddle or wooden spoon, slice through the rice at a 45-degree angle to break up any lumps, while slowly pouring the vinegar mixture over the rice, distributing evenly. Continue to slice, lifting and turning the rice from the outside to the center.

Fan the rice so that it cools to body temperature, turning it occasionally, about 8 minutes. Cooling gives a good flavor, texture, and gloss to the rice. If the rice becomes too cold, it hardens, so do not refrigerate .

To stop the rice from drying out, keep it covered with a damp cloth while making the sushi.

MAKES 4 CUPS

NIGIRI SUSHI

Felix and Monti, together again, bringing sushi to the people! In the Japanese tradition, actually handling the raw fish is a job reserved for the greatest sushi masters. An apprentice might prepare nothing but the sushi rice for, literally, years before being allowed to touch the handle of a fish knife.

But Westerners love sushi, and more and more of us make it at home, so we're not at all daunted by the thought of whether we're doing it "right." And this recipe removes any mystery about making individual pieces of nigiri sushi. The word *nigiri* means "hand-formed" and beginners in Japan typically shape nigiri sushi into a ball of rice with the fish wrapped around it, the classic oblong shape considered too difficult for any but master sushi chefs.

For most Americans, the only real concern is not how precisely our rice is shaped but how fresh our fish is. Be sure to ask for "sushi-grade" fish at your local market—and be prepared to pay for it. It doesn't come cheap, but it's worth it.

---

4 large shrimp, deveined

4 slices (2 x 1 x ¼ inch) sashimi-grade ahi tuna

4 slices (2 x 1 x ¼ inch) sashimi-grade salmon

4 slices (2 x 1 x ¼ inch) sashimi-grade yellowtail

1½ teaspoons prepared wasabi plus more for serving

About 2¼ cups Sushi Rice (page 121)

Pickled ginger

Soy sauce

Bring a medium saucepan of salted water to a simmer and prepare a medium bowl of ice water. Starting at the head end, slide a skewer down the length of each shrimp. Cook the shrimp in the water for 1 minute. Drain and submerge the shrimp in the ice water to cool. Drain well. Remove the skewers and peel the shrimp, leaving the tail end intact. Using a sharp knife, cut each shrimp along the belly to butterfly it, then flatten it.

Place 1 fish slice or 1 shrimp across the middle joints of your fingers, with your hand palm side up. Spread about ⅛ teaspoon of wasabi over the center of the fish slice. Moisten your other hand and squeeze about 2 tablespoons rice into a football shape that is about the size of the fish slice. Place the shaped rice on the fish.

With the hand holding the fish, curl your fingers to cup the fish and rice, and at the same time, with two fingers from your other hand, gently press the rice to adhere to the fish. Turn the sushi over and repeat this pressing motion. Using your thumb and middle finger, press the sides of the fish so that they cling to the sides of the rice. Set the nigiri on a plate, rice side down. Repeat until you have made 16 nigiri. Serve immediately with the pickled ginger, soy sauce, and wasabi.

Recipe courtesy of
**FELIX FANG AND
MONTI CARLO**

SERVES 4

While the term "sushi grade" sounds authoritative, and is

certainly bandied about when referring to fish used for sushi, it is in fact relatively meaningless. In other words, while the FDA has extremely stringent standards for the safe handling of fish for sale to the public, "sushi grade" is not a technical term. When you ask for sushi-grade fish from a reputable fishmonger, what you will likely get is an extremely high-end piece of very recently caught fish, but also one that has likely spent as many as 7 days in your fishmonger's freezer.

This is not a matter for concern. "Fresh" is a buzzword when it comes to any kind of fish except the kind that you're going to eat raw. Freezing the fish kills any potential for harmful bacteria, allowing you to safely consume your sushi. The fish can be stored at a very low temperature (-31°F) for 24 hours or at a higher temperature (-4°F) for a week. This regimen is cold enough, and long enough, to destroy any possible pathogens or parasites.

Anyone selling you sushi-grade fish at the price it's likely to command will also usually be happy to tell you precisely where the fish came from and how it's been treated. The best sushi-grade fish is actually line-caught by fishermen who immediately "spike" or kill the fish and rapidly transfer it to a commercial freezer at the appropriate temperature. (By the way, it's the "line-caught" part of the equation that costs you so much, not the trouble of freezing it.)

If for any reason you feel suspicious about the quality of a piece of fish that you intend to eat raw, or if you want to eat a piece of raw fish that you've caught yourself (and you other-wise feel safe about its provenance), place it in a home freezer chest that's set to -4°F. The box freezer that's part of your refrigerator will not get that cold, but a chest freezer usually can (some can get much colder). Freeze your fish for 7 days. After that, bring the fish to room temperature, and it will be safe to eat raw.

UNI AND ROCK SHRIMP SUSHI
WITH UNI AIOLI AND SHAVED FENNEL-MICROGREEN SALAD

L ong before the Sushi challenge, Stacey Amagrande expressed interest in making sushi, so when she found a sea urchin in the bottom of her Mystery Box, it wasn't surprising that she decided to turn it into a sushi component. She did surprise the judges by using uni in the aioli she made, adding a little chili oil to spark it up. She also used uni in the spicy ginger dressing she tossed with the microgreen salad. Aioli drizzled over the rock shrimp and avocado sushi added one more layer of creaminess, and a fillet of uni draped over the salad was a visual reminder of the flavors that infused each bite.

It's not a traditional Japanese sushi, but the judges considered it a restaurant-quality sushi dish. They ranked Stacey at the top of the challenge for her professionalism in layering the uni flavors through the dish.

FOR THE AIOLI

- 1 large egg yolk
- 1 teaspoon kosher salt
- ½ teaspoon cayenne
- 3 uni fillets (sea urchin roe)
- 3 tablespoons fresh lemon juice
- ½ teaspoon chili oil
- 3 tablespoons olive oil

FOR THE ROCK SHRIMP

- ⅓ cup fresh blood orange juice, strained
- 2 teaspoons soy sauce
- 1 teaspoon toasted sesame oil
- 1 teaspoon peeled, grated fresh ginger
- 12 ounces rock shrimp, peeled and deveined

FOR THE SALAD

- 1 small fennel bulb, shaved paper thin
- 1 cup wasabi microgreens
- 1 cup rainbow microgreens
- ½ cup corn shoots, coarsely chopped
- 4 fresh basil chiffonade
- ½ teaspoon peeled, grated fresh ginger
- ½ small avocado, peeled, pitted, and diced
- 4 uni fillets (sea urchin roe)

FOR THE SUSHI

- 4 dried nori sheets
- 3 cups Sushi Rice (page 121)
- About 2 teaspoons rice vinegar
- About 1 teaspoon wasabi paste
- 1½ small avocados, peeled, pitted, and sliced
- 4 sugar snap peas, stringed and slivered
- 8 fresh basil leaves
- 12 uni fillets (sea urchin roe), halved lengthwise

TO MAKE THE AIOLI: Combine the egg yolk, salt, and cayenne in a small food processor and process until smooth. Add the uni, lemon juice, and chili oil and blend until smooth. With the machine running, gradually blend in the olive oil, pouring it in a very thin, slow stream, until smooth and thick. Cover and refrigerate.

TO MAKE THE ROCK SHRIMP: Combine the orange juice, soy sauce, sesame oil, and ginger in a large, heavy-bottomed sauté pan. Bring to a simmer. Add the shrimp and cook for 2 minutes. Remove the pan from the heat and set aside to cool completely. Discard the cooking liquid. Reserve half of the shrimp for the sushi and half for the salad. Cover separately and refrigerate.

TO MAKE THE SALAD: Combine the fennel, microgreens, corn shoots, basil, and the reserved shrimp in a large wide bowl. Whisk together the ginger and 2 tablespoons of the aioli in a small bowl. Cover the salad and ginger-aioli dressing separately, and refrigerate until ready to serve.

TO MAKE THE SUSHI: Just before serving, lay a bamboo sushi mat on the work surface so that the slats run horizontally. Place 1 nori sheet on the mat with the long side facing you. With dampened hands, spread about ¾ cup of the rice onto it, leaving a ½-inch border along the top edge.

Lightly spritz some of the vinegar over the rice. Spread a small bit of wasabi paste horizontally across the center of the rice. Arrange 3 avocado slices overlapping slightly in a horizontal line over the wasabi paste. Top them with one-fourth of the snap peas and about one-fourth of the shrimp. Drizzle 2 teaspoons of aioli over. Top with 2 basil leaves. Grasp the edges of the nori and mat from the side facing you, lift the nori and mat slightly, and roll the nori evenly and tightly away from you, pressing down slightly with each quarter turn.

Seal the roll with a drop of water on the far edge of the nori, press the seam closed, and transfer the roll to a cutting board. Make 3 more rolls in the same manner. Trim the ends of the rolls and cut each roll crosswise into 6 pieces.

Arrange the sushi pieces, cut side up, on 4 plates. Spoon some aioli atop the sushi. Lay 1 piece of uni and 1 thin slice of avocado on each piece of sushi.

Just before serving the salad, use your fingers or chopsticks to gently toss it with the ginger-aioli dressing to coat lightly. Gently toss in the diced avocado. Mound the salad alongside the sushi on the plates. Top each salad with an uni fillet and serve immediately.

SERVES 4

Recipe courtesy of
STACEY AMAGRANDE

ESCOLAR
WITH WHIPPED AVOCADO AND CRISPY PLANTAINS

Because he'd won the previous challenge, Joshua Marks got to chose one of Graham's dishes for his fellow contestants to attempt. His choice was quickly nicknamed Presidential Sashimi, because this beautiful presentation of escolar, a type of fatty white tuna, is a dish that was served to President Obama at Graham's Chicago restaurant. The way Graham serves it at the restaurant, with a passion fruit sorbet scooped on at the end, is far more complex than the version that Christine Ha ultimately won with. Graham's original recipe is one that you'll likely make only if you're a professional cook, but it's fascinating to compare the two versions.

ESCOLAR

- 1 pound sashimi-grade escolar, cleaned
- 2 passion fruit
- 1 tablespoon crushed cocoa nibs
- 1 tablespoon extra-virgin olive oil
- Fleur de sel

WHIPPED AVOCADO

- 1 cup cilantro
- ½ cup flat-leaf parsley
- 1 shallot, peeled
- ½ tablespoon chopped jalapeño chile pepper (wear plastic gloves when handling)
- 1 clove garlic
- 1 cup ice water
- 2 avocados
- 2 limes
- Salt

CRISPY PLANTAINS

- 3 cups canola oil
- 2 green plantains
- ½ tablespoon ancho powder
- Salt

ESCOLAR

Trim any fat from the escolar and slice into ⅛-inch planks.

Cut the passion fruit in half and scoop out the flesh and seeds with a spoon. Discard the husk and reserve the seeds.

Arrange the fish on plates. Dust lightly with the cocoa nibs, and sprinkle with the oil, fleur de sel, and passion fruit seeds.

WHIPPED AVOCADO

In a blender, combine the cilantro, parsley, shallot, chile pepper, garlic, and ice water. Puree until smooth.

Cut the avocados in half and remove the pit. With a spoon, scoop the avocado into the blender and puree until smooth.

Cut the limes and squeeze the juice into the blender. Season the mixture with salt.

Pass the puree through a fine-mesh strainer and reserve in a squeeze bottle.

CRISPY PLANTAINS

Heat the canola oil in a saucepan to 325°F.

With a sharp paring knife, remove the skin of the plantains and rinse the flesh with cold water. Cut the plantain into three segments. With a Japanese mandoline, cut long ribbons out of the plantains. Rinse the ribbons in cold water and shake dry.

Fry the ribbons in the oil until crispy, then drain. Toss in a bowl with the ancho powder and salt.

Place a ribbon of plantain over the fish. Squeeze a few dollops of the whipped avocado on the plate.

SERVES 6

PRESIDENTIAL SASHIMI

In their efforts to replicate Graham's complex sashimi dish, Christine Ha and Frank Mirando both won. Their versions were similar in terms of the essentials, but Christine added a little sour cream to her avocado mousse to smooth and lighten it and astonished the judges with the visual presentation. Don't hesitate to plate it up according to her directions below.

FOR THE AVOCADO MOUSSE

- 1 firm but ripe avocado, peeled and pitted
- 1½ tablespoons fresh lemon juice
- 1 tablespoon sour cream
- ½ teaspoon wasabi powder
- About 1 teaspoon kosher salt

FOR THE PLANTAIN CHIPS

- Canola oil
- 1 small green plantain
- Kosher salt

FOR THE TUNA

- 16 slices (2 x 1½ x ¼) white tuna
- 2 radishes, sliced into paper-thin rounds
- 1 scallion (dark green part only), very thinly sliced on a sharp bias
- 2 passion fruits

Recipe courtesy of
CHRISTINE HA

- About 1 tablespoon cocoa nibs
- About 2 teaspoons Maldon sea salt
- 2 teaspoons extra-virgin olive oil

TO MAKE THE AVOCADO MOUSSE: Combine the avocado, lemon juice, sour cream, wasabi, and 1 teaspoon of the salt in a small food processor and blend until smooth. Season to taste with more salt. Transfer the mousse to a pastry bag fitted with a small plain tip and refrigerate.

TO MAKE THE PLANTAIN CHIPS: Heat 1 to 2 inches of oil in a medium, heavy-bottomed saucepan over medium heat to 375°F. Peel the plantain, then cut it in half lengthwise. Cut one half on a sharp bias into 16 paper-thin slices. Using a round cookie cutter, cut each slice into half-moons. Cover and refrigerate the leftover plantain half for another use. Working in batches, fry the slices until golden brown, about 3 minutes. Using a slotted spoon, transfer the chips to paper towels to drain. Season with salt.

TO ASSEMBLE THE TUNA: Lay 4 tuna slices on each of 4 plates. Pipe a small mound of the avocado mousse alongside each slice. Lay 1 radish slice against each mound of mousse and garnish with the scallion. Cut the passion fruits in half and spoon their pulp, juice, and seeds over the tuna. Sprinkle with the cocoa nibs and sea salt. Drizzle the oil evenly and serve immediately with the plantain chips.

SERVES 4

WINE PAIRING This delicate seafood crudo dish calls for a lighter-style wine that won't overpower it. An Arneis from the great Italian winemaking region of Piedmont is an excellent choice. Once used primarily to soften the great Nebbiolo wines, today it is a stand-alone varietal. These wines are lighter weight and aromatic, making them the perfect complement to raw white tuna. Look for one that is aged in steel with no oak.

Tracy Kontos

A disastrous salmon dish led to Tracy Kontos's exit from *MasterChef* Season 2. During the time she'd been a contestant, she had lost her corporate sales job, so her departure from the competition left her with some big choices to make.

"Luckily, upon my exit from the show, the judges presented me with opportunities to work in their kitchens," Tracy says. "Since I had lost my job, I knew this was a pivotal moment in my life. Decisions needed to be made, and the winning factor was that I loved to cook. In the end, I knew I wanted to cook for the rest of my life.

"With that said, I had never spent time in a professional kitchen, so I thought it best to start with an apprenticeship or 'staging' position. Immediately after the show had ended, I jumped in headfirst to the offers the judges had made. My first offer from Graham led me to Chicago for a chance to learn at [his] restaurant. Needless to say, the experience was life-changing. As eclectic as the man himself, Graham's restaurant was inspiring. Next, I was on to NYC to visit Del Posto, a restaurant of Joe Bastianich's. Del Posto was perhaps one of the most captivating experiences I've had yet. The size of the kitchen and staff is enormous, and you can hardly believe a kitchen like that exists! Both restaurants taught me that a commitment to innovation, perfection, flavor, and execution would undoubtedly need to be the base of my career. I'll forever be grateful to Graham and Joe.

"From NYC, I decided to make the move from my home in Florida to California. Former contestant Alejandra Schrader and I decided to open our own private chef company. Cucina Cocina was launched in 2011 and has been going strong ever since."

SALMON REDEMPTION SALAD

I made my dramatic exit out of the *MasterChef* kitchen all due to this little fish. So, ever since that moment, I vowed I would perfect salmon in every way possible! Here's my favorite way to enjoy it. Poaching in olive oil keeps the salmon moist and complements the flavor of the fish nicely. Believe it or not, olive oil poaching does not make the fish greasy. It's a foolproof way to perfect fish for those who are intimidated."

FOR THE SALMON

- 6 (5-ounce) boneless, skinless salmon fillets
- 4 cups (or more) olive oil, as needed
- 12 sprigs fresh thyme
- 4 cloves garlic, peeled and bruised
- 8 whole black peppercorns
- 1 orange

  Kosher salt and freshly ground black pepper

  Fresh oregano, for garnish

  Fresh chives, thinly sliced, for garnish

FOR THE VINAIGRETTE

- 2 tablespoons fresh orange juice
- 2 tablespoons minced shallots
- 2 tablespoons white wine vinegar
- 1½ teaspoons finely grated orange zest
- ½ teaspoon kosher salt
- ¼ teaspoon coarsely ground black pepper
- ¼ cup olive oil

FOR THE SALAD

- 2 cups mixed baby greens
- 1 cup shaved fennel (paper thin)
- ¼ cup finely julienned watermelon radishes
- ¼ cup fresh basil chiffonade
- ¼ cup fresh mint chiffonade
- ¼ cup fresh fennel fronds
- 2 tablespoons fresh oregano leaves
- 1 orange, segmented

  Kosher salt and freshly ground black pepper

SALMON REDEMPTION SALAD

(continued)

TO MAKE THE SALMON: Let the salmon stand at room temperature for 30 minutes.

Combine the oil, thyme, garlic, and peppercorns in a large, heavy-bottomed skillet just wide enough to hold the salmon in a single layer without touching. Using a vegetable peeler, remove the zest from the orange and add to the oil, reserving the orange. Heat the oil over medium-low heat to 175°F.

Season the salmon on both sides with salt and pepper, then lay the salmon in a single layer in the oil, ensuring that it is completely covered by the oil. The temperature of the oil will drop, so increase the heat slightly (never above medium-low) just until it reaches 175°F again, then reduce the heat to maintain the temperature.

Cook until the fish is completely opaque on top, about 10 minutes. Using a flexible metal spatula, remove the salmon from the oil and transfer it to a plate lined with paper towels to drain.

TO MAKE THE VINAIGRETTE: Whisk the orange juice, shallots, vinegar, zest, salt, and pepper in a medium bowl to blend. Gradually add the oil in a slow stream, whisking until well blended.

TO MAKE THE SALAD: Toss the greens, fennel, radishes, basil, mint, fennel, oregano, and orange segments in a large bowl to blend. Just before serving, toss the salad with enough vinaigrette to coat. Season the salad to taste with salt and pepper and serve immediately.

TO SERVE: Arrange the salmon on a serving platter, and top it with the oregano and chives. Cut the reserved orange in half and squeeze the juice over the salmon. Sprinkle with salt and serve immediately with the salad.

SERVES 6

SPRING VEGETABLE TERRINE
WITH PRAWN MOUSSE, PEA PUREE, AND MICROGREEN SALAD

For the Michelin Star challenge, while the Girls Team made the elegant Thai Seafood Soup (page 117), the Boys Team took an entirely different approach. This elaborate seafood-flavored appetizer is, in fact, a vegetable terrine, with jumbo asparagus and multicolored heirloom carrots (orange, yellow, purple) set in an intense gelée made of seafood broth. The scallops, mussels, and spot prawns have given up their flavor to the court bouillon that will become the jelly to hold the terrine together. The prawn tails become a creamy mousse, and the peas are a sweet puree that pulls all the flavors together. It's an incredibly refined dish, something you'd expect to find in a four-star restaurant. And here's how you can do it at home.

FOR THE GELÉE

- 1 bunch jumbo asparagus, bottoms trimmed, spears peeled
- 5 thin carrots (assorted colors), peeled
- 6 prawns with heads
- 6 mussels
- 3 sea scallops
- 2 large sprigs fresh tarragon
- 2 large sprigs fresh lemon thyme
- ½ fennel bulb, sliced
- ¼ cup fumé blanc or other dry white wine
- 4¼ cups water
- 1 (¼-ounce) envelope unflavored powdered gelatin

FOR THE PRAWN MOUSSE AND PEA PUREE

- 1 cup heavy cream
  Kosher salt
- 1 cup frozen peas, thawed

FOR THE MICROGREEN SALAD

- 2 cups microgreens
- 1 tablespoon extra-virgin olive oil
- 1 teaspoon fresh lemon juice
  Kosher salt and freshly ground black pepper

TO MAKE THE GELÉE: Line a 12 x 9 x 1-inch rimmed baking sheet with plastic wrap so there are no seams and the plastic wrap extends up the sides of the baking sheet.

Prepare a medium bowl of ice water. Cook the asparagus in a medium saucepan of boiling salted water until crisp-tender, about 3 minutes. Fish out the asparagus and submerge in the bowl of ice water to cool completely. Drain well and refill the bowl with ice. Add the carrots to the same pot of boiling water and cook until crisp-tender, about 4 minutes. Drain, then submerge them in the bowl of ice water to cool completely. Drain well.

Cut the carrots and asparagus crosswise into ¼-inch-thick rounds. Arrange the rounds in a single layer on the prepared baking sheet. Cover the baking sheet and set it on a level rack in the refrigerator while preparing the gelée.

Remove the heads and shells from the prawns, and set the tails aside to use for the mousse. Place the prawn heads and shells in a large, heavy-bottomed saucepan. Add the mussels, scallops, tarragon, thyme, fennel, wine, and 4 cups of the water. Bring to a boil over high heat. Reduce the heat to medium-low and simmer gently for 15 minutes. Strain the broth through a fine-mesh sieve into a large bowl, then cover and keep hot. You should have 2¾ cups of broth. If you have more, simmer the broth until it is reduced to 2¾ cups. If you have less, add enough water to equal 2¾ cups.

Place the remaining ¼ cup water in a small bowl. Sprinkle the gelatin over and set aside until the gelatin softens, about 10 minutes. Stir the softened gelatin into the hot broth until it is completely dissolved. Cool slightly. Pour the gelée over the carrot and asparagus rounds, then adjust the vegetables so they are evenly dispersed and well arranged. Refrigerate until set, at least 1 hour.

TO MAKE THE PRAWN MOUSSE AND PEA PUREE: Bring the cream to a boil in a small, heavy-bottomed saucepan over high heat. Add the reserved peeled prawn tails to the cream and remove the pan from the heat. Cover and set aside until the prawns are cooked, turning them over after the first 3 minutes to ensure that they cook evenly, about 7 minutes. Using a slotted spoon, transfer the prawns to a blender (preferably a very powerful one, such as a Vitamix) and puree, adding enough of the cream to form a smooth puree. Season the mousse to taste with salt. Transfer the mousse to a squeeze bottle or piping bag and refrigerate.

Cook the peas in a small saucepan of boiling salted water until tender, about 2 minutes. Drain, then submerge them in a bowl of ice water to cool. Drain well. Transfer the peas to a small food processor and blend well, adding a pinch of salt and enough water to form a smooth puree. Strain the puree through a fine-mesh sieve into a small bowl. Transfer the puree to another squeeze bottle and refrigerate.

TO MAKE THE MICROGREEN SALAD: Toss the microgreens in a medium bowl with the oil and lemon juice, then season to taste with salt and pepper.

TO SERVE: Cut the gelée into eight 4 x 3-inch rectangles and lay them on 8 plates. Mound the microgreen salad alongside the gelée. Pipe the prawn mousse and pea puree alongside the gelée and serve immediately.

SERVES 8

SPRING VEGETABLE TERRINE
(continued)

Recipe courtesy of
**FRANK MIRANDO
AND JOSHUA MARKS**

INDIAN CATFISH IN COCONUT-LEEK BROTH
WITH GARAM MASALA EGGPLANT

Catfish doesn't figure much in New York kitchens, and Frank Mirando wasn't sure he had ever even cooked catfish before he was faced with a whole one in the *MasterChef* kitchens. His version is miles away from the breaded and deep-fried catfish favored in the deep South, where catfish is far more regularly caught and cooked. (If you're not accustomed to seeing catfish too often in your neck of the woods, try another meaty white fish such as halibut.) The potent Indian spices and the creamy coconut broth turned out to be an ideal pairing with the meaty white fish, however, and the fried eggplant slices tossed with spicy-sweet garam masala add body and heartiness to the dish.

FOR THE FISH

- 2   (1½ to 1¾-pound) whole catfish, cleaned and gutted
- 1   teaspoon brown mustard seeds
- ¼   cup all-purpose flour
- 2   tablespoons cornstarch
- 1   teaspoon ground coriander
- 1   teaspoon ground cumin
- 1   teaspoon turmeric
- ⅓   cup unsweetened coconut milk, whisked to blend

FOR THE COCONUT-LEEK BROTH

- 5   cloves garlic
- 5   (1-inch) pieces fresh ginger, peeled
- 1   teaspoon kosher salt plus more for seasoning
- 1   tablespoon whole black peppercorns
- 3   leeks, very thinly sliced
- 2   tablespoons canola oil
- 1   shallot, thinly sliced
- 2   red jalapeño chile peppers, thinly sliced (wear plastic gloves when handling)
- 1   teaspoon brown mustard seeds
- 1   teaspoon ground coriander
- 1   teaspoon ground cumin
- 1⅓ cups unsweetened coconut milk, whisked to blend

FOR THE EGGPLANT AND SCALLIONS

- 1   Chinese eggplant, cut crosswise on a bias into ⅛-inch-thick slices
- 1   tablespoon kosher salt plus more for seasoning
- 1   teaspoon garam masala
- 1   teaspoon canola oil plus more for frying
- 4   scallions, trimmed

    Freshly ground black pepper

- 4   small sprigs fresh flat-leaf parsley
- 2   tablespoons fresh lime juice
- 1   orange

TO MAKE THE FISH: Remove the 2 fillets from each catfish (you should have about 1 pound of bones). Set aside the fish bones and heads for making the broth. Remove and discard the skin from the fillets, then cover and refrigerate.

Stir the mustard seeds in a small, heavy-bottomed sauté pan over medium heat until toasted and fragrant, about 3 minutes. Grind the seeds in a spice grinder or mortar and pestle. Mix the ground seeds with the flour, cornstarch, coriander, cumin, and turmeric on a small baking sheet to blend. Pour the coconut milk in a wide shallow bowl. Set the milk and flour mixture aside to coat the fish just before frying and serving.

TO MAKE THE BROTH: Combine the reserved fish bones and heads, garlic, ginger, salt, peppercorns, and 2 of the leeks in a large, heavy-bottomed pot. Add enough water to nearly cover, about 6 cups. Bring to a boil and simmer until reduced to about 4 cups, about 30 minutes. Strain the broth and discard the solids.

Heat the oil in a large, heavy-bottomed saucepan over medium heat. Add the shallot, jalapeños, mustard seeds, coriander, and cumin. Sauté until the shallot is tender, about 3 minutes. Add the coconut milk, broth, and the remaining leek. Simmer until the broth is reduced to 3 cups, about 30 minutes. Spoon off the excess fat from the top of the broth. Season to taste with salt and keep warm.

TO MAKE THE EGGPLANT AND SCALLIONS: Meanwhile, preheat the oven to 500°F.

Arrange the eggplant slices in a single layer on a large baking sheet. Sprinkle the salt over the eggplant and set aside until the excess water from the eggplant is exuded, about 15 minutes. Rinse off the excess liquid and salt, then pat dry with paper towels. Sprinkle the garam masala over the eggplant and toss gently to coat.

Heat 2 inches of oil in a large, heavy-bottomed skillet (preferably cast-iron) over high heat until it registers 350°F on a deep-fry thermometer. Working in batches, fry the eggplant slices until they are golden brown, about 3 minutes. Using a slotted spoon, transfer the eggplant to a baking sheet lined with paper towels to absorb the excess oil. Return the oil to 350°F (for cooking the fish).

INDIAN CATFISH IN COCONUT-LEEK BROTH
(continued)

Place the scallions on a baking sheet and coat them with 1 teaspoon of the oil. Season with salt and pepper. Roast until the scallions are tender and slightly charred, about 7 minutes.

TO COOK THE FISH: Dredge the catfish fillets in the bowl of coconut milk to coat lightly, then dredge them in the flour mixture to coat lightly. Place 2 fillets in the pan with the hot oil, and fry until golden and just cooked through, about 5 minutes total. Using the slotted spatula, transfer the fillets to a rack set over paper towels to drain briefly. Return the oil to 350°F and fry the remaining fillets in the same manner.

TO SERVE: Ladle the broth into 4 wide shallow bowls. Place the catfish in the bowls and drape the eggplant slices over. Top with the scallions and parsley. Drizzle the lime juice over, grate some orange zest over, and serve immediately.

SERVES 4

Recipe courtesy of
FRANK MIRANDO

SPANISH-STYLE GRILLED SPOT PRAWNS WITH PAELLA BASMATI AND SALSA VERDE

Shrimp paella is a classic in Spanish cooking, with the little crustaceans nestled into the hot rice just at the end of cooking, so the steaming paella turns them just pink and opaque, not overcooked and tough. Becky Reams cleverly played off the paella method of serving shrimp, making a paella-style base of fragrant rice, including the traditional seasoning of saffron threads, but she grilled the spot prawns and served them on top of the rice, so that they were the highlight, not the garnish. The meaty, lobsterlike flesh of spot prawns stands up well to the pungent Salsa Verde, and the roasted tomatoes around the plate help marry the sweetness of the prawns with the flavorful rice.

FOR THE PRAWNS

- 8 large live spot prawns (with roe; about 1¾ pounds total)
- About 1 tablespoon extra-virgin olive oil
- 2 tablespoons unsalted butter
- 1 teaspoon minced fresh flat-leaf parsley
- Kosher salt

PRAWN STOCK

- 6 live spot prawns (about 14 ounces)
- 5 cups water
- ½ cup assorted fresh herb stems (such as parsley, chives, cilantro, and tarragon)
- 2 scallions, chopped
- ½ shallot
- 2 cloves garlic
- Pinch of kosher salt

FOR THE RICE

- 6 vine-ripened tomatoes, quartered and then halved
- 4 large cloves garlic, bruised, plus 2 cloves garlic, minced
- ¼ cup plus 2 tablespoons extra-virgin olive oil
- Kosher salt and freshly ground black pepper
- 2 tablespoons minced shallot
- 1 cup basmati rice
- ¼ teaspoon saffron threads
- ½ cup Chardonnay
- About 2 cups Prawn Stock
- 4 tablespoons (½ stick) unsalted butter, diced

FOR THE VINAIGRETTE

- 2 tablespoons fresh lemon juice
- 1 tablespoon Prawn Stock
- ¼ cup extra-virgin olive oil
- 1 tablespoon prawn roe
- Kosher salt

SALSA VERDE

- ½ cup very coarsely chopped fresh flat-leaf parsley
- ¼ cup very coarsely chopped fresh chives
- ¼ cup very coarsely chopped fresh cilantro
- ¼ cup very coarsely chopped fresh tarragon
- ¼ cup extra-virgin olive oil
- ¼ cup Prawn Stock
- 1 teaspoon finely grated lemon zest (from ½ lemon)
- 2 tablespoons fresh lemon juice
- 1 clove garlic, minced
- ½ teaspoon red-pepper flakes
- Pinch of kosher salt plus more to taste

TO MAKE THE PRAWNS: Gently scrape any roe from under the prawn tails and set it aside. Pierce the prawns between the eyes through the head to instantly kill them. Turn the prawns belly side up and cut them in half. Cover the prawns and roe separately and refrigerate until ready to use.

Just before serving, brush the rack of a barbecue grill with the oil and prepare the grill for high heat; or preheat an indoor grill pan over high heat.

Melt the butter in a small bowl and stir in the parsley. Brush the parsley butter over the prawn flesh and season with salt. Lay the prawns, flesh side down, on the grill and set a pan on top to weight down the prawns. Cook until grill marks form, 1 to 2 minutes, then turn the prawns over and cook until just cooked through but still juicy and tender, about 1 minute.

TO MAKE THE PRAWN STOCK: Peel the prawns and remove the heads. Refrigerate the prawn flesh for another use. Place the shells and heads in a large, heavy-bottomed saucepan. Add the water, herb stems, scallions, shallot, and garlic to the pan and bring the water to a simmer over high heat. Reduce the heat to medium-low. Cover and simmer for 45 minutes.

Strain the stock through a fine-mesh sieve into an 8-cup measuring cup or medium bowl, pressing on the solids to extract as much liquid as possible. Discard the solids. You should have about 4 cups of stock.

TO MAKE THE RICE: Preheat the oven to 450°F. Toss the tomatoes and the bruised garlic cloves with ¼ cup of the oil and season with salt and pepper. Arrange the tomatoes on a baking sheet and roast until they are tender and lightly caramelized, about 30 minutes.

Meanwhile, heat a medium, heavy-bottomed saucepan over medium-high heat. Add the remaining 2 tablespoons oil and the shallot, and sauté until translucent, about 2 minutes. Add the minced garlic and ½ teaspoon salt and sauté until fragrant, about 30 seconds. Add the rice and stir until it is toasted, about 2 minutes. Crumble the saffron and stir it into the rice. Add the wine and simmer until it evaporates completely, about 2 minutes. Stir in the stock. Cover and simmer gently over medium-low heat until the liquid is absorbed and the rice is almost tender, about 15 minutes.

Remove the pan from the heat. Scatter the butter pieces over the rice, then fluff the rice with a fork. Cover and set the pan aside (off the heat) until the rice is tender, about 10 minutes. Season to taste with salt and pepper.

SPANISH-STYLE GRILLED SPOT PRAWNS

(continued)

Recipe courtesy of
BECKY REAMS

TO MAKE THE SALSA VERDE: Combine all the ingredients in a small food processor. Process until the herbs are very finely chopped. Season to taste with more salt.

TO MAKE THE VINAIGRETTE: Whisk the lemon juice and stock in a medium bowl to blend. Gradually whisk in the oil, then add the roe and whisk until the roe breaks apart. Season to taste with salt. Set aside.

TO SERVE: Mound the rice in the centers of 4 plates. Top with the roasted tomatoes. Arrange the prawns on top. Spoon some Salsa Verde over the shrimp. Drizzle the vinaigrette around and top with some reserved prawn roe. Serve immediately.

SERVES 4

 **MYSTERY BOX** / California Spot Prawns

They're strange little creatures, and any contestant not

from the West Coast had very possibly never heard of them before: spot prawns. They are found in the North Pacific from Alaska down to about San Diego, and they're only fished from very deep waters. They tend to hang out in the rocky caverns of the ocean's floor, a good 700 feet down.

For this challenge, the contestants' Mystery Boxes actually contained an aquarium. The producers had found particularly large spot prawns, and in the bottom of each aquarium was a giant spot prawn, almost like a little lobster.

Why the aquarium? More than perhaps any other seafood, spot prawns must be live when you get them. As soon as they die, an enzyme is released in their heads that spreads through the body and begins to degrade the meat. So while you might be able to source frozen cooked spot prawns at a fishmonger, the fresh ones tend to hug the West Coast, the only place where they grow and also where they can be found live in aquariums at fish shops.

Live, their torsos seem almost to glow. They have striped legs and tentacles and a few spots distributed on their torsos. Cooked, the shells turn bright red, more like a regular shrimp. Spot prawns are actually the largest shrimp harvested in the United States, which perhaps in some way accounts for the flavor that makes them so noteworthy as dinner: The flesh is particularly sweet and meaty, so they're really more like an exquisite little lobster than a shrimp.

SPOT PRAWN CEVICHE

A lthough any fresh fish can be prepared as a ceviche, a meaty or oily fish such as sea bass, mackerel, or tuna is often used in traditional South American preparations. The only given is that lime juice and salt are always in the recipe, both to season and "cook" the ceviche through the chemical interaction of the acid with the fish, which turns it opaque. David Martinez took advantage of the spot prawn's meaty tail by preparing it very simply with lime and salt, then slicing it thin to serve on a garlicky basil puree made with a stock from the heads. The flavors were carefully layered to echo each other, and the sharp pico de gallo definitely offers additional bite to the lime-drenched prawns.

16	live spot prawns (about 2 pounds total)
1	teaspoon kosher salt plus more for the pico de gallo
½	cup plus 3 tablespoons fresh lime juice
3	tablespoons olive oil
1	tomato, finely diced
½	red onion, finely diced
1	jalapeño chile pepper, finely diced (wear plastic gloves when handling)
3	tablespoons finely chopped fresh cilantro
12	cloves garlic, minced
4	large fresh basil leaves, minced
½	cup water
1½	teaspoons white balsamic vinegar
1	avocado, peeled, pitted, and diced
	Cilantro sprigs, for garnish

Remove the heads and shells from the prawns and reserve them. Toss the peeled prawns, salt, ½ cup lime juice, and 1 tablespoon of the oil in a glass baking dish to coat. Set aside until the prawns are opaque on the outside but still translucent in the center, turning the prawns after the first 30 minutes, about 1 hour.

Combine the tomato, onion, jalapeños, chopped cilantro, and the remaining 3 tablespoons lime juice in a medium bowl. Season the pico de gallo generously with salt.

Heat the remaining 2 tablespoons oil in a medium, heavy-bottomed saucepan over medium heat. Add the reserved prawn heads and shells, the garlic, and basil and sauté until the garlic is tender, about 2 minutes. Add the water and bring the mixture to a simmer. Reduce the heat to medium-low and simmer gently for 20 minutes, pressing on the prawn heads occasionally. Transfer the prawn heads to a bowl and set aside to cool slightly. When cool enough to handle, squeeze the prawn heads to extract as much liquid as possible into the saucepan, then discard the heads. Transfer the mixture to a blender, add the vinegar, and puree until smooth. Transfer the puree to a bowl and refrigerate until cold.

Spoon the puree in the centers of 4 plates. Cut the prawn tails crosswise and on a slight bias into thin slices, and arrange them over the puree. Spoon the pico de gallo on top. Top with the avocado, then garnish with the cilantro sprigs and serve.

SERVES 4

Recipe courtesy of
DAVID MARTINEZ

CLAY POT CATFISH
WITH PICKLED CARROTS AND CUCUMBERS

Here it is, the recipe everyone has been waiting for from Season 3. Catfish is such a humble fish, a bottom feeder that can taste muddy if not cooked properly. Christine Ha didn't try to gussy it up with a four-star presentation. Instead, she gently brought out the best in it.

She dressed it with some potent Asian flavors—garlic, fish sauce, scallions, and cilantro—and, the magic touch, a little dark caramel that she poured over the fish before braising it in its modest clay pot. This classic technique in Vietnamese cooking brings out the best in a meaty slab of catfish. (If your fishmonger doesn't have these thicker catfish "steaks," ask for fillets instead.) And her presentation, on a fragrant heap of jasmine rice, with a mound of tangy quick-pickled vegetables, hit all the right notes.

FOR THE PICKLED CARROTS AND CUCUMBERS

- 2 small carrots, peeled and thinly sliced
- 2 small cucumbers, thinly sliced into rounds
- ½ cup rice vinegar
- 6 tablespoons sugar
- 2 tablespoons kosher salt

FOR THE FISH

- ¼ cup canola oil
- 2 small shallots, sliced
- 2 cloves garlic, minced
- 1 teaspoon cayenne
- 4 (1- to 1½-inch-thick) skinless catfish steaks
- ¼ cup sugar
- 2 tablespoons plus ½ cup water
- 2 tablespoons fish sauce
- 3 cups steamed jasmine rice
- 2 scallions, thinly sliced
- Cilantro sprigs, for garnish
- Lemon wedges

CLAY POT CATFISH

(continued)

TO MAKE THE PICKLED CARROTS AND CUCUMBERS: Toss the carrots, cucumbers, vinegar, sugar, and salt in a large bowl. Cover and refrigerate.

TO MAKE THE FISH: Heat the oil in a large, heavy-bottomed sauté pan over medium-high heat. Add the shallots and garlic and sauté just until fragrant, about 1 minute. Stir in the cayenne. Add the catfish and cook until they are golden brown on both sides but still raw in the center. Transfer the catfish to a clay pot. Be sure your clay pot is approved for stovetop cooking. Pour off the oil from the pan and spoon the shallots and garlic over the fish in the pot.

Stir the sugar and 2 tablespoons of the water in a small, heavy-bottomed saucepan over low heat until the sugar dissolves. Brush down the sides of the pan with a very wet pastry brush to remove any sugar granules. Increase the heat to medium-high and cook, swirling the pan constantly but not stirring the sugar mixture, until the sugar dissolves and becomes golden brown, about 5 minutes. Stir in the remaining ½ cup water.

Pour the caramel sauce over the fish in the pot. Add the fish sauce and put the pot over very low heat. Simmer, uncovered, until reduced by about half, about 15 minutes.

TO SERVE: Mound the steamed rice in 4 wide bowls. Set the catfish steaks on top of the rice and spoon the sauce over the fish. Set the bowls on a large plate. Mound the pickled carrots and cucumbers on the plate. Sprinkle the scallions over the fish and pickles, and garnish with the cilantro, as desired. Serve immediately with lemon wedges.

SERVES 4

Recipe courtesy of
CHRISTINE HA

TEMPURA-STYLE SHRIMP
WITH THAI COCONUT BROTH AND SPICED YUCCA CHIPS

The whole point of tempura is to get it as crisp, light, greaseless, and dry as possible, right? Becky Reams turns that assumption on its ear by floating her coconut-coated tempura shrimp in a bowl of tangy, Thai-flavored broth. It's a stunning visual trick—hot, freshly fried shrimp dipped in a creamy coconut sauce mixed with spicy Sriracha and set afloat on little cucumber rafts—but the result really works. Have everything ready to go before you even think of dipping a shrimp in the tempura batter.

This dish tastes best when the crispness of the batter is just starting to melt into the creamy and spicy coconut broth, a clever melding of all sorts of flavors and textures. The spiced yucca chips give you an added buzz, thanks to their coating of Szechuan peppercorns, which set your tongue to tingling.

FOR THE SHRIMP STOCK

- 1 pound large shrimp
- 7 cups water
- 1 (2-inch) piece fresh ginger, peeled and halved
- 1 shallot, halved lengthwise
- 3 tablespoons sake
- 2 teaspoons kosher salt

FOR THE SRIRACHA-COCONUT SAUCE

- 1 can (13.5 ounces) unsweetened coconut milk (not shaken or stirred)
- 1 tablespoon Sriracha
- ½ teaspoon fish sauce
- ½ teaspoon finely grated lime zest

FOR THE THAI COCONUT BROTH

- 1 tablespoon canola oil
- 4 cloves garlic, minced

- 1 Fresno chile pepper, thinly sliced (wear plastic gloves when handling)
- ½ serrano chile pepper, thinly sliced (wear plastic gloves when handling)
- 2 scallions (white and pale green parts only), sliced
- 4 teaspoons peeled, grated fresh ginger
- 1 teaspoon grated lime zest
- 3 tablespoons fresh lime juice
- ½ teaspoon fish sauce

FOR THE TEMPURA-STYLE SHRIMP

- Canola oil
- 1 cup store-bought tempura batter mix
- 3 tablespoons finely grated dried coconut (unsweetened)
- About 1 cup ice-cold sparkling water
- Kosher salt

SPICED YUCCA CHIPS

- 1 (4-ounce) piece yucca root, peeled
- 1½ teaspoons Szechuan peppercorns
- ¾ teaspoon brown mustard seeds
- ¾ teaspoon whole coriander seeds
- ¼ teaspoon cayenne
- Canola oil
- Kosher salt

FOR THE GARNISH

- 1 cucumber, peeled, seeded, and cut into batons
- ¼ cup fresh cilantro
- 1 Fresno chile pepper, very thinly sliced into rounds (wear plastic gloves when handling)

TEMPURA-STYLE SHRIMP

(continued)

TO MAKE THE SHRIMP STOCK: Peel the shrimp and set the shells in a large saucepan. Devein the shrimp, place them in a bowl, then cover and refrigerate until ready to use.

Add the water, ginger, shallot, sake, and salt to the saucepan. Bring the water to a boil over high heat, then reduce the heat and simmer gently until the stock is reduced to 5 cups, about 30 minutes. Strain the stock into a bowl, pressing on the solids to extract as much liquid as possible. Discard the shells and set the stock aside.

TO MAKE THE SRIRACHA-COCONUT SAUCE: Spoon ¼ cup of the thick coconut cream off the top of the coconut milk in the can and put it in a large bowl. Add the Sriracha, fish sauce, and zest to the bowl and whisk to blend. Cover and set the sauce aside. Reserve the remaining coconut milk for the Coconut Broth.

TO MAKE THE THAI COCONUT BROTH: Heat the oil in a large, heavy-bottomed saucepan over medium-high heat. Add the garlic, chile peppers, and scallions and sauté until fragrant and the garlic just begins to brown lightly, about 1 minute. Stir in the ginger, lime zest, lime juice, fish sauce, and the reserved coconut milk. Simmer until the mixture thickens and is reduced by about one-third, about 5 minutes.

Add the shrimp stock and simmer until the sauce is reduced to 3½ cups, about 15 minutes. Strain the broth through a fine-mesh sieve into a small saucepan. Rewarm the broth before serving.

TO MAKE THE TEMPURA-STYLE SHRIMP: Heat 3 inches of oil in a large wok or pot over medium-high heat until a deep-fry thermometer registers 375°F. Adjust the heat to maintain the temperature.

In a large bowl, stir the tempura mix, coconut, and enough sparkling water to form a thin, slightly lumpy batter. Working in batches, dip the reserved shrimp in the batter to coat lightly (the batter should coat the shrimp but be transparent). Fry the shrimp until they are just cooked through and pale golden, about 2 minutes. Using a mesh strainer or slotted spoon, remove the shrimp from the oil and place them on paper towels to drain the excess oil. While the shrimp are still hot, season them with salt. Allow the temperature of the oil to return before frying each batch.

TO MAKE THE SPICED YUCCA CHIPS: Using a mandoline or vegetable slicer, cut the yucca root into paper-thin round slices. Soak them in a large bowl of ice water for 5 to 15 minutes. Drain and arrange the slices in a single layer on paper towels. Pat them with more towels to dry thoroughly.

Stir the peppercorns, mustard seeds, and coriander seeds in a small, heavy-bottomed sauté pan over medium heat until very fragrant and toasted, about 1 minute. Grind the toasted spices in a mortar and pestle. Mix in the cayenne.

Heat 2 inches of oil in a large wok or pot over medium-high heat until a deep-fry thermometer registers 375°F. Adjust the heat to maintain the temperature. Working in batches, fry the yucca slices until they are a pale tan color and crisp, about 2 minutes. Using a mesh strainer or slotted spoon, remove the yucca chips from the oil and place them on paper towels to drain the excess oil. While the chips are still hot, season them with salt and the toasted spices. Serve warm or at room temperature.

TO SERVE: Arrange the cucumber batons in the centers of 6 wide shallow bowls. Pour the hot broth into the bowls. Garnish with the cilantro and fresh chile slices. Dip the sides of the hot fried shrimp into the Sriracha-coconut sauce to coat lightly. Arrange the shrimp on top of the cucumber batons so that they are not submerged in the broth. Garnish with the spiced yucca chips and serve immediately.

SERVES 6

Recipe courtesy of
BECKY REAMS

WINE PAIRING

Riesling loves spicy dishes. Choose one that is on the sweeter side to help contrast with the spice of the yucca chips. These wines tend to be *terroir* expressive, so characteristics vary, however most are fruity aromatic whites with hints of apple. Colder climates produce the best bottles, and there are currently a number of great producers throughout upstate New York.

THAI CRAB TRIO

Crab lovers beware: The hot, spicy, sweet-and-sour flavors of classic Thai cooking are ideally suited to the sweet meatiness of crabmeat, playing up the delicate flavor rather than smothering it. Once you try these Thai variations on a crab theme, you may never be able to go back to ordinary crab cakes with cracker crumbs and lemon. Joshua Marks served this dish as almost a buffet, on a plate that held a small bowl of curry, the dressed crab salad, and the sweet chili-and-lime-inflected crab cake. Jasmine rice, with its heady perfume, and a dipping sauce of chili, lime, and garlic completed the presentation. Even if you opt to prepare only one component of this tempting Thai trio, you won't be sorry.

FOR THE CRAB THAI CURRY PASTE

- 1 tablespoon olive oil
- 1 lemongrass stalk, finely chopped
- 2 Fresno chile peppers, seeded and diced (wear plastic gloves when handling)
- 1 (1-inch) piece fresh ginger, peeled and chopped
- 4 cloves garlic, chopped
- 1 shallot, chopped
- 4 cilantro sprigs with stems, chopped

  Juice of ½ lime

FOR THE CURRIED CRAB

- 1 tablespoon olive oil
- ½ red bell pepper, seeded and diced
- 1 (1-inch) piece fresh ginger, peeled and chopped
- 1 Fresno chile pepper, diced (wear plastic gloves when handling)
- ½ shallot, minced

- 2 cloves garlic, minced
- 2 tablespoons dry white wine
- 1 (13.5-ounce) can unsweetened coconut milk, stirred to blend
- 1 cup vegetable stock
- ½ teaspoon fish sauce

  Cayenne

  Red-pepper flakes

  Thai red curry powder
- 1 (4-ounce) container lump crabmeat, drained

  Large pinch minced fresh cilantro

  Fresh basil, thinly sliced, for garnish

FOR THE CRAB CAKES

- ½ cup Thai sweet chili sauce

  Juice of 2 limes
- 4 cloves garlic, minced
- 3 tablespoons olive oil
- 2 teaspoons minced fresh cilantro
- 2 large eggs, beaten to blend

- 4 (4-ounce) containers lump crabmeat, drained

  Kosher salt and freshly ground black pepper
- ½ cup panko (Japanese) bread crumbs
- 2 tablespoons unsalted butter

  Thai red curry powder

FOR THE SALAD

- 2 cups packed watercress, coarsely chopped
- ½ (4-ounce) can lump crabmeat, drained
- ½ red bell pepper, seeded and diced
- 2 tablespoons Thai sweet chili sauce

  Juice of ½ lime
- 2 fresh basil leaves, smashed
- 1 tablespoon olive oil

STEAMED JASMINE RICE

- 2 cups water
- 1 cup jasmine rice

THAI CRAB TRIO

(continued)

TO MAKE THE CRAB THAI CURRY PASTE: Heat the oil in a large, heavy-bottomed sauté pan over medium heat. Add the lemongrass, chile peppers, ginger, garlic, shallot, and cilantro sprigs and sauté until the shallots and garlic are tender, 3 to 5 minutes. Transfer the mixture to a food processor and puree until a smooth pastelike puree forms. Blend in the lime juice. Transfer the curry paste to a container, then cover and refrigerate until cold.

TO MAKE THE CURRIED CRAB: Heat the oil in a large wok over medium heat. Add the bell pepper, ginger, chile pepper, shallot, and garlic and sauté until the shallot is translucent, about 2 minutes. Add the curry paste and sauté until caramelized, about 2 minutes. Add the wine and simmer for 5 minutes. Add the coconut milk, stock, and fish sauce and simmer until reduced by half, about 20 minutes. Season to taste with the red-pepper flakes, and curry powder. Stir in the crabmeat and cilantro.

TO MAKE THE THAI SPICED CRAB CAKES: Whisk the chili sauce, lime juice, and garlic in a small bowl to blend. Whisk in the olive oil to blend. Set half of the sauce aside to serve as a dipping sauce for the crab cakes. Mix the remaining sauce with the chopped cilantro, then the eggs. Stir in the crabmeat. Season with salt and pepper.

Using a 3-inch-diameter ring mold, form the crabmeat mixture into 4 crab cakes. Coat the crab cakes in the panko, then cover and refrigerate until cold.

Melt the butter in a large, heavy-bottomed nonstick sauté pan over medium-high heat. Add the crab cakes and cook until they are golden brown and heated through, about 4 minutes per side. Sprinkle with curry powder.

TO MAKE THE SWEET CHILI CRAB SALAD: Combine the watercress, crabmeat, and bell pepper in a large bowl. Whisk the chili sauce, lime juice, and basil leaves in a medium bowl to blend. Whisk in the oil until emulsified.

TO MAKE THE STEAMED JASMINE RICE: Bring the water to a boil in a medium, heavy-bottomed saucepan over high heat. Stir in the rice, cover, and simmer until the rice is tender and the water is absorbed, about 20 minutes.

TO SERVE: Spoon the curried crab into 4 small bowls and set them in the centers of 4 rectangular plates. Set 1 crab cake beside the bowl on each plate. Drizzle the dressing over the salad and toss to coat, then mound the salad on the opposite side of the plate. Garnish the curried crab with the sliced basil and the crab cakes with cilantro leaves. Serve immediately with the reserved dipping sauce and steamed rice.

Recipe courtesy of
JOSHUA MARKS

SERVES 4

SHRIMP ÉTOUFFÉE

Étouffée means "smothered," as any fan of Cajun cooking knows, and Joshua Marks didn't skip any of the classic vegetables in the sauce that smothered his shrimp. This is a finely honed version of the traditional preparation, and even though a stick of butter may seem generous for a pound of shrimp...well, the dish would miss it if you used less. To get the roux to a medium golden color and cook it properly, you need this volume of butter and flour. And it's true to the spirit of generations of generous, open-handed Cajun cooks, who aren't known for starting a dish with merely a tablespoon or two of butter!

Once the wine and stock have gone in, the sauce simmers till it's thick and smooth. At this point, your étouffée is pretty much ready, so don't add the shrimp until the rice is cooked and your guests are seated at the table. It doesn't take long to smother the shrimp once they go in.

½ cup (1 stick) butter

½ cup all-purpose flour

2 celery stalks, diced

1 red bell pepper, seeded and diced

1 yellow bell pepper, seeded and diced

1 Vidalia onion, diced

1 jalapeño chile pepper, seeded and diced (wear plastic gloves when handling)

3 cloves garlic, minced

¼ cup white wine

4 cups chicken stock

1 tablespoon Cajun seasoning

1 pound jumbo shrimp, peeled and deveined

3¼ cups water

2 cups jasmine rice

Chopped cilantro, for garnish

Melt the butter in a large, heavy-bottomed pot, over medium-high heat. Add the flour and whisk to combine. Constantly whisk the roux, being careful not to let it burn, until a medium brown color is reached, 12 to 15 minutes. Add the celery, bell peppers, onion, jalapeños, and garlic and sauté for 5 minutes. Add the wine and cook another 1 to 2 minutes. Add the stock and Cajun seasoning. Bring to a boil, then lower the heat and simmer another 15 to 20 minutes, stirring occasionally. Add the shrimp and cook until it is cooked through, 4 to 5 minutes.

Meanwhile, bring 3¼ cups water to a boil in a medium pot. Add the rice and stir. Cover, lower the heat, and cook until the rice is done, 15 minutes.

Mound the rice in the center of a plate, and pour the shrimp mixture all around, garnishing with the cilantro.

SERVES 4

Recipe courtesy of
JOSHUA MARKS

DIRTY NEW ENGLAND LOBSTER

Husband of fellow contestant Anna Rossi, AJ Rossi hails from Boston, so it's not surprising that the New Englander knows his way around a lobster. Each lobster is split and lightly sautéed, then broiled until the edges of the shells just char. The pan juices are flamed with a hefty dose of smooth-sweet bourbon, then finished with shallots, half a pound (yes—two sticks!) of butter, and a big fistful of fresh herbs. This heavenly elixir is spooned all over the hot broiled lobster. Wherever it hails from, this is an over-the-top luxury dish in the best possible way.

2 (1½-pound) live lobsters

6 tablespoons peanut oil

½ cup bourbon

2 tablespoons dry white wine

¼ cup minced shallots

1 cup (2 sticks) unsalted butter, cut into pieces

¼ cup chopped fresh chives

2 tablespoons chopped fresh tarragon

2 tablespoons chopped fresh flat-leaf parsley, plus sprigs for garnish

Kosher salt and freshly ground black pepper

Preheat the broiler.

Lay 1 lobster, stomach side down, on the cutting board. Firmly insert the tip of a chef's knife into the base of the lobster head and cut through the head to split it in half (this kills the lobster instantly). Cut the lobster tail in half, forming 2 halves. Remove the tomalley (liver) and coral (the eggs, in females only), and set them aside to use later. Working over a bowl to collect any juices, remove the claws. Crack the claws, but leave them intact. Cut the tail meat through the shells into 6 pieces total. Repeat with the second lobster.

Heat 2 large, heavy-bottomed broilerproof sauté pans over high heat. Add the oil to the hot pans, then lay the lobster pieces, meat side down, in the pans and cook until the shells turn slightly pink and juices form, about 2 minutes. Stir the tomalley and coral (if using) into the juices that form, and cook for 2 minutes.

Turn the lobster pieces over and place the pans under the broiler. Broil the lobster pieces until the shell edges are slightly charred, about 3 minutes. Remove the pans from the broiler and set them on the stove over medium-high heat. Add the bourbon and carefully ignite the bourbon in the pans. Shake the pans gently, then carefully add the wine and shallots. Reduce the heat to low and cook until the flames subside and the liquids reduce slightly, about 2 minutes. Arrange the lobster pieces on a platter. Stir the butter, chives, tarragon, and chopped parsley into the sauce in the pans and stir until the butter melts, about 1 minute. Season the sauce to taste with salt and pepper.

Spoon the sauce over the lobster pieces, garnish with the parsley sprigs if desired, and serve immediately.

Recipe courtesy of
AJ ROSSI

SERVES 4

JOHN DORY
WITH ROASTED ALMOND SAUCE AND ASPARAGUS

A whole John Dory is an extremely bony and awkward fish, especially because of its poisonous barbs; even restaurant chefs consider it one of the most difficult fish to clean and fillet. When Monti Carlo was faced with this daunting task, she was less than enthusiastic. But once she got over her fear of those nasty barbs, she wielded her filleting knife with skill and professionalism. Her preparation, enriched with finely chopped almonds and heavy cream in a rich sauce, was just the icing on the cake and an excellent way to bring out the best of a fillet of John Dory. Try to see if your fishmonger will do the dirty work for you!

FOR THE SAUCE

- ½ cup blanched almonds
- 1½ tablespoons extra-virgin olive oil
- ½ cup dried bread crumbs
- ½ onion, chopped
- 4 cloves garlic, chopped
- 1 teaspoon sweet paprika
- ¼ cup chopped fresh cilantro
- ¼ cup chopped fresh flat-leaf parsley
- ½ cup dry white wine
- 1 cup fish stock
- ½ cup heavy cream
- Kosher salt

FOR THE ASPARAGUS

- 32 thin asparagus spears, trimmed
- 1 tablespoon olive oil
- Pinch of red-pepper flakes
- Kosher salt and freshly ground black pepper

FOR THE FISH

- ½ cup all-purpose flour
- ½ teaspoon kosher salt
- ¼ teaspoon cayenne
- ¼ teaspoon sweet paprika
- 4 (6-ounce) skinless John Dory fillets
- 4 tablespoons olive oil
- 4 tablespoons (½ stick) unsalted butter
- 4 sprigs fresh flat-leaf parsley
- 4 lemon slices

TO MAKE THE SAUCE: Preheat the oven to 400°F. Spread the almonds on a heavy baking sheet and roast in the oven until golden brown, about 8 minutes. Transfer to a food processor. Leave the oven on and increase the temperature to 500°F (for the asparagus).

Heat ½ tablespoon of the oil in a medium, heavy-bottomed sauté pan over medium heat. Add the bread crumbs and stir until golden brown, about 5 minutes. Transfer to the food processor with the almonds.

Heat the remaining 1 tablespoon oil in the same sauté pan over medium heat. Add the onion and garlic and sauté until tender, about 5 minutes. Add the paprika and sauté 1 minute. Transfer to the food processor. Add the cilantro and parsley to the food processor and process the almond mixture until the nuts are finely chopped. Add the wine and blend until a thick paste forms.

Combine the almond mixture and fish stock in a medium, heavy-bottomed saucepan and simmer over medium-high heat until reduced by half, about 10 minutes. Strain the sauce through a fine-mesh sieve into a small saucepan, pressing to extract as much liquid as possible. Whisk the cream into the sauce and simmer until reduced to a creamy consistency that thinly coats the back of a spoon, about 2 minutes. Season to taste with salt.

TO MAKE THE ASPARAGUS: Place the asparagus on a large heavy baking sheet. Drizzle the oil over the asparagus and sprinkle with the red-pepper flakes. Season with salt and pepper. Roast until the asparagus are crisp-tender and begin to brown, about 5 minutes.

TO MAKE THE FISH: Meanwhile, mix the flour, salt, cayenne, and paprika in a wide shallow dish. Dredge the fillets in the flour mixture to coat lightly and shake off any excess flour.

Heat 2 tablespoons of the oil in each of 2 large, heavy-bottomed skillets over medium-high heat. Add 2 fillets to each pan and cook until golden brown on the bottom, about 2 minutes. Turn the fillets over and add the butter to the pans. Cook, basting the fish with the melted butter, until the fish is golden brown on the bottom and just cooked through, about 1½ minutes.

TO SERVE: Weave the asparagus on 4 plates. Top with the fillets. Spoon the sauce around the fish. Garnish with the parsley sprigs and lemon slices, and serve immediately.

SERVES 4

Recipe courtesy of
MONTI CARLO

CRISPY-SKIN ROCKFISH
WITH CAULIFLOWER PUREE, CHARDONNAY EMULSION, HERB OIL, AND PICKLED RADISHES

R ockfish are no beauty queens. They're more like some sort of fantastic sea monster than a regular fish, and they're challenging to clean and bone. Not only did Becky Reams rise to the challenge in her inimitable way, but the judges agreed that her crisp-skinned fish, served on a velvety cauliflower puree and brightened with glowing green herb oil, was one of the very best dishes of the entire fish challenge. The green cauliflower that she used, available in gourmet and organic markets, gives the finished dish a beautiful color, but you could use the golden yellow cauliflower that also turns up in specialty markets or the regular white kind. They will all taste equally good.

PICKLED RADISHES

- ½ cup Champagne vinegar
- ½ cup Chardonnay
- ⅓ cup sugar
- 2½ teaspoons freshly ground black pepper
- 1 teaspoon kosher salt
- 2 purple radishes, very thinly sliced
- 2 red radishes, very thinly sliced
- 2 white radishes, very thinly sliced

FOR THE HERB OIL

- 1 tablespoon coarsely chopped fresh flat-leaf parsley
- ½ cup packed 1-inch pieces fresh chives

  Scant ½ cup olive oil

  Kosher salt

FOR THE CAULIFLOWER PUREE

- 1 head green cauliflower, cut into large florets
- 1 cup water
- 3 tablespoons unsalted butter
- ¼ cup heavy cream
- ½ teaspoon kosher salt
- ½ teaspoon freshly ground black pepper

FOR THE CHARDONNAY EMULSION

- 1 tablespoon canola oil
- 1 large shallot, minced
- ½ cup Chardonnay
- ½ cup (1 stick) chilled unsalted butter, diced
- 3 large egg yolks
- 1 teaspoon Champagne vinegar

  Kosher salt

FOR THE FISH

- 4 (5- to 6-ounce) rockfish fillets with skin, scaled

  Kosher salt and freshly ground black pepper

  All-purpose flour

- 3 tablespoons canola oil

  Chopped fresh chives, for garnish

TO MAKE THE PICKLED RADISHES: Combine the vinegar, Chardonnay, sugar, pepper, and salt in a small saucepan and bring to a simmer over high heat. Add the radishes, reduce the heat to medium, and simmer for 2 minutes. Pour the mixture into a bowl and set aside to cool completely. Cover and refrigerate until cold. Remove the radishes from the pickling liquid to serve.

TO MAKE THE HERB OIL: Cook the parsley and chives in a small saucepan of boiling salted water for 1 minute. Drain, reserving the cooking liquid for the cauliflower puree. Transfer the herbs to a bowl of ice water and set aside until cold. Drain well and pat the herbs dry.

Combine the herbs and oil in a blender and blend until the herbs are almost pureed and the oil is green, about 2 minutes. Strain the herb oil through a fine-mesh sieve and season to taste with salt.

TO MAKE THE CAULIFLOWER PUREE: Combine the cauliflower and water in a large, heavy-bottomed saucepan over high heat. Cover and steam until most of the water evaporates and the cauliflower is tender, about 12 minutes. Pour off any excess water. Add 1 tablespoon of the butter and cook until the cauliflower begins to brown, about 3 minutes. Add the cream and the remaining 2 tablespoons butter. Using an immersion blender, puree the cauliflower mixture, adding about ¼ cup of the reserved herb cooking liquid 1 tablespoon at a time, to form a smooth and semi-thick puree. Season with salt and pepper. Strain the puree through a fine-mesh sieve into a small saucepan. Cover and rewarm over low heat before serving.

TO MAKE THE CHARDONNAY EMULSION: Heat the oil in a small, heavy-bottomed saucepan over medium-high heat. Add the shallot and sauté until it begins to brown, about 2 minutes. Add the wine and simmer until reduced to 2 tablespoons, about 13 minutes. Remove the pan from the heat and gradually whisk in the butter to form a creamy sauce.

Blend the egg yolks in a small food processor. With the machine running, slowly add the hot butter-shallot mixture, blending until smooth and creamy and scraping down the sides of the work bowl as needed. Mix in the vinegar. Season to taste with salt.

To keep the emulsion warm, transfer it to a small metal bowl set over a saucepan of very hot, but not simmering, water and whisk occasionally.

CRISPY-SKIN ROCKFISH

(continued)

TO MAKE THE FISH: Using a sharp knife, score the skin on the fillets. Season the skin liberally with salt and pepper, pressing the seasoning into the cuts. Dredge the fillets through flour to coat lightly, shaking off any excess flour.

Heat the oil in a large, heavy-bottomed sauté pan over high heat. Lay the fillets, skin side down, in the hot pan and cook until the skin is crisp and dark golden, about 7 minutes. Turn the fillets over and cook 1 minute. Using the slotted spatula, transfer the fillets to a plate lined with paper towels to absorb the excess oil.

TO SERVE: Spoon the cauliflower puree in a swipe across the centers of 4 plates. Spoon a line of the emulsion alongside the cauliflower puree. Lay the fish fillets, skin side up and perpendicular, atop the puree and emulsion. Drain the pickled radishes and place about 3 slices on each plate. Drizzle the herb oil in a circle around the outer edge of the plates. Sprinkle a few chive slices on the plate and serve immediately.

SERVES 4

Recipe courtesy of
BECKY REAMS

HALIBUT WITH TOMATO MARMALADE, ROASTED FENNEL, AND SMOKED EGGPLANT PUREE

Halibut is an especially dense and meaty white fish, and chefs love it because it's prone to staying moist and is far less likely to be overwhelmed by other flavors than, say, flounder or brook trout. The smoky eggplant puree and the intense tomato "marmalade" in Graham's exciting dish—not to mention the anise scent of the roasted fennel—would overwhelm a lesser fish, but with halibut, they merely pull together to magnify its star power. Again, this is one of Graham's recipes written in the casual shorthand he would give to his prep chefs. It will titillate your senses and dazzle you with its complexity, but may not tempt you into the kitchen unless you're a professional chef with equipment such as hotel pans, a Vita-Prep, and a dehydrator at your beck and call. It's a fascinating glimpse behind the scenes at a top restaurant, and if you're a serious home cook, it can only increase your respect for what the pros do every day.

SMOKED EGGPLANT PUREE

Soak 2 cups of applewood chips in water to cover for 24 hours.

2 eggplant halves drizzled with olive oil and placed on roasting rack to bake for 20 min at 375 or until golden brown. A little char will not hurt.

Pull eggplant and allow to cool.

Strain wood chips and place in a hotel pan lined with aluminum foil.

On stove top (low flame) bring chips to a smoke. Place a greased perforated pan on top of smoking hotel pan. Add eggplant face up and cover for 30 min. Adjust flame to allow smoke to continue.

Remove eggplant from smoker and cool.

Scoop the flesh of the eggplant into Vita-Prep.

Add 3 tablespoons of honey, 2 tablespoons of any nice sherry vinegar, and 1 tablespoon lemon juice.

Puree till smooth and salt to taste

TOMATO MARMALADE

10 roma tomatoes peeled and seeded. Reserve skins for tomato powder.

In a large pot add 1 cup sugar, 1 cup red wine vinegar, and the tomatoes.

Cook on low flame for several hours until liquid has been fully evaporated.

Make sure to stir regularly. If any buildup occurs on the bottom, change pot.

Finish with salt and a pinch of red-pepper flakes.

TOMATO POWDER

Place all reserved tomato skins in dehydrator for 24 hours.

Using a coffee or spice grinder buzz skins till powder. Sift through a strainer.

FENNEL

1 large fennel bulb peeled and cut into 12 equal pieces, reserve fronds for garnish.

In a large sauté pan with olive oil almost to a smoke, brown fennel on both sides.

Remove fennel from pan and allow residual heat to finish the cooking.

In a 425 oven for 5 minutes toast 1 tablespoon fennel seed till golden brown.

Cool and grind to a coarse powder.

HALIBUT

6 oz portion x 6

Pat fish with towel to absorb any moisture. The drier the fish the better the sear.

Salt fish liberally.

In a large sauté pan with blend oil, almost to a smoke place fish presentation side down and cook till edges seem to be browning. Add 1 tablespoon of butter to pan and place in a 400 degree oven for 2 minutes.

Remove fish from oven and using a spatula gently flip each fish allowing the bottom side to just kiss the oil before removing from pan. Finish by dusting the halibut with toasted fennel.

SERVES 6

BUTTERMILK FRIED CHICKEN
WITH CREAMED KALE

T he orange zest and juice in the marinade was the first hint that Christine Ha intended her fried chicken to be more than a little out of the ordinary, but it was the creamed kale that clinched the deal. Used to thinking of leafy greens as the healthiest of vegetables? Simmer them in ¾ pound of cream cheese and a cup of heavy cream, and you may think a little differently! The sturdy, strongly flavored greens take remarkably well to this treatment, however, and even if it's not your everyday preparation, try it at least once. The cherry tomatoes add color and a little pop of acid at the end of the cooking time, and the blood oranges on the finished plate indicate that this is not ordinary fried chicken. For the best flavor, marinate the chicken overnight.

FOR THE CHICKEN

- 1½ cups buttermilk
- 2 oranges, zested and juiced
- 1 tablespoon plus 2 teaspoons kosher salt
- 1 teaspoon freshly ground black pepper
- 8 chicken drumsticks
  Canola oil
- 1¼ cups all-purpose flour
- 1¼ cups cornmeal
- 4 teaspoons garlic powder
- 4 teaspoons onion powder
- 4 teaspoons sweet paprika
- ½ teaspoon cayenne

FOR THE CREAMED KALE

- 2 pounds kale, stems and ribs removed, leaves coarsely chopped
- 1 tablespoon canola oil
- 3 large shallots, thinly sliced
- 3 cloves garlic, minced
- 12 ounces cream cheese
- 1 cup heavy cream
- ½ teaspoon kosher salt plus more to taste
- ½ teaspoon freshly ground black pepper plus more to taste
- 8 ounces cherry tomatoes, halved
- 1 blood orange, cut into wedges

TO MAKE THE CHICKEN: Whisk the buttermilk, orange zest and juice, 1 tablespoon of the salt, and ½ teaspoon of the black pepper in a large bowl to blend. Add the chicken and turn to coat. Cover and refrigerate for at least 30 minutes and up to 1 day, rotating the drumsticks to marinate evenly.

Position a rack in the center of the oven and preheat the oven to 250°F. Set a cooling rack in a large shallow baking pan. Heat 1½ inches of oil in a large, heavy-bottomed skillet over medium heat to 350°F.

Mix the flour, cornmeal, garlic powder, onion powder, paprika, cayenne,

BUTTERMILK FRIED CHICKEN

(continued)

and the remaining 2 teaspoons salt and ½ teaspoon black pepper in a large resealable plastic bag. Drain the chicken in a colander and discard the marinade. Add the chicken, one piece at a time, to the bag and shake to coat well. Tap off the excess flour mixture and transfer the chicken pieces to a sheet of waxed paper.

Add 4 drumsticks to the hot oil and cook, turning occasionally with tongs, until golden brown and cooked through, about 10 minutes. Transfer the chicken to the rack in the baking pan and keep warm in the oven. Return the oil to 350°F before frying the remaining 4 chicken drumsticks.

TO MAKE THE CREAMED KALE: Prepare a large bowl of ice water. Cook the kale in a large pot of boiling salted water until wilted, about 2 minutes. Drain, then submerge the kale in ice water to cool completely. Drain well.

Heat the oil in a large, heavy-bottomed skillet over medium heat. Add the shallots and garlic and sauté until fragrant and tender, about 1 minute. Add the cream cheese, cream, salt, and pepper and stir to blend. Add the kale and bring to a simmer. Reduce the heat to medium-low, cover, and simmer until the kale is tender, stirring occasionally, about 15 minutes. Stir in the tomatoes, then cover and cook until they are heated through and tender, stirring occasionally, about 10 minutes. Season to taste with more salt and pepper.

Divide the creamed kale among 4 serving bowls and set each on a plate. Place 2 drumsticks on each plate and serve with the blood orange wedges.

SERVES 4

Recipe courtesy of
CHRISTINE HA

ROAST CHICKEN
WITH RED PEPPER GRITS AND COLLARD GREENS

With all this Southern cooking going on, it's not surprising that Paula Deen showed up to do a little taste-testing. And David Martinez's red pepper grits had her raving. Paula showed up *in* the Mystery Box of Southern ingredients, so the contestants knew they'd better turn their culinary thoughts south of the Mason-Dixon line.

David's unusual technique involved cooking the grits in a strained light vegetable broth he'd made of onion, garlic, and red bell pepper. Once the grits were cooked, he blended the vegetables that he'd removed from the broth and stirred this red puree into the grits with a hefty dose of butter. The result was creamy with a kick, a wonderful base for smoky collards, roast chicken, and crisp onion rings, all topped with an unusual sauce that includes juicy sweet blackberries and Worcestershire sauce.

FOR THE GRITS

- 9 cups water
- 1 red bell pepper, seeded and cut into large chunks
- ½ onion, cut into large chunks
- 4 cloves garlic, peeled
- 1 cup corn grits
- 6 tablespoons (¾ stick) unsalted butter

  About 1 teaspoon kosher salt

FOR THE FRIED ONIONS

  Canola oil

- 1 small onion, very thinly sliced (⅛-inch-thick)
- 1 cup buttermilk
- 1 cup all-purpose flour
- 1 teaspoon salt

FOR THE CHICKEN AND SAUCE

- 6 tablespoons olive oil
- 4 small chicken legs (thigh and drumstick)
- 4 small boneless chicken breasts (with skin)

  Kosher salt and freshly ground black pepper

- ½ cup finely diced onion
- 6 cloves garlic, minced
- 12 ounces fresh blackberries
- ¼ cup Worcestershire sauce
- ¾ cup water
- 2 tablespoons cold unsalted butter, diced

COLLARD GREENS WITH SMOKY BACON

- 8 cups water
- 1 lemon, zested and juiced
- 1 teaspoon kosher salt
- 2 pounds collard greens, center stems and ribs discarded, leaves cut into ¾-inch-wide ribbons
- 4 ounces applewood-smoked bacon slices, cut into ½-inch pieces
- ½ onion, coarsely chopped
- 3 cloves garlic, minced
- 3 cups chicken stock
- 1 teaspoon light brown sugar

  Kosher salt and freshly ground black pepper

ROAST CHICKEN

(continued)

TO MAKE THE GRITS: Combine the water, bell pepper, onion, and garlic in a large, heavy-bottomed saucepan and bring to a boil over high heat. Reduce the heat to medium-low and simmer until the vegetables are tender, about 15 minutes. Using a slotted spoon or sieve, remove the vegetables from the cooking liquid and transfer them to a blender. You should have about 7 cups of cooking liquid remaining.

Gradually whisk the grits into the bell pepper cooking liquid and bring to a simmer. Reduce the heat to medium-low and simmer gently until the grits are very tender and the mixture thickens, stirring frequently, about 50 minutes. If the grits thicken too much too quickly, add enough hot water to loosen the mixture as needed.

Puree the cooked vegetables until smooth. Stir the puree and butter into the grits. Season with the salt.

TO MAKE THE FRIED ONIONS: Heat 2 inches of oil in a heavy, deep frying pan over medium heat to 375°F. Combine the onion and buttermilk in a medium bowl and set aside for 15 minutes, stirring occasionally. Drain well in a colander.

Mix the flour and salt in a wide shallow bowl. Dredge the onion rings in the flour to coat, then place them on a baking sheet. Working in batches, fry the onions until they are crisp and golden brown, 2 to 3 minutes per batch. Using a slotted spoon, remove the fried onions from the oil and transfer to paper towels to drain the excess oil.

TO MAKE THE CHICKEN AND SAUCE: Meanwhile, preheat the oven to 450°F. Heat 3 tablespoons of the oil in a large, heavy-bottomed ovenproof skillet over medium-high heat. Season the chicken with salt and pepper. Place the chicken legs, skin side down, in the skillet and cook until golden brown on the bottom, about 8 minutes. Turn the chicken over and transfer the skillet to the oven. Using a second ovenproof skillet, repeat with the remaining 3 tablespoons oil and chicken breasts.

Roast the chicken until it is cooked through, about 20 minutes for the legs and 15 minutes for the breasts. Transfer the chicken pieces to a baking sheet and tent with foil to keep them warm while making the sauce.

Place both of the skillets over medium-high heat. Add the onion and garlic to one skillet and sauté until fragrant, about 1 minute. Add the blackberries and Worcestershire sauce and bring to a simmer. Add the water to the second skillet and stir to scrape up any browned bits, then add the liquid to the pan with the berries. Simmer until the berries are tender and the sauce reduces by half, about 17 minutes. Remove the skillet from the heat and whisk in the butter. Season the sauce to taste with salt and pepper.

TO MAKE THE COLLARD GREENS AND SMOKY BACON:
Combine the water, lemon zest and juice, and salt in a large, heavy-bottomed pot and bring to a boil over high heat. Add the greens and cook until wilted, about 7 minutes. Drain.

Cook the bacon in a large, heavy-bottomed skillet over medium heat until the fat renders and the bacon is golden, about 5 minutes. Add the onion and garlic and sauté until the onion is translucent, about 2 minutes. Stir in the greens and chicken stock. Bring to a simmer, then reduce the heat to medium-low and simmer gently until the greens are very tender and most of the liquid evaporates, about 45 minutes.

Stir in the brown sugar and cook until the greens are thinly coated with the cooking liquid, about 2 minutes. Season to taste with salt and pepper.

TO SERVE: Pour the grits onto 4 plates. Mound the collard greens in the center. Place the chicken pieces alongside the greens. Spoon the sauce over the chicken and greens. Top with the onion rings.

SERVES 4

Recipe courtesy of
DAVID MARTINEZ

WINE PAIRING

If you're in the mood for a red wine but have a dish that traditionally pairs with a white, an Oregon Pinot Noir is a great alternative. Light- to medium-bodied with cherry and berry fruit flavors, the name is synonymous with the great Burgundy winemaking region in France, but stellar examples are coming out of Oregon's Willamette Valley. They are not too tannic and more delicate than the big oaky Cabernet Sauvignons or California Zinfandels, which could drown out the flavors of the roast chicken.

ROAST CHICKEN AND BISCUITS
WITH PAN GRAVY AND FRIED GREEN TOMATOES AND OKRA

Chicken and biscuits sounds like down-home cooking, but Becky Reams ensured that this dish was anything but. From the chicken stock prepared solely to enrich the gravy, to the chicken fat used to braise the breasts while roasting, to the homemade buttermilk used to raise the biscuits, she carefully layered and reinforced the flavors at every step. You might consider the fried green tomatoes and fried okra to be gilding the lily—it's like every bit of classic Southern cooking packed onto one plate—but when you spoon on the creamy jalapeño sauce, you'll know she got the balance just right.

Note that this recipe starts with a whole chicken that you joint, reserving the wingtips and back (and feet, if your chicken was *very* whole) for stock. If you prefer, you can jump ahead in the recipe by starting with two jointed chickens and 8 cups of stock.

FOR THE CHICKEN

- 2 (3- to 3½-pound) whole chickens
- 6 bacon slices, coarsely chopped
- 1 onion, cut into large chunks
- 2 heads garlic, cloves separated
- 10 cups cold water
- 2 tablespoons extra-virgin olive oil
- Kosher salt and freshly ground black pepper

FOR THE GRAVY

- 1 onion, finely diced
- 3 tablespoons all-purpose flour
- 3 tablespoons unsalted butter, softened
- Dash of hot sauce
- Dash of Worcestershire sauce

- ½ teaspoon freshly ground black pepper
- Pinch of cayenne
- Kosher salt

HOMEMADE BUTTERMILK BISCUITS

- 3 cups all-purpose flour
- 4 teaspoons baking powder
- 1 teaspoon kosher salt
- ½ cup (1 stick) cold unsalted butter, diced
- 1½ cups plus 1 tablespoon Homemade Buttermilk (page 177)
- 1 large egg, beaten to blend

FOR THE CREAMY JALAPEÑO SAUCE

- 3 ounces cream cheese, at room temperature
- ⅓ cup jalapeño pepper jelly

FOR THE TOMATOES AND OKRA

- ½ cup corn grits
- ¼ cup all-purpose flour
- 2 teaspoons freshly ground black pepper
- 1 teaspoon kosher salt plus more to taste
- ½ teaspoon cayenne
- ½ cup Homemade Buttermilk (page 177)
- ½ teaspoon hot pepper sauce
- 1 pound green tomatoes (about 4 medium), cut into ½-inch-thick slices
- ¾ cup olive oil
- 12 okra pods, cut on a bias into ½-inch-thick slices

ROAST CHICKEN AND BISCUITS

(continued)

TO MAKE THE CHICKEN: Cut off the wings and feet (if attached) of each chicken, then remove the backbones. Next, cut the chickens into 4 pieces so you have 2 boneless breasts and 2 leg pieces (thigh and drumstick connected). Refrigerate the breasts and leg pieces.

Heat a large, heavy-bottomed stockpot over medium-high heat. Combine the chicken wings, feet, and all bones in the pot. Add the bacon, onion, and half of the garlic and cook until the chicken pieces brown, about 12 minutes. Fill the pot with the water, adding more if needed to cover the chicken. Bring the water to a simmer, then reduce the heat to medium-low and simmer, skimming any foam off the top of the stock as necessary, about 1½ hours.

Strain the stock into an 8-cup measuring cup or bowl and discard the solids. You should have about 8 cups of stock. Skim off any excess fat from the top of the stock. Reserve 2½ cups of the stock for the gravy, then cover and refrigerate the remaining stock for another use.

Preheat the oven to 450°F.

Place the reserved leg pieces on a large heavy baking sheet. Rub the olive oil all over the chicken pieces and sprinkle with salt and pepper. Scatter the remaining garlic cloves between the chicken pieces. Roast until some fat has rendered, about 15 minutes. Spoon off 3 tablespoons of the rendered fat from the baking sheet and reserve it for the gravy.

Add the breasts to the baking sheet and brush the chicken with the remaining fat in the pan. Return the pan to the oven and continue roasting the chicken legs and breasts until the skin is crisp and golden brown and the chicken is cooked through but still juicy inside, about 20 minutes.

TO MAKE THE GRAVY: Heat the reserved 3 tablespoons rendered fat in a large, heavy-bottomed sauté pan over medium heat. Add the onion and sauté until tender and pale golden, about 3 minutes. Mix the flour and butter in a small bowl to form a paste. Whisk the paste into the onions and stir for 2 minutes. Add the reserved 2½ cups chicken stock and whisk to blend. Bring the mixture to a simmer, then continue simmering until the gravy thickens, about 5 minutes.

While the gravy comes to a simmer, transfer the roasted chicken pieces to a carving board and set them aside. Stir any accumulated juices and loosen any browned bits from the bottom of the baking sheet and add them to the gravy. Add the hot sauce, Worcestershire sauce, black pepper, and cayenne to the gravy and season to taste with salt.

TO MAKE THE HOMEMADE BUTTERMILK BISCUITS: Preheat the oven to 425°F. Line a heavy baking sheet with parchment paper.

Combine the flour, baking powder, and salt in a food processor and pulse to blend. Add the butter and pulse until pea-size pieces of butter still remain. Add 1½ cups of the buttermilk and pulse just until blended.

Transfer the dough to a floured work surface and gently gather the dough into a ¾-inch-thick disk. Do not knead the dough. Using a floured 2½-inch round biscuit cutter, cut out the biscuits, gathering and reshaping the dough scraps to cut out 12 biscuits total. Place the biscuits on the baking sheet and brush the tops with the remaining 1 tablespoon buttermilk.

Bake for 10 minutes, then quickly brush the tops with the beaten egg and continue baking until the biscuits are golden, about 12 minutes. Serve warm.

TO MAKE THE CREAMY JALAPEÑO SAUCE: Beat the cream cheese and jelly in a small bowl to blend. Set aside.

TO MAKE THE TOMATOES AND OKRA: Whisk the grits, flour, black pepper, salt, and cayenne in a shallow baking dish to blend. Place the buttermilk in another shallow bowl and stir in the hot pepper sauce.

Working in batches, dredge the tomato slices in the flour mixture to coat, then dip them in the buttermilk mixture to coat. Coat the tomato slices again with the flour mixture, pressing firmly to adhere, then arrange the slices in a single layer on a baking sheet.

Heat ½ cup of the oil in a cast-iron skillet over medium heat. Fry the tomato slices until golden brown, about 3 minutes per side. Transfer the tomatoes to a rack set over paper towels to drain the excess oil.

Heat the remaining ¼ cup oil in the skillet. Coat the okra slices in the flour mixture, then fry until golden brown, about 3 minutes. Transfer to a plate lined with paper towels to drain the excess oil. Sprinkle the hot fried tomatoes and okra with salt to taste.

TO SERVE: Split 4 biscuits and set each bottom on a plate. Remove the skins from the chicken breasts and slice the breasts. Arrange the slices over the biscuit bottoms. Spoon a generous amount of gravy over the chicken breasts, then set the skins on top. Lean the biscuit tops alongside. Place 1 chicken leg piece on each plate. Spoon some of the jalapeño sauce on the opposite side of the plate. Place the fried tomatoes over the sauce, then spoon a dollop of the sauce on top of the tomatoes. Sprinkle the fried okra pieces over the tomatoes and serve immediately.

SERVES 4

HOMEMADE BUTTERMILK

2 cups whole milk

2 tablespoons fresh lemon juice

Combine the milk and lemon juice in a small bowl and set aside until the mixture curdles, about 5 minutes. Stir to blend.

MAKES ABOUT 2 CUPS

Recipe courtesy of
BECKY REAMS

Alejandra Schrader

Like several other contestants, Alejandra

Schrader was inspired to follow a new career path after her time on *MasterChef*. She had worked in architecture and urban planning, but the allure of a food career pulled her from the drawing board to the kitchen, where she has continued her commitment to wellness, community, and the environment. Alejandra says: "I've started a private chef business, Cucina Cocina, along with fellow Season 2 alumna Tracy Kontos. We offer our services to a vast array of clients, including a major motion picture studio, individuals, and private companies. Guided by business mentors Mary Sue Milliken and Susan Feniger, we make it a point to be involved with our communities and participate in nonprofit events.

"I have continued to create figure-friendly, fresh, and flavorful dishes for my blog, *Cook Global. Eat at Home!* where I share conscious recipes from all over the world as well as cooking tips with all my friends and fans.

"I have done a number of public appearances and cooking segments on shows like *Access Hollywood Live*, *Café CNN*, and *Primera Edicion UNIVISION*. I have also been in magazines like *InTouch Weekly* and *Taste of Home*. I have been involved in many prestigious food events such as Food and Wine Festival Palm Desert, Malibu Food & Wine Festival, and Taste of Chicago, the largest food festival in the world. *MasterChef* has opened so many doors for me!"

STUFFED PEPPERS
WITH TURKEY, BROWN RICE, AND FONTINA CHEESE

This is healthy comfort food, easy enough for a weeknight supper and satisfying enough for a weekend session in the kitchen. The creamy fontina, ideal for melting, pulls all the tastes together. "This recipe is simple, fast, and easy to make," says Alejandra. "It is light and low in calories. However, this one-pot meal is full of flavor and pizzazz!"

FOR THE TOMATO SAUCE

- 4 large tomatoes (about 1½ pounds), blanched, peeled, and roughly chopped
- ½ cup low-sodium chicken broth
- ½ onion, coarsely chopped
- 1 celery stalk, coarsely chopped
- 4 cloves garlic
- 2 tablespoons tomato paste

  Kosher salt and freshly ground black pepper

FOR THE PEPPERS

- ½ cup minced shallots
- 3 cloves garlic, minced
- 1 large egg, beaten to blend
- 1½ teaspoons kosher salt plus more for seasoning
- 1 teaspoon ground cumin
- 1 teaspoon smoked paprika
- ¾ teaspoon freshly ground black pepper plus more for seasoning
- 1½ pounds ground turkey (85% lean)
- 1 cup cooked brown rice
- 6 ounces fontina cheese, cubed
- 1 zucchini, finely diced
- 1 pound baby Yukon Gold potatoes, halved
- ½ onion, thinly sliced
- 3 tablespoons olive oil
- 6 assorted bell peppers

FOR THE CILANTRO CREMA

- 1½ cups loosely packed fresh cilantro
- ½ cup Mexican crema
- 2 tablespoons fresh lemon juice
- ½ teaspoon cayenne

  Kosher salt

Recipe courtesy of
Alejandra Schrader

TO MAKE THE TOMATO SAUCE: Combine the tomatoes, broth, onion, celery, garlic, and tomato paste in a blender and blend on high until smooth, about 30 seconds. Strain the sauce into a small, heavy-bottomed saucepan. Bring to a simmer over medium-high heat. Reduce the heat to low, cover, and simmer for 10 minutes to allow all the flavors to blend. Season to taste with salt and pepper.

TO MAKE THE PEPPERS: Preheat the oven to 375°F.

Combine the shallots, garlic, egg, salt, cumin, paprika, and pepper in a large bowl. Add the turkey, rice, cheese, and zucchini and mix just to blend. Set aside.

Arrange the potatoes and onion over the bottom of a 13 x 9-inch baking dish. Season with salt and pepper and toss with the oil. Cut the tops off the bell peppers and remove the seeds. Stuff the peppers with the turkey mixture, mounding slightly. Cover with the pepper tops, then place the peppers in the baking dish.

Pour the tomato sauce over the peppers. Bake until the filling is cooked through, the peppers are tender and beginning to char, and the potatoes are tender, about 1 hour. Remove the dish from the oven and let the peppers rest for at least 5 minutes before serving.

TO MAKE THE CILANTRO CREMA: Combine the cilantro, crema, lemon juice, and cayenne in a blender and blend until smooth. Season to taste with salt.

TO SERVE: Place 1 pepper in the centers of 6 plates or shallow bowls. Arrange the potatoes alongside the peppers and top with the sliced onion. Spoon some of the tomato sauce over the peppers and serve with the cilantro crema.

SERVES 6

STUFFED PEPPERS
(continued)

WINE PAIRING

Often overshadowed by the Piedmont region's more famous Nebbiolo grape, Barberas are an excellent choice for this dish. They have a vegetal edge to complement the peppers, and enough structure to stand up to the complexity of flavors. The characteristics can differ depending on the methods of production used, so look for one that is meant to be drunk young and has been aged in steel, as opposed to one with a lot of oak influence.

SOUTHERN-INSPIRED CHICKEN GALANTINE WITH ROASTED
POTATO AND GREEN TOMATO–RED PEPPER CHUTNEY

I f you have good knife skills in the kitchen, if you carefully hone your blades each time before you cut, and if you're always the person asked to carve at family holidays, this recipe contains the perfect task for you: removing the skin from a 6½-pound chicken in a single piece (or as large a single piece as possible). The chicken skin must be large enough that you can cut out four good-size rectangles, which you will later use to roll around the filling that you'll make from the chicken. As demonstrated by Frank Mirando, this is no mean feat.

Work slowly and use your fingertips as much as your knife blade. Gently loosening and massaging the skin away from the meat will help you make fewer cuts as you work to separate it entirely from the chicken. The resulting chicken rolls are sliced and fanned out on the plate. Served with crisp, golden-roast potato skins and accented with a tangy green tomato–red pepper chutney, this is a dish designed to impress.

FOR THE CHICKEN

- 1 (6½-pound) chicken
- 4 ounces bacon
- 2 tablespoons unsalted butter
- ½ cup finely diced onion
- ½ cup finely diced and seeded red bell pepper
- 1 clove garlic, minced
- 1 tablespoon Worcestershire sauce
- 1 large egg
- Grated zest of 1 lemon
- 3 tablespoons canola oil

FOR THE POTATOES

- 6 red-skinned potatoes (about 2 pounds), cut into ¾ inch pieces
- 1 tablespoon olive oil
- 2 tablespoons unsalted butter, melted
- 1 teaspoon kosher salt
- 1 teaspoon freshly ground black pepper
- ½ teaspoon cayenne
- 1 small lemon, zested and juiced

GREEN TOMATO–RED PEPPER CHUTNEY

- 1 tablespoon olive oil
- 1 green tomato, cut into ½-inch pieces
- 1 red bell pepper, seeded and cut into ½-inch pieces
- ½ onion, diced
- 1 clove garlic, minced
- ¼ cup water
- 3 tablespoons jalapeño pepper jelly
- 1 tablespoon packed light brown sugar
- 2 teaspoons grated lemon zest (from 1 lemon)
- ¼ cup fresh lemon juice
- 1 teaspoon cayenne
- Kosher salt

TO PREPARE THE CHICKEN: Carefully remove the skin from the chicken, keeping it intact as much as possible. Lay the skin on a cutting board and cut out 4 rectangles, each about 6 inches x 5 inches. Lay the chicken skins flat on a baking sheet, cover and refrigerate until ready to use.

Remove the thighs and drumsticks from the chicken and reserve the remaining chicken for another use. Debone the drumsticks and thighs, then coarsely chop the meat. Grind the chopped meat with the bacon through a meat grinder. Freeze the ground meat until cold, at least 30 minutes.

Melt the butter in a large, heavy-bottomed sauté pan over medium heat. Add the onion, bell pepper, and garlic and sauté until tender, about 3 minutes. Add the Worcestershire sauce and cook until slightly reduced, about 3 minutes. Transfer the mixture to a medium bowl and freeze just until cold, about 30 minutes.

Add the cold ground meat to the cold bell pepper mixture and mix with a fork to blend. Mix in the egg and lemon zest. Spoon the meat mixture in a log down the center of each chilled piece of chicken skin. Roll up the skins around the meat, forming sausage-like rolls. Wrap 3 pieces of twine around each log and tie them loosely to secure the skins. Cover and refrigerate for at least 1 hour.

Preheat the oven to 450°F. Heat the oil in a large, heavy-bottomed ovenproof sauté pan over medium-high heat. Add the chicken rolls and cook until browned on all sides, about 8 minutes. Transfer the pan to the oven and roast until an instant-read thermometer registers 160°F. Keep the oven on.

TO MAKE THE POTATOES: Toss them in a large bowl with the oil, butter, salt, black pepper, and cayenne to coat. Transfer the potatoes to a heavy baking sheet and roast until crisp and golden, turning as necessary, about 25 minutes.

TO MAKE THE GREEN TOMATO-RED PEPPER CHUTNEY: Heat the oil in a small, heavy-bottomed saucepan over medium heat. Add the tomato, bell pepper, onion, and garlic and sauté until the pepper is tender, about 8 minutes. Add the water, jelly, brown sugar, lemon zest, lemon juice, and cayenne. Simmer gently until the mixture reduces slightly and thickens, stirring often, about 15 minutes. Season to taste with salt.

TO SERVE: Remove the kitchen twine from the chicken rolls. Using a sharp knife, trim the ends of the chicken rolls, then cut the rolls crosswise into thick slices. Arrange the slices on 4 plates. Spoon the potatoes and chutney alongside. Sprinkle the lemon zest over the potatoes and squeeze some juice over. Serve immediately.

SERVES 4

Recipe courtesy of
FRANK MIRANDO

INDIAN CURRY CORNISH HEN

I f you're in the habit of buying a can of something marked "curry powder," throw it away and make a proper, Indian-style spice mixture. A laundry list of spices is toasted in a dry skillet to bring all the essential oils to the fore. When it's ground in a coffee or spice grinder, you'll be astonished at how fragrant and enticing a curry powder can be. Cornish hens, which are really a sort of miniature chicken, are usually roasted whole, but Joshua Marks's clever twist was to quarter them and braise them with a creamy, flavorful yogurt sauce, including a hefty dose of that homemade curry powder. Served with aromatic basmati rice, this dish makes ordinary chicken curry look downright dull.

FOR THE CURRY POWDER

- 3   green cardamom pods
- 2   whole cloves
- 1   teaspoon caraway seeds
- 1   teaspoon coriander seeds
- 1   teaspoon whole black peppercorns
- 1   teaspoon yellow mustard seeds
- ½   teaspoon red-pepper flakes
- 1½ teaspoons sweet paprika
- 1½ teaspoons turmeric
- 1   teaspoon ground ginger

FOR THE YOGURT SAUCE

- 1   tablespoon canola oil
- 2   shallots, minced
- 1   (2-inch) piece fresh ginger, peeled and minced
- 2   cloves garlic, minced
- 1   Fresno chile pepper, minced (wear plastic gloves when handling)
- 1   cup plain Greek yogurt

FOR THE HENS AND STOCK

- 2   (1½-pound) Cornish game hens, quartered, backbones and wings tips removed and reserved
- 6   cups chicken stock

    Kosher salt
- 2   tablespoons canola oil

    Fresh cilantro leaves, for garnish

FOR THE BASMATI RICE

- 1   cup basmati rice
- 1   teaspoon kosher salt
- ½   cup finely chopped fresh cilantro

TO MAKE THE CURRY POWDER: Stir the cardamom, cloves, caraway, coriander, peppercorns, mustard seeds, and red-pepper flakes in a small, heavy-bottomed dry skillet over medium heat until toasted, about 7 minutes. Set the toasted spices aside to cool, then grind them in a spice grinder or a clean coffee grinder. Transfer the ground spices to a small bowl, then stir in the paprika, turmeric, and ginger. Set the curry powder aside.

INDIAN CURRY CORNISH HEN

(continued)

TO MAKE THE YOGURT SAUCE: Heat the oil in a large, heavy-bottomed sauté pan over medium heat. Add the shallots, ginger, garlic, and chile pepper and sauté until tender and translucent, about 2 minutes. Set aside to cool. Place the yogurt in a medium bowl and stir in the shallot mixture. Reserve the skillet.

TO MAKE THE HENS AND STOCK: Combine the hen backbones and wing tips and the chicken stock in a large, heavy-bottomed saucepan and bring to a simmer over high heat. Reduce the heat to medium and simmer until the stock reduces to 4½ cups, about 45 minutes. Strain the stock through a fine-mesh sieve into an 8-cup liquid measuring cup or large bowl. Spoon off the excess fat.

Meanwhile, season the game hen quarters with salt, then sprinkle 2½ tablespoons of the curry powder all over to coat. Heat the oil in the reserved skillet over medium-high heat. Add half of the hen pieces to the skillet and cook until they are golden brown, about 2 minutes per side. Transfer the hen pieces to a baking sheet, and repeat with the remaining hen pieces.

Add ½ cup of the hen stock to the skillet and stir to scrape up any browned bits. Stir in the yogurt sauce, 2 cups of the hen stock, and 1 teaspoon of the curry powder. Bring the sauce to a simmer. Return the hen pieces, bone side down, to the skillet, and reduce the heat to medium-low. Simmer gently until the hen pieces are cooked through, turning the thigh pieces occasionally, about 20 minutes. Transfer the hen pieces to a clean baking sheet and tent with foil to keep warm.

Continue simmering the sauce until it has thickened slightly, about 5 minutes. Return the hen pieces to the skillet and turn to coat with the sauce and rewarm, if necessary.

TO MAKE THE RICE: Combine 2 cups of the hen stock with the rice and salt in a medium, heavy-bottomed saucepan and bring to a simmer over medium-high heat. Reduce the heat to medium-low, cover, and simmer gently until the liquid is absorbed and the rice is almost tender, about 15 minutes. Remove the pan from the heat and fluff the rice with a fork. Cover and set the pan aside (off the heat) until the rice is tender, about 10 minutes. Add the cilantro and fluff with a fork to mix it in.

TO SERVE: Use a 3-inch ring mold to form the rice on 4 plates. Divide the hen pieces among the plates, and spoon the sauce over and around the pieces. Garnish with the cilantro leaves.

Recipe courtesy of
JOSHUA MARKS

SERVES 4

HOISIN DUCK
WITH ROASTED DAIKON PUREE AND CRISPY BAMBOO RICE

Bamboo rice is a short-grained white rice that's been infused with the juice of young bamboo shoots. The result is rice with a jade-green color and an elusive aroma reminiscent of green tea. When cooked, bamboo rice tends to be moist and sticky, so it can be readily formed into rectangular rice cakes here, each coated with sesame seeds and shallow-fried until crisp. It's a striking accompaniment to the duck, which is coated in a hoisin sauce that is, remarkably, homemade!

Most people cooking Asian food buy the thick, sweet, bottled hoisin sauce at Asian markets, but the team's version allows a cook to use the best ingredients and to simmer the sauce to the desired thickness. The mild, creamy daikon puree sets off the more potent flavors of the duck, and the quick-pickled daikon and cucumbers add tang and crunch. The Girls Team created this refined dish for the Michelin Star challenge—and it's as if someone ran classic Asian ingredients through traditional French methods.

FOR THE DAIKON PUREE

- 1 daikon radish (about 11 ounces), peeled and cut into 1-inch pieces
- 2 tablespoons canola oil
  Kosher salt
- 1¼ cups heavy cream
- 1 cup whole milk

FOR THE HOISIN SAUCE

- ½ cup blood orange juice
- ½ cup pure maple syrup
- ½ cup red miso
- 3 tablespoons rice vinegar
- 1 tablespoon canola oil
- 1 tablespoon Chinese five-spice powder
- 1 teaspoon toasted sesame oil
- ½ teaspoon Sriracha sauce
- 1 clove garlic, minced

FOR THE DUCK

- 6 (6-ounce) boneless duck breasts
  Kosher salt and freshly ground black pepper
- 2 tablespoons duck fat
- 6 shiitake mushrooms, stemmed and sliced
- 1 bunch Chinese broccoli, ends trimmed

CRISPY BAMBOO RICE CAKES

- 2 cups water
- 1 cup bamboo rice
- 1 teaspoon kosher salt
- 2 tablespoons black sesame seeds
- 3 tablespoons canola oil

PICKLED DAIKON AND CUCUMBERS

- 1 cup rice vinegar
- ⅓ cup sugar
- 2 Thai chile peppers, thinly sliced (wear plastic gloves when handling)
- 2 cloves black garlic
- 1 daikon radish (about 10 ounces), peeled and cut into ½-inch cubes
- 1 Persian cucumber, peeled and cut into ½-inch cubes

TO MAKE THE DAIKON PUREE: Preheat the oven to 375°F. Toss the daikon with the oil in a large bowl to coat, then transfer the daikon to a baking sheet and season with salt. Roast until it begins to brown, about 35 minutes.

Transfer the daikon to a medium, heavy-bottomed saucepan, then add the cream and milk and bring to a simmer over medium-high heat. Reduce the heat to medium-low and simmer until the daikon is tender, about 10 minutes. Using a slotted spoon, transfer the daikon to a food processor and puree until smooth, adding about ¼ cup of the cooking liquid to form a thick puree. Strain the puree through a fine-mesh sieve into another saucepan and season to taste with salt. (Discard the cream and milk used for cooking, or reserve it for another use.)

TO MAKE THE HOISIN SAUCE: Stir all the sauce ingredients in a medium, heavy-bottomed saucepan and bring to a simmer over medium-high heat. Reduce the heat to medium and simmer until the sauce reduces slightly, about 7 minutes. Strain the sauce through a fine-mesh sieve into a small saucepan and rewarm before serving.

TO MAKE THE DUCK: Season the duck breasts with salt and pepper. Place the breasts, skin side down, in a large heavy skillet, then set the skillet over medium-high heat. Cook until golden brown on the bottom, about 6 minutes. Turn the breasts over and continue cooking until an instant-read thermometer register 125°F when inserted into the thickest part of the breast, basting the duck with the pan drippings, about 3 minutes. Transfer the duck breasts to a carving board, tent with foil, and set aside for 5 minutes. Pour off the pan drippings and return the skillet to the stove.

Heat the skillet over medium-high heat. Once the pan is very hot, add the drippings, then the mushrooms and broccoli. Season with salt and sauté until tender, about 2 minutes.

TO MAKE THE CRISPY BAMBOO RICE CAKES: Combine the water, rice, and salt in a medium, heavy-bottomed saucepan and bring to a boil over high heat. Reduce the heat to medium-low, cover, and simmer gently until the rice is almost tender and the water is absorbed, about 15 minutes. Fluff the rice with a fork, then cover and set aside off the heat until the rice is tender, about 10 minutes.

HOISIN DUCK
(continued)

HOISIN DUCK
(continued)

Transfer the rice to a small baking sheet and form it into a 9 x 8-inch rectangle, pressing to compact it. Cool completely, then cover and refrigerate until cold. Cut the rice into four 4 x 3-inch rectangles. Coat the rice cakes with the sesame seeds.

Heat the oil in a large, heavy-bottomed frying pan over high heat. Fry the rice cakes until they are golden brown and heated through, about 2 minutes per side.

TO MAKE THE PICKLED DAIKON AND CUCUMBERS: Combine the vinegar, sugar, chile peppers, and black garlic in a medium, heavy-bottomed saucepan and bring to a simmer, stirring to dissolve the sugar. Remove the saucepan from the heat and add the daikon and cucumber. Cover and set aside to cool slightly. Transfer the mixture to a container and refrigerate until cold, at least 3 hours.

TO SERVE: Spoon the daikon puree onto 6 plates. Arrange the rice cakes at an angle on top of the puree. Cut the duck into ½-inch-thick slices and lay them over the rice cakes. Drizzle the hoisin sauce around the plate and over the duck. Place the mushrooms and broccoli alongside the duck. Garnish with the pickled daikon and cucumbers.

SERVES 6

Recipe courtesy of
THE GIRLS TEAM
(Becky Reams and Christine Ha)

FIVE-SPICE DUCK BREAST
WITH SWEET POTATO AND EGGPLANT CHIPS

D uck's dark flesh has a certain natural sweetness, and Felix Fang played it up from all sides without making it cloying. From the dark rum and maple syrup in the duck's sauce to the sweet potato chips to the chile-inflected peanut sauce, so many of these components have their own natural sweetness that, taken together, they bring out the very best in the duck breast.

FOR THE CHILE EMULSION

- 6 large egg yolks
- 1 tablespoon water

  Juice of 2 lemons
- 1 Fresno chile pepper, seeded and coarsely chopped (wear plastic gloves when handling)
- 2 teaspoons balsamic vinegar

  Kosher salt

FOR THE PEANUT SAUCE

- ½ cup roasted shelled unsalted peanuts
- 4 teaspoons chopped fresh marjoram
- 2 jalapeño chile peppers, seeded (wear plastic gloves when handling)

  Kosher salt

FOR THE VEGETABLES

- 2 bunches kale, center stem removed
- 2 Chinese eggplants
- 2 slender sweet potatoes, peeled

  About ½ cup olive oil

  Kosher salt

FOR THE DUCK

- 4 large boneless duck breasts
- 2 teaspoons Chinese five-spice powder
- 1 cup dark rum
- ¼ cup pure maple syrup
- 2 teaspoons all-purpose flour

TO MAKE THE CHILE EMULSION: Combine the egg yolks and water in a food processor and mix until smooth. Blend in the lemon juice and the Fresno chile. Blend in the vinegar and then season to taste with salt. Strain and discard the chile pepper. Cover and set the emulsion aside at room temperature.

TO MAKE THE PEANUT SAUCE: Combine the peanuts, marjoram, and jalapeños in a food processor, and puree until smooth and a pestolike consistency forms. Season to taste with salt and set aside.

TO MAKE THE VEGETABLES: Cook the kale in a large pot of boiling water until wilted, about 45 seconds. Drain and transfer the kale to a bowl of ice water. Once cold, drain the kale and squeeze out as much liquid as possible. Set aside at room temperature.

Preheat the oven to 350°F. Line a large heavy baking sheet with parchment paper.

Cut the eggplants and sweet potatoes crosswise on a bias into ⅛-inch-thick ovals. Cook the eggplants and potatoes in a pot of boiling salted water for 1 minute. Drain and transfer to a bowl of ice water to cool completely. Drain and pat dry with a towel. Lightly coat the disks with the oil and arrange them in a single layer on the prepared baking sheet. Season with salt and roast until they are slightly browned on both sides, 8 to 10 minutes, turning them over as necessary. Transfer the baking sheet to a cooling rack.

TO PREPARE THE DUCK: As soon as the vegetables go into the oven, score the duck breast skins and sprinkle with the five-spice powder. Lay the breasts, skin side down, in a large, heavy-bottomed sauté pan. Set the cold pan over medium heat and slowly cook the duck until the skin is dark brown and nicely caramelized, about 8 minutes. Turn the breasts over and cook to medium-rare doneness, about 2 minutes. Transfer to a plate and let rest.

Set the sauté pan over medium heat. Slowly add the flour, whisking constantly until well blended. Add the rum and maple syrup and whisk to blend. Simmer until the sauce thickens slightly, about 2 minutes. Strain the sauce if necessary.

TO SERVE: Arrange the kale leaves in a circular pattern on 4 plates. Slice the duck breasts on the bias and arrange them over the kale. Place the eggplant and sweet potato chips alongside the duck. Spoon the rum sauce over the duck and vegetables. Spoon the peanut sauce alongside. Divide the emulsion among small serving ramekins and set them on the plates alongside the duck and vegetables.

SERVES 4

FIVE-SPICE DUCK BREAST
(continued)

Recipe courtesy of
FELIX FANG

RIBEYE STEAKS
WITH WHISKEY-CHILE BUTTER

Ancho chiles aren't particularly hot, but they have a very rounded, full, and fruity flavor that pairs wonderfully with beef. For the Cowboy Challenge, the Red Team extracted the flavor from an ancho in warm butter, then made an emulsion with a hit of rounded Kentucky bourbon and some cold butter to firm up the sauce. It's so good with the grilled steak that rather than wondering if 11 tablespoons of butter is too much, you may find yourself wondering if it's remotely enough. Spoon some sweet potatoes and green beans alongside the steak, and you'll have a winning combination.

FOR THE WHISKEY-CHILE BUTTER

- 1 dried ancho chile pepper, cut into 6 pieces (wear plastic gloves when handling)
- 11 tablespoons cold unsalted butter
- 2 tablespoons Kentucky bourbon whiskey

  Kosher salt

FOR THE STEAKS

- 1 tablespoon kosher salt
- 1½ teaspoons freshly ground black pepper
- 1½ teaspoons garlic powder
- 1 teaspoon paprika
- ¾ teaspoon ancho chile powder
- ¾ teaspoon New Mexico chile powder
- ¾ teaspoon ground cumin
- 4 (12-ounce) boneless ribeye steaks (1½ inches thick)

TO MAKE THE WHISKEY-CHILE BUTTER: Combine the ancho chile and 6 tablespoons of the butter in a small, heavy-bottomed saucepan and simmer over medium-low heat without stirring until the butter has melted. Spoon off the foam that rises to the top of the butter. Remove the pan from the heat and let infuse for 30 minutes. Discard the chile. Pour the clarified butter into a measuring cup, leaving the milky solids in the pan.

Place the bourbon in a small deep bowl. Using an immersion blender, gradually beat the clarified butter into the bourbon in a very slow, thin stream until all the butter is incorporated. Gradually add the remaining 5 tablespoons of cold butter, 1 tablespoon at a time. Season the chile butter to taste with salt.

TO MAKE THE STEAKS: Prepare the barbecue grill for medium-high heat. Mix the salt, black pepper, garlic powder, paprika, chile powders, and cumin in a small bowl to blend. Season the steaks with the spice mixture. Grill the steaks for 6 to 7 minutes per side for medium-rare doneness, or until an instant-read thermometer registers 120°F when inserted into the thickest part of the steak. Set aside for 5 to 10 minutes.

Place the steaks on 4 plates. Spoon some whiskey butter on top of the steaks and serve immediately.

SERVES 4

Recipe courtesy of
THE RED TEAM
(Monti Carlo, Becky Reams, Joshua Marks, Felix Fang)

PAN-SEARED T-BONE STEAKS
WITH PEACH-TARRAGON SAUCE AND ROASTED CORN AND CABBAGE

For one of the Mystery Box challenges, each contestant was given a box with some corn, cabbage, watermelon, peaches, tarragon, and a T-bone steak—all purchased at low prices. The challenge was to pull together a meal that gave no hint of bargain shopping. Frank Mirando's perfectly seared steak would have been good simply placed on the bed of the roasted corn and cabbage side dish he created. But then he caramelized peaches in the pan juices and transformed them into a creamy sauce accented by the fresh tarragon, and this grace note pulled the entire dish sharply into focus.

FOR THE STEAKS

- 2 tablespoons kosher salt
- 2 teaspoons smoked paprika
- 2 teaspoons sugar
- 1 teaspoon cayenne
- 1 teaspoon freshly ground black pepper
- 2 (1-pound) T-bone steaks
- 4 tablespoons unsalted butter

FOR THE CORN/CABBAGE

- 2 ears corn, husks removed
- 5½ cups water
- 3 lemons, zested and juiced
- 1 teaspoon kosher salt
- 6 cups shredded green cabbage
- 1 tablespoon unsalted butter
- ¼ cup sugar
- 1½ teaspoons smoked paprika
- Kosher salt

FOR THE SAUCE

- 1 tablespoon unsalted butter
- 2 peaches, pitted and cut into cubes
- ½ cup water
- ¼ cup sour cream
- 3 tablespoons chopped fresh tarragon
- 1 lemon, zested and juiced
- Kosher salt

- Fresh tarragon leaves, for garnish

TO MARINATE THE STEAKS: Mix the salt, paprika, sugar, cayenne, and black pepper in a small bowl to blend. Rub the spice mixture all over the steaks, then wrap the steaks in plastic and set aside to marinate.

TO MAKE THE CORN/CABBAGE: Preheat a broiler. Broil the corn until it is slightly charred all over. Set the corn aside to cool, then cut the kernels off the cob and set aside.

Combine 5 cups of the water, the juice and zest from 1 lemon, and the salt in a large, heavy-bottomed pot and bring to a boil over high heat. Add the cabbage and cook until it begins to wilt, about 1 minute. Drain well and place the cabbage in a bowl of ice water to cool completely. Drain well.

Melt the butter in a large, heavy-bottomed sauté pan over medium-high heat. Add the cabbage and sugar and cook until it begins to brown. Add the corn kernels, zest from 2 lemons, and paprika. Increase the heat to high and sauté until caramelized, then add the remaining ½ cup water and stir to deglaze the pan. Simmer until the cabbage is tender and the water has reduced, then remove the pan from the heat and stir in the juice from 2 lemons. Season the cabbage to taste with salt.

TO COOK THE STEAKS: Heat a cast-iron skillet over high heat. Add 2 tablespoons of the butter to the skillet, then add 1 steak and cook until browned and crusty on each side and cooked to desired doneness, about 3 minutes per side for medium-rare. Transfer the steak to a plate and repeat with the remaining 2 tablespoons butter and steak. Set the steaks aside for 10 minutes. Return the skillet to the stove.

TO MAKE THE SAUCE: Pour off the excess butter from the skillet, then add 1 tablespoon butter and the peaches. Cook until the peaches begin to caramelize, then add the water and stir to deglaze the pan. Transfer the mixture to a food processor and pulse until smooth. Add the sour cream, tarragon, lemon zest and juice, and blend until smooth. Strain the sauce through a fine-mesh sieve into a bowl. Season the sauce to taste with salt.

TO SERVE: Spoon the sauce onto 4 plates. Cut the steaks into slices and arrange them on top of the sauce. Mound the cabbage mixture on top of the steaks. Garnish with the fresh tarragon leaves and serve.

SERVES 4

Recipe courtesy of
FRANK MIRANDO

GRILLED T-BONE
WITH CORN SAUCE, PEACH-WATERMELON CHUTNEY, AND BRAISED CABBAGE WITH WATERMELON

To accompany her T-Bone, Tanya Noble, a sociology student from Austin, Texas, made braised cabbage and a sauce with corn and sour cream. Her master touch seemed to draw on her hometown cuisine: She was born and raised in Jakarta, and there's definitely a hint of her Indonesian heritage in the tangy-sweet chutney made of peaches and watermelons. The sauce is not too sweet, not too sharp; it uses a little lemon juice instead of the harsher vinegars that many chutneys use. Her chutney brings together all the flavors of summer in a sauce, making this T-bone meal taste like a holiday picnic.

FOR THE STEAKS

- 4 tablespoons olive oil
- 1 tablespoon smoked paprika
- 1 teaspoon kosher salt
- ½ teaspoon cayenne
- ½ teaspoon freshly ground black pepper
- 1 sprig fresh tarragon, chopped
- 2 (1-pound) T-bone steaks

FOR THE CORN SAUCE

- 2 ears corn, husks removed
- ¼ cup olive oil
- 2 tablespoons sour cream
- 1 teaspoon kosher salt

  Cayenne

FOR THE BRAISED CABBAGE

- ½ cup olive oil
- 2 teaspoons kosher salt plus more for seasoning
- 1 teaspoon cayenne
- 1 teaspoon freshly ground black pepper
- 1 small head green cabbage, cut into 1-inch-thick slices
- ½ cup thinly sliced watermelon
- 2 tablespoons fresh lemon juice
- 2 sprigs fresh tarragon, chopped

PEACH-WATERMELON CHUTNEY

- ¼ cup (½ stick) unsalted butter
- 2 tablespoons olive oil
- 4 firm but ripe peaches, pitted and cubed
- ½ cup chopped watermelon
- ¼ cup sugar
- ¼ cup water
- 1 tablespoon fresh lemon juice
- 1 teaspoon kosher salt

  Cayenne

TO MARINATE THE STEAKS: Whisk 2 tablespoons of the oil with the paprika, salt, cayenne, black pepper, and tarragon in a baking dish. Add the steaks and turn to coat. Cover and refrigerate for at least 30 minutes and up to 1 day.

TO MAKE THE CORN SAUCE: Cook the corn in a large pot of boiling salted water until tender, about 2 minutes. Remove the corn from the water and drain well. Cut the kernels off the cobs and transfer the kernels to a blender. Add the oil, sour cream, and salt. Pulse until blended, then strain the puree through a fine-mesh sieve into a small bowl, pressing on the solids. Discard the solids. Season the corn sauce to taste with cayenne.

TO BRAISE THE CABBAGE: Preheat the oven to 350°F. Whisk the oil, salt, cayenne, and black pepper in a large baking dish to blend. Add the cabbage slices and toss to coat. Transfer the baking dish to the oven and braise the cabbage for 15 minutes. Core the cabbage and cut the cabbage into thin slices.

TO COOK THE STEAKS AND FINISH THE CABBAGE: Heat a large cast-iron pan over medium-high heat. When the pan is hot, add the remaining 2 tablespoons oil, and when the oil is nearly smoking, add the steaks and cook until browned on both sides and cooked to desired doneness, about 5 minutes per side for medium-rare. Transfer the steaks to a cutting board, tent with foil, and set aside to rest. Return the pan to the stove.

Heat the cast-iron pan over medium heat. Add the braised cabbage and sauté until tender and wilted. Toss the cabbage with the watermelon, lemon juice, and tarragon. Season to taste with salt.

TO MAKE THE PEACH-WATERMELON CHUTNEY: Melt the butter with the oil in a large, heavy-bottomed saucepan over medium heat. Add the peaches, watermelon, sugar, water, lemon juice, and salt and cook until the peaches are tender, about 12 minutes. Transfer the mixture to a food processor and puree until almost smooth. Season the chutney to taste with cayenne.

TO SERVE: Trim the fat off the steaks, then slice the steaks on a bias. Spoon some chutney onto 4 plates and lay the steak slices over the chutney. Mound the warm cabbage mixture alongside the steak slices. Drizzle the corn sauce over the steaks and serve.

SERVES 4

Recipe courtesy of
TANYA NOBLE

JOE'S PORCINI STEAK RUB

Porcini dust is like a magic ingredient, bringing depth and complexity of flavor, adding earthiness and a rich nuttiness to foods. Best of all, it adds an explosive savor of *umami*, the Japanese word for the fifth basic taste, the meaty, savory mouthfeel that makes food satisfying. If you can't find it in gourmet stores, you can make your own by grinding dried porcini mushrooms in a coffee or spice grinder until they're a fine powder. Mixed with sugar, salt, garlic, and red-pepper flakes, Joe Bastianich's spice rub is a flavor bomb, all you need to rub on a steak before cooking for the perfect seasoning.

⅓ cup porcini dust

⅓ cup sugar

⅓ cup kosher salt

6 cloves garlic, minced

Red-pepper flakes

Combine the porcini dust, sugar, salt, garlic, and red-pepper flakes to taste in a small bowl.

To use, rub the mixture generously on both sides of steaks and allow to rest for 10 minutes before cooking. Use the rub the same day, and discard any leftovers.

MAKES 1 GENEROUS CUP, ENOUGH FOR 6 TO 8 STEAKS

FILETS THREE WAYS

The Pressure Tests really made the contestants sweat. When Joshua Marks landed with a filet Pressure Test, he had a short amount of time and a limited amount of steak to impress the judges with his technique. Filet mignon is a particularly buttery piece of beef, and if it's not well cooked, it can taste downright mushy. With these precise directions, you can cook a filet to perfection, whether you want it rare, medium-rare, or well done.

3 (8-ounce) beef filet mignon steaks (each about 1½ inches thick)

Kosher salt and freshly ground black pepper

3 tablespoons olive oil

6 tablespoons unsalted butter

3 sprigs fresh thyme

2 sprigs fresh rosemary

3 large cloves garlic, unpeeled and bruised

TO COOK 1 STEAK UNTIL WELL DONE: Preheat the oven to 450°F. Season 1 steak with salt and pepper. Heat a 10-inch heavy skillet (preferably cast-iron) over medium-high heat. Add 1 tablespoon of the oil to the hot skillet, then lay the steak in the skillet and cook until browned, about 2 minutes per side. Add 2 tablespoons of the butter and all of the thyme, then transfer the skillet to the oven and finish cooking the steak until an instant-read thermometer registers 135°F when inserted into the center of the steak, about 8 minutes. Occasionally baste the steak with the pan drippings, turning it over after the first 5 minutes. Transfer the steak to a plate and set aside for 5 minutes before serving to allow the internal temperature to continue rising to 140°F.

TO COOK 1 STEAK UNTIL MEDIUM-RARE: Preheat the oven to 450°F. Season 1 steak with salt and pepper. Heat a 10-inch heavy skillet (preferably cast-iron) over medium-high heat. Add 1 tablespoon of the oil to the hot skillet, then lay the steak in the skillet and cook until browned, about 2 minutes per side. Add 2 tablespoons of the butter and all of the rosemary, then transfer the skillet to the oven and roast until an instant-read thermometer registers 120°F when inserted into the center of the steak, about 6 minutes. Occasionally baste the steak with the pan drippings, turning it over after the first 3 minutes. Transfer the steak to a plate and set aside for 5 minutes before serving to allow the internal temperature to continue rising to 125°F.

TO COOK 1 STEAK UNTIL RARE: Season 1 steak with salt and pepper. Heat a 10-inch heavy skillet (preferably cast-iron) over medium-high heat. Add 1 tablespoon of the oil to the hot skillet, then lay the steak in the skillet and cook until browned, about 2 minutes per side. Reduce the heat to medium, then add 2 tablespoons of the butter and all of the garlic. Cook on the stove until an instant-read thermometer registers 115°F when inserted into the center of the steak, about 4 minutes. Occasionally baste the steak with the melted butter, turning it over after the first 2 minutes. Transfer the steak to a plate and set aside for 5 minutes before serving to allow the internal temperature to continue rising to 120°F.

SERVES 3

Recipe courtesy of
JOSHUA MARKS

GRILLED NY STRIP STEAK
WITH SMOKY SPICY-SWEET BARBECUE SAUCE

When the Blue Team was considering what to make for cowboys on a dude ranch, a NY strip steak seemed like the right kind of hearty evening meal for people who'd been wrangling cattle all day. The steaks themselves have a potent spice rub complemented by the layered flavors of the very spicy barbecue sauce. Try the same sauce on a burger for a real taste sensation. The Blue Team served this up with Garlic Mashed Potatoes (page 107) and Grilled Corn on the Cob (page 106). The recipe uses some big steaks, so if you make enough side dishes and carve up your steaks, you can serve a party.

FOR THE BARBECUE SAUCE

- 2 tablespoons unsalted butter
- ½ onion, diced
- 2 bacon slices, cut into ½-inch pieces
- 3 tablespoons packed light brown sugar
- 1 tablespoon chopped chipotle chile peppers in adobo sauce
- 1½ teaspoons garlic powder
- 1 teaspoon chili powder
- 1 teaspoon ground cumin
- 1 teaspoon sweet paprika
- 1 teaspoon kosher salt
- ½ teaspoon freshly ground black pepper
- ¼ teaspoon cayenne
- 1 cup ketchup
- ½ cup apple cider vinegar
  Kosher salt

FOR THE STEAKS

- 2 teaspoons chili powder
- 2 teaspoons ground cumin
- 2 teaspoons garlic powder
- 2 teaspoons onion powder
- 2 teaspoons sweet paprika
- 2 teaspoons packed light brown sugar
- 1 teaspoon ground cinnamon
- 1 teaspoon freshly ground black pepper
- 6 (14- to 16-ounce) New York strip steaks, trimmed (about 1½ inches thick)
- 2 tablespoons kosher salt

TO MAKE THE BARBECUE SAUCE: Melt 1 tablespoon of the butter in a medium, heavy-bottomed saucepan over medium-high heat. Add the onion, bacon, brown sugar, chipotle chile, garlic powder, chili powder, cumin, paprika, salt, black pepper, and cayenne. Cook until the onion is tender and the brown sugar dissolves, about 10 minutes. Add the ketchup, vinegar, and the remaining 1 tablespoon butter. Bring the sauce to a boil, then reduce the heat and simmer until the flavors blend and the mixture reduces slightly, about 10 minutes. Season the sauce to taste with salt. Cool the sauce slightly.

Working in batches if necessary, puree the sauce in a blender until smooth. Transfer the sauce to a saucepan and warm before serving.

TO MAKE THE STEAKS: Prepare a barbecue grill for medium-high heat. Mix the chili powder, cumin, garlic powder, onion powder, paprika, brown sugar, cinnamon, and pepper in a small bowl to blend. Generously season the steaks on both sides with the salt. Evenly coat the steaks with the spice mixture.

Grill the steaks until they are cooked to the desired doneness, about 5 minutes per side for medium-rare. Transfer the steaks to plates and let rest 5 minutes.

Divide the sauce among 6 plates. Top each with a steak. Serve immediately.

NOTE: The steaks are large, so they can be cut into slices to serve up to 12 people, if desired.

SERVES 6

Recipe courtesy of
THE BLUE TEAM
(Frank Mirando, Christine Ha, David Martinez, Stacey Amagrande)

WINE PAIRING

A big classic steak calls for a big classic American wine: A California Zinfandel is your best bet every time! The characteristics of Zinfandels vary depending on the climate in which they are grown, but California typically turns out big, juicy, jammy Zinfandels with high alcohol contents, with bold berry flavors, that pack enough punch in flavor to hold their own against the steak.

STEAK TACOS
WITH BELL PEPPERS, GUACAMOLE, AND PICO DE GALLO

For the Food Truck challenge, the Red Team decided to make tacos. It makes sense if you're trying to prep food quickly: The meat and vegetables can be tossed with spices and a little oil and grilled as needed. Home cooks can do the same. Everything can be sliced up and left to marinate earlier in the day; the pico de gallo and even the guacamole can be made in advance. For the guacamole, be sure to cover it tightly with plastic wrap, pressing the plastic against the surface of the guacamole. When you're ready, the grilling is short work and you can be eating in minutes.

FOR THE STEAK

- 1½ teaspoons smoked paprika
- 1 teaspoon chili powder
- 1 teaspoon garlic powder
- 1 teaspoon ground coriander
- ¾ teaspoon ground cumin
- 1 teaspoon kosher salt
- 1 small lemon
- 1 lime
- 1½ pounds flank steak
- 4 teaspoons canola oil

FOR THE VEGETABLES

- 2 teaspoons canola oil
- ½ teaspoon dried oregano
- ½ teaspoon ground cumin
- ½ teaspoon sweet paprika
- ½ teaspoon kosher salt
- 2 green bell peppers, seeded and cut into ¾-inch strips
- 1 onion, cut into ¾-inch strips

- 1 jalapeño chile pepper, seeded and cut into ¼-inch pieces (wear plastic gloves when handling)

FOR THE PICO DE GALLO

- 2 tomatoes (1 pound total); 1 quartered, 1 diced
- 1 medium white onion; ½ coarsely chopped, ½ finely diced
- ½ jalapeño chile pepper, coarsely chopped (wear plastic gloves when handling)
- 2 cloves garlic, finely chopped
- 2 tablespoons minced fresh cilantro
- 1 teaspoon kosher salt

FOR THE GUACAMOLE

- 2 avocados, peeled and pitted
- 1 large clove garlic, minced
- 2 tablespoons finely chopped fresh cilantro
- 2 tablespoons minced scallion

- 2 tablespoons fresh lime juice
- 1 tablespoon seeded, minced jalapeño chile pepper (wear plastic gloves when handling)
- 1 teaspoon (or more) kosher salt

  Freshly ground black pepper

FOR THE TACOS

- 8 corn tortillas, warm

  Pico de Gallo

  Guacamole

- ½ cup crumbled Cotija cheese

STEAK TACOS

(continued)

TO PREPARE THE STEAK: Mix the paprika, chili powder, garlic powder, coriander, cumin, and salt in a large bowl. Using a Microplane grater, grate the zest from the lemon and lime into the spice mixture, then squeeze about 2 tablespoons of juice from each into the spice mixture. Stir to blend. Cut the steak into ¾-inch strips, then add them to the spice mixture and toss to coat.

TO PREPARE THE VEGETABLES: Whisk the oil, oregano, cumin, paprika, and salt in a medium bowl to blend. Add the bell peppers, onion, and jalapeño and toss to coat.

TO GRILL THE STEAK AND VEGETABLES: Heat 2 teaspoons of the oil in a large, heavy-bottomed skillet over high heat. Add half of the steak strips and cook until brown on the outside and medium-rare, about 3 minutes. Transfer the steak to a small baking dish. Repeat with the remaining 2 teaspoons oil and steak strips. Tent with foil to keep warm. Toss the steak strips in the dish to coat with their juices before serving.

Heat the same skillet over medium-high heat. Add the vegetables and cook until they are crisp-tender and slightly charred, about 6 minutes.

TO MAKE THE PICO DE GALLO: Combine the quartered tomato, coarsely chopped onion, jalapeño, and garlic in a food processor and pulse until the tomato is finely chopped and the mixture is juicy. Transfer the mixture to a medium bowl. Stir in the diced tomato, diced onion, cilantro, and salt. Set aside at room temperature for at least 30 minutes and up to 1 hour to allow all the flavors to blend.

TO MAKE THE GUACAMOLE: Using a fork, coarsely mash the avocados in a medium bowl. Mix in the garlic, cilantro, scallion, lime juice, jalapeño, and 1 teaspoon salt. Season the guacamole to taste with more salt and black pepper. Serve immediately or press a sheet of plastic wrap directly on the surface of the guacamole and refrigerate for up to 2 hours.

TO SERVE: Divide the steak and vegetables among the warm tortillas. Using a slotted spoon, spoon some of the pico de gallo over the tacos. Top each with some guacamole and sprinkle with the Cotija. Serve the remaining pico de gallo and guacamole alongside.

SERVES 4

Recipe courtesy of
THE RED TEAM
(Stacey Amagrande, Becky Reams, Frank Mirando, Tali Clavijo)

PANAMANIAN SPICED BEEF MOFONGO

Mofongo is a dish of fried green plantains, mashed and usually mixed with meat or seafood. It's ubiquitous throughout Puerto Rico, the Dominican Republic, and Cuba. Historians speculate that it actually stems from recipes that Africans brought to Spanish New World colonies, since the dish so closely mimics the starchy *fufu* that's found in many countries throughout Africa.

When faced with a heap of meat in the Ground Beef challenge, Joshua Marks turned to a Panamanian version of the dish that has meatballs stirred into the mashed plantains. It is definitely a heavy, hearty dish, ideal for cooler weather, but he lightened it with a bright mango puree and a crisp jicama slaw, along with a little fried squid on top to acknowledge the time-honored place seafood also has in a dish of *mofongo*.

FOR THE PLANTAINS

- ¼ cup canola oil
- 2 green plantains, peeled and cut into ¼-inch slices
- 1½ teaspoons ground cinnamon
- 1½ teaspoons kosher salt
- 1 teaspoon cayenne
- 2 cloves garlic, minced
- 1 sprig fresh oregano
- ¼ cup olive oil

FOR THE MEATBALLS

- 1 pound ground beef
- 1½ teaspoons garlic powder
- 1½ teaspoons onion powder
- 1 teaspoon cayenne
- 1 teaspoon curry powder
- ½ teaspoon chili powder
- ½ teaspoon kosher salt

- ½ teaspoon smoked paprika
- ¼ teaspoon ground white pepper
- Vegetable oil

FOR THE MANGO PUREE

- 2 mangoes, peeled, pitted, and coarsely chopped
- ½ cup orange juice
- ½ habanero chile, sliced (where plastic gloves when handling)

FOR THE JICAMA SLAW

- 1 small jicama, peeled and julienned
- ¼ red onion, thinly sliced
- ½ habanero chile, sliced (where plastic gloves when handling)
- 1 teaspoon chopped fresh cilantro
- Juice of ½ lime
- ½ teaspoon chili powder
- 2 tablespoons olive oil

FOR THE TEMPURA SQUID

- Canola oil
- 1 cup all-purpose flour
- ½ teaspoon smoked paprika
- ½ teaspoon kosher salt
- 1 cup ice-cold club soda
- 1 cleaned squid body, sliced into ½-inch-wide rings

- Chopped fresh cilantro, for garnish
- Smoked paprika, for garnish

PANAMANIAN SPICED BEEF MOFONGO

(continued)

TO MAKE THE PLANTAINS: Heat the canola oil in a large, heavy-bottomed skillet over medium-high heat. Fry the plantain slices until they're golden brown, about 2 minutes. Transfer the fried plantains to paper towels to drain. Mix the cinnamon, salt, and cayenne in a large bowl to blend. Add the hot fried plantains and toss to coat. Set aside to cool. Using a mortar and pestle, mash the plantains with the garlic, oregano, and olive oil.

TO MAKE THE MEATBALLS: Preheat the oven to 400°F. Mix the beef with the garlic powder, onion powder, cayenne, curry, chili powder, salt, paprika, and white pepper. Form the beef into 4 balls. Heat ¼ inch of vegetable oil in a large, heavy-bottomed skillet over medium-high heat. Add the meatballs and cook until they are browned all over, about 5 minutes. Transfer the meatballs to a baking sheet. Bake until the meatballs are cooked through, about 12 minutes.

Mold the mofongo into 4 small bowls or ramekins. Place a cooked meatball inside each.

TO MAKE THE MANGO PUREE: Combine the mangoes, orange juice, and habanero in a blender and puree until smooth. Strain the puree through a fine-mesh sieve into a small, heavy-bottomed saucepan. Simmer the sauce over medium-high heat until reduced by one-third, about 10 minutes. Set aside.

TO MAKE THE JICAMA SLAW: Toss the jicama, onion, habanero, and cilantro in a medium bowl. Whisk the lime juice and chili powder in a medium bowl to blend. Gradually add the oil, whisking constantly to emulsify. About 15 minutes before serving, toss the jicama mixture with the dressing to coat.

TO MAKE THE SQUID TEMPURA: Heat 1 inch of canola oil in a large, heavy-bottomed saucepan over medium-high heat to 375°F. Stir the flour, paprika, and salt in a large bowl to blend. Add the club soda and stir to form a thin, slightly lumpy tempura batter. Toss the squid rings in the batter to coat lightly. Remove the squid from the batter, allowing any excess batter to drip back into the bowl. Fry the squid until the tempura is crisp and golden, about 3 minutes. Using a slotted spoon, remove the squid tempura from the oil and transfer to paper towels to drain the excess oil.

TO SERVE: Spoon the mango puree onto 4 plates. Invert the mofongo meatball onto the plate atop the sauce. Mound the jicama slaw alongside the mofongo and top with the squid tempura. Garnish with the cilantro and smoked paprika and serve immediately.

Recipe courtesy of
JOSHUA MARKS

SERVES 4

BARBECUE PORK CHOPS

P ork chops can be tough to cook. They go from too pink in the middle to perfectly cooked to almost inedibly dry in the blink of an eye, all the while looking nothing but golden brown on the exterior. Even when perfectly cooked, pork chops on their own can be a little unexciting. But pork loves barbecue sauce and chops are no exception. The judges all agreed it was the sauce that won this challenge, where the teams had to feed the troops at Camp Pendleton, a Marine Corps base near San Diego. The sauce has all the flavors of a classic, smoky, tomato-based sauce in perfect balance here, including a shot of ballpark yellow mustard to brighten the flavors and just enough chipotle to add some smoky heat without a lot of burn. You'll be making up batches of this sauce even when you're not cooking chops.

FOR THE PORK CHOPS

½ cup apple cider vinegar

2 tablespoons kosher salt

2 tablespoons sugar

2 tablespoons chopped fresh basil

2 tablespoons chopped fresh flat-leaf parsley

2 tablespoons chopped fresh oregano

1 tablespoon dried Italian seasoning

4 (2- to 2½-inch-thick) bone-in center-cut pork chops

FOR THE BARBECUE SAUCE

1½ cups ketchup

1 onion, grated

¾ cup packed light brown sugar

½ cup yellow mustard

¼ cup mild-flavored molasses

¼ cup Worcestershire sauce

2 tablespoons garlic powder

1 tablespoon chopped chipotle chiles in adobo sauce

2 teaspoons freshly ground black pepper

TO MARINATE THE PORK CHOPS: Whisk the vinegar, salt, sugar, basil, parsley, oregano, and Italian seasoning in a glass baking dish to blend. Add the pork chops and turn to coat. Cover and marinate for 10 minutes.

MEANWHILE, TO MAKE THE BARBECUE SAUCE: Combine the ketchup, onion, brown sugar, mustard, molasses, Worcestershire sauce, garlic powder, chipotle, and black pepper in a large, heavy-bottomed saucepan over medium heat. Simmer, stirring occasionally, until the sauce thickens and reduces slightly, about 12 minutes.

TO GRILL THE PORK CHOPS AND SERVE: Prepare a barbecue grill for high heat. Grill the pork chops until an instant-read thermometer registers 145°F when inserted into the center, about 4 minutes per side. Transfer the pork chops to plates and slather with the barbecue sauce. Let rest for 5 minutes before serving.

Recipe courtesy of
THE RED TEAM
(Stacey Amagrande, Monti Carlo, Helene Leeds, Mike Hill, Anna Rossi, Joshua Marks, Ryan Umane, David Martinez)

SERVES 4

PAN-ROASTED PORK CHOPS
WITH MUSHROOMS AND POMEGRANATE GASTRIQUE

For the Blue Moon challenge, eight contestants who had already been eliminated got a second chance. Each of the eight was allowed to go into the pantry and to choose one ingredient, and then every contestant had to make something using those ingredients. During the judging, Ryan, a contestant from New York, did not get handed another white apron, but his pan-roasted pork chops are a worthy recipe, a great treatment for pork chops and easy enough for a weeknight supper. "Gastrique" may sound like something you won't find outside the confines of a French restaurant, but it's really just a simple reduction of fruit juice, sugar, and vinegar, a perfect tangy sauce for pork.

FOR THE GASTRIQUE

- 1 cup fresh pomegranate juice (from 2 pomegranates; see Tip opposite page)
- 1 celery stalk, diced
- ½ cup water
- ½ cup sugar
- ¼ cup white wine vinegar
- 2 tablespoons unsalted butter

  Kosher salt

FOR THE MUSHROOMS

- 3 tablespoons olive oil
- 2 celery stalks, thinly sliced
- 4 portobello mushrooms, gills scraped, caps sliced
- 2 tablespoons unsalted butter
- 1 tablespoon white wine vinegar

  Kosher salt and freshly ground black pepper

- 2 tablespoons fresh lemon juice

FOR THE PORK

- 4 (1½-inch-thick) bone-in, center-cut pork chops

  Kosher salt and freshly ground black pepper

  All-purpose flour

- 4 tablespoons olive oil
- 4 tablespoons (½ stick) unsalted butter

TO MAKE THE GASTRIQUE: Combine the pomegranate juice, celery, water, and ¼ cup of the sugar in a small, heavy-bottomed saucepan and simmer gently until reduced by half, about 25 minutes.

Cook the remaining ¼ cup sugar in another small, heavy-bottomed saucepan over medium heat without stirring until it melts and turns a golden brown color, swirling the pan to brown the sugar evenly, about 8 minutes. Slowly add the vinegar and pomegranate reduction. Simmer until the sauce has a syrupy consistency, about 7 minutes. Whisk in the butter to blend. Strain the sauce and season to taste with salt.

TO MAKE THE MUSHROOMS: Heat the oil in a large, heavy-bottomed sauté pan over medium-high heat. Add the celery and sauté until translucent, about 3 minutes. Add the mushrooms and butter and toss to coat. Sauté until the mushrooms are tender, about 3 minutes. Stir in the vinegar. Season to taste with salt and pepper. Drizzle with the lemon juice.

TO MAKE THE PORK: Preheat the oven to 450°F. Season the pork chops with salt and pepper. Dredge the chops in flour to coat lightly and shake off any excess flour.

Meanwhile, heat 2 large, heavy-bottomed skillets (preferably cast-iron) over high heat. Once hot, add 2 tablespoons of the oil then 2 pork chops to each skillet and cook until golden brown, about 3 minutes per side. Add the butter to the skillets and transfer the skillets to the oven. Roast the pork chops until an instant-read thermometer registers 145°F when inserted into the center, about 5 minutes. While the pork chops roast, occasionally baste them with the pan drippings. Transfer the pork chops to a carving board and let rest for 5 to 10 minutes.

TO SERVE: Mound the mushrooms in the centers of 4 plates. Slice the pork chops and set them on top of the mushrooms. Pour any accumulated juices from the pork over the chops. Spoon the gastrique around and serve.

TIP: To make fresh pomegranate juice, cut 2 pomegranates in half crosswise, then remove the seeds from the pomegranates and pound the seeds in a mortar with a pestle until their juice exudes. Strain the mixture through a fine-mesh sieve into a bowl, pressing on and discarding the solids. You should have about 1 cup of juice.

SERVES 4

Recipe courtesy of
RYAN UMANE

STUFFED LAMB SADDLE
WITH ROASTED BABY VEGETABLES
AND ISRAELI COUSCOUS

L amb saddle is something you will likely need to request from a butcher. The lamb saddle is basically the entire lamb loin, the part where you get all those beautiful chops, but still encircled in a layer of creamy fat. It's not an inexpensive piece of meat; but for a luxury, high-end meal, it's as tender and juicy as a piece of lamb can be.

This is the main dish that the Boys Team created for the Michelin Star challenge, so they garnished the plate with exquisitely turned baby vegetables, roasted just to tenderness, and creamy large pearls of Israeli couscous, napped with an aromatic tomato sauce spiced with ras el hanout. It's a Moroccan spice mixture whose name literally means "best in shop." The exact spices used can vary dramatically, including up to 100 different ingredients. It generally contains about a dozen ground spices, such as turmeric, cinnamon, cardamom, chile, cloves, coriander, cumin, nutmeg, black and white peppercorns, mace, and star anise. If you can't find a ready-made mixture, make your own by combining ¼ teaspoon of each desired spice.

FOR THE LAMB AND JUS

- 1 (6½-pound) lamb saddle
- 2 teaspoons olive oil
- 1 onion, very coarsely diced
- 2 celery stalks, very coarsely diced
- 2 medium carrots, peeled and very coarsely diced
- 6 cups lamb stock
- 6 cups water
- 2 large sprigs fresh thyme
- 1 fresh bay leaf
- 18 thin slices prosciutto
- ½ teaspoon jalapeño chile powder
  Kosher salt and freshly ground black pepper
- 2 tablespoons goat milk butter

FOR THE FILLING

- 1 tablespoon olive oil
- 2 ramps, bulbs and slender pink stems finely diced
- 2 cloves garlic, minced
- 2 cups plain Greek yogurt
- ¾ cup pine nuts, toasted
- ½ cup golden raisins
- ¼ cup minced fresh mint
- ½ teaspoon jalapeño chile powder
- ½ teaspoon kosher salt

FOR THE VEGETABLES

- 8 baby purple potatoes (about 1¼- to 1½-inch-diameter)
- 8 baby Yukon Gold potatoes (about 1¼- to 1½-inch-diameter)
- 3 cloves garlic, peeled
- 3 sprigs fresh thyme
- 3 tablespoons olive oil
  Kosher salt and freshly ground black pepper
- 8 baby golden beets (about 1¼- to 1½-inch-diameter)
- 8 baby red beets (about 1¼- to 1½-inch-diameter)
- 16 petite carrots, peeled
- 8 baby spring onions, halved lengthwise

1   pound cherry tomatoes

3   tablespoons extra-virgin
olive oil

Kosher salt and freshly
ground black pepper

4   red jalapeño chiles, seeded
and coarsely chopped (use
plastic gloves when
handling)

2   shallots, coarsely chopped

2   cloves garlic, coarsely
chopped

1   cup fumé blanc or other dry
white wine

1   tablespoon ras el hanout

1   cup Israeli couscous

TO PREPARE THE LAMB SADDLE AND JUS: Using a boning knife, remove the chine bone (backbone) that runs down the center of the saddle and between the 2 loins and 2 tenderloins, being careful not to cut through the outer layer of fat that keeps the saddle intact (the tenderloins will detach). Set the bone aside. Trim most of the outer layer of fat and trim any sinew from the saddle and tenderloins.*

Heat the oil in a large, heavy-bottomed stockpot over medium-high heat. Add the bone and meaty trimmings and cook until browned, about 8 minutes. Add the onion, celery, and carrots. Add the lamb stock, water, thyme, and bay leaf, and bring to a simmer. Reduce the heat to medium-low and simmer gently, about 2½ hours. Strain the stock through a fine-mesh sieve into an 8-cup bowl, and discard the solids. Skim the fat.

Simmer the stock in a medium, heavy-bottomed saucepan over medium-high heat until reduced to 1 cup, about 1 hour. Cover and set aside.

TO MAKE THE FILLING: Heat a small, heavy-bottomed sauté pan over medium-low heat. Add the oil, ramps, and garlic and sauté until tender, about 2 minutes. Transfer to a medium bowl and cool completely. Mix in the yogurt, pine nuts, raisins, mint, chile powder, and salt.

TO STUFF AND ROAST THE SADDLE: Lay the prosciutto slices in a single layer over an 18 x 14-inch sheet of plastic wrap so that they overlap slightly and cover the plastic sheet completely. Season the lamb with chile powder, salt, and pepper, then spoon 1¼ cups yogurt mixture down the center. Reserve the remaining yogurt mixture to serve with the saddle. Lay the tenderloins over the filling, then fold the saddle together. Lay the lamb on the sheet of prosciutto and wrap the prosciutto tightly around the lamb to cover completely, folding in the ends. Cover and refrigerate at least 45 minutes and up to 1 day.

Preheat the oven to 400°F. Set the saddle on a rack in a roasting pan. Roast until an instant-read thermometer registers 120°F when inserted into the thickest part of the meat, about 45 minutes. Transfer the saddle on the rack to a carving board and set aside for 15 minutes.

Add the reduced lamb stock to the roasting pan and stir to scrape up any browned bits and pan drippings. Strain the jus into a small saucepan and set aside.

MEANWHILE, TO PREPARE THE VEGETABLES: Coat the potatoes, garlic, and thyme with 1 tablespoon of the oil in a medium

STUFFED LAMB SADDLE

(continued)

bowl. Season with salt and pepper. Arrange the mixture over half of a large heavy baking sheet.

Coat the beets in the same bowl with 1 tablespoon of the oil. Season with salt and pepper and arrange over the other half of the baking sheet.

Coat the carrots and spring onions on another large heavy baking sheet with the remaining 1 tablespoon oil. Season with salt and pepper.

Roast all the vegetables until they are tender and beginning to brown, jostling the pans and turning the vegetables occasionally to ensure they brown evenly, about 25 minutes.

TO MAKE THE ISRAELI COUSCOUS WITH RAS EL HANOUT– TOMATO SAUCE: Preheat the broiler. Coat the tomatoes on a small heavy baking sheet with 1 tablespoon of the oil and season with salt and pepper. Broil the tomatoes until they blister and begin to char, about 8 minutes.

Heat the remaining 2 tablespoons oil in a medium, heavy-bottomed saucepan over medium-high heat. Add the chiles, shallots, and garlic and sauté until tender, about 3 minutes. Add the broiled tomatoes and wine. Bring to a simmer, then reduce the heat to medium-low. Cover and simmer gently until the tomatoes are very tender, about 15 minutes. Stir in the ras el hanout. Transfer the mixture to a blender and puree until smooth. Strain the mixture through a fine-mesh sieve and return it to the saucepan. Season the sauce to taste with salt.

Meanwhile, cook the couscous in a large saucepan of boiling salted water until tender but still firm to the bite, about 5 minutes. Drain the couscous and arrange on a small baking sheet to cool.

When ready to serve, bring the sauce to a simmer over medium heat. Add the couscous and stir just until heated through, about 2 minutes. Serve immediately.

TO SERVE: Bring the jus to a simmer. Remove the pan from the heat and whisk in the goat butter. Season the jus to taste with salt and pepper.

Spoon the couscous onto the center of 8 plates. Cut the lamb crosswise into eight 1-inch-thick slices. Lay 1 slice alongside the couscous on each plate. Arrange the roasted vegetables on the plates. Spoon a dollop of the reserved yogurt mixture on each plate. Spoon the jus around and serve immediately.

* Alternatively, ask your butcher to fabricate the saddle up to this point, then cut the chine bone in half and reserve the bones and all the meaty trimmings for you.

Recipe courtesy of
**FRANK MIRANDO
AND JOSHUA MARKS**

SERVES 8

CARIMAÑOLAS WITH THREE SALSAS

The Legs challenge required the contestants to cook with some sort of leg: chicken legs, frog legs, lamb legs. Joshua Marks was fortunate enough to get the leg of lamb as his challenge, and he reached for the exciting flavors of the Caribbean to bring out the best in it. *Carimañolas* are yuca fritters popular in Panama and Colombia. It's stuffed with meat or cheese, or both, and deep-fried. Joshua made a spicy mixture from cubed lamb and served it up with three different salsas and a crispy jicama slaw. Carimañolas make a very filling main dish, but they're also a great finger food to eat with cocktails.

FOR THE CARIMAÑOLAS

- 8 ounces well-trimmed leg of lamb meat, cut into ½-inch pieces

  Kosher salt and freshly ground black pepper

- 1½ teaspoons Madras curry powder
- 1 teaspoon cayenne
- 1 teaspoon smoked paprika
- 1 tablespoon olive oil
- 3 cups beef stock
- 1 yuca root (1¼ pounds), peeled and cut into ¾-inch pieces

  Canola oil

FOR THE MANGO SALSA

- 1 mango, peeled, pitted, and coarsely chopped
- ¼ cup orange juice
- ½ small habanero chile, seeded and chopped (wear plastic gloves when handling)

  Small pinch of cayenne

  Kosher salt

FOR THE SALSA ROJA

- 2 vine-ripened tomatoes, quartered
- 1 Fresno chile pepper, halved (wear plastic gloves when handling)
- 2 cloves garlic, with skin on
- 1 tablespoon canola oil

  Pinch of Madras curry powder

FOR THE SALSA VERDE

- 3 tomatillos, husked and quartered
- 1 poblano chile pepper, seeded and quartered (wear plastic gloves when handling)
- 1 jalapeño chile pepper, halved (wear plastic gloves when handling)
- 1 tablespoon canola oil
- ¼ cup loosely packed fresh cilantro
- 1½ tablespoons fresh lime juice

FOR THE JICAMA SLAW

- 1 cup finely julienned jicama
- ½ cup finely julienned red onion
- 2 tablespoons fresh lime juice
- 1 teaspoon olive oil
- ¼ teaspoon chile powder
- ¼ teaspoon kosher salt
- ⅓ cup micro cilantro, for garnish

TO MAKE THE CARIMAÑOLAS: Season the lamb with salt and pepper, then season it with the curry powder, cayenne, and smoked paprika. Heat the oil in a large heavy pressure cooker over medium-high heat. Add the lamb and cook until browned, about 8 minutes. Add the beef stock and stir to scrape up the browned bits. Cover and seal the pressure cooker. Bring the pressure to 15 psi over high heat, then reduce the heat to medium-low and cook for 20 minutes. Turn off the heat and set aside for 10 minutes. Release the pressure from the cooker. Set aside until the mixture is cool. Drain the excess liquid, keeping just enough to moisten the meat.

Meanwhile, cook the yuca in a large saucepan of boiling salted water until tender, about 18 minutes. Drain. Press the yuca through a potato ricer into a medium bowl. Season to taste with salt. Cool completely.

Using 2 tablespoons for each carimañola, form the yuca puree into a cup in the palm of your hand. Spoon about 1 generous teaspoon of the lamb into the yuca cup, then pinch the yuca opening together to enclose the filling. Roll the carimañola between the palms of your hands to form it into a ball. Repeat to make 18 total. Cover and refrigerate.

TO MAKE THE MANGO SALSA: Combine the mango, orange juice, habanero, and cayenne in a blender and puree until smooth. Strain the puree through a fine-mesh sieve into a small bowl. Season to taste with salt. Cover and refrigerate until cold.

TO MAKE THE SALSA ROJA AND SALSA VERDE: Preheat the oven to 500°F. Toss the tomatoes, Fresno chile, garlic, and oil in a medium bowl to coat. Arrange the mixture over half of a large heavy baking sheet. Coat the tomatillos, poblano, and jalapeño with the oil in the same medium bowl, then arrange them on the other half of the baking sheet. Sprinkle the mixtures with salt, and roast until the tomatoes and tomatillos are tender and beginning to caramelize on the bottom but are still quite juicy, about 15 minutes.

Remove the skin from the roasted garlic, then combine the tomato mixture in a blender. Add the curry powder and puree until smooth. Strain the puree through a fine-mesh sieve into a small bowl.

Combine the tomatillo mixture in a clean blender or small food processor. Add the cilantro and lime juice, then puree until smooth. Strain the puree through a fine-mesh sieve into a small bowl.

TO COOK THE CARIMAÑOLAS: Heat 2 inches of oil in a large, heavy-bottomed frying pan over medium heat to 375°F. Fry the carimañolas until golden brown and heated through, about 5 minutes. Using a slotted spoon, transfer the carimañolas to a plate lined with paper towels to drain.

TO MAKE THE SLAW: Just before serving, toss all the ingredients in a medium bowl.

TO SERVE: Spoon 1 tablespoon of each of the 3 salsas in separate pools onto each of 4 plates. Set 1 carimañola on top of each pool of salsa. Mound the jicama salsa alongside, garnish with the micro cilantro, and serve immediately.

SERVES 6

CARIMAÑOLAS
(continued)

Recipe courtesy of
JOSHUA MARKS

GRILLED VENISON MEDALLIONS
WITH BOURBON-MUSHROOM REDUCTION AND CREAMED POTATOES

Venison can be tough to cook, quite literally. It's an extremely lean meat that dries out like shoe leather if it cooks too long, and it generally takes a real pro to bring out its best. Mike Hill had cooked some admirable dishes during the competition, but this dish was his zenith. Mike is—as he'll be the first to tell you—a cowboy from Atlanta; he actually rode into his audition on horseback, and his fellow contestants quickly dubbed him "Cowboy Mike." So perhaps it's to be expected that he has such a good hand with cooking meat from out on the range. Certainly this dish was perfection: moist and tender veal medallions, creamy potatoes, rich and meaty reduction infused with bacon, shallots, and bourbon. The judges were downright shocked at the quality, and roundly proclaimed Mike's dish worthy of five stars in any restaurant. For all that, it's a surprisingly straightforward recipe and worth seeking out venison just to make this.

FOR THE VENISON

- 6 tablespoons bourbon
- 6 tablespoons packed light brown sugar
- 6 tablespoons soy sauce
- 6 tablespoons Worcestershire sauce
- 1 teaspoon garlic powder
- ½ teaspoon freshly ground black pepper
- 1 (1-pound) venison tenderloin

FOR THE CREAMED POTATOES

- 3 russet (baking) potatoes, peeled and cut into 1-inch cubes
- ½ cup heavy cream, warm
- 4 tablespoons (½ stick) unsalted butter, at room temperature

  Kosher salt and freshly ground black pepper

FOR THE REDUCTION SAUCE

- 4 bacon slices, finely diced
- ½ shallot, minced
- 1 clove garlic, minced
- 8 ounces shiitake mushrooms, stemmed and halved
- ¼ cup bourbon

SAUTÉED GREEN BEANS AND SHALLOTS

- 12 ounces green beans, ends trimmed
- 2 tablespoons unsalted butter
- 3 tablespoons finely diced shallots

  Kosher salt and freshly ground black pepper

TO MARINATE THE VENISON: Whisk the bourbon, brown sugar, soy sauce, Worcestershire sauce, garlic powder, and black pepper in a baking dish to blend. Transfer ½ cup of the marinade to a small, heavy-bottomed saucepan and set aside for the reduction sauce. Add the venison tenderloin to the marinade in the baking dish and turn to coat. Cover and refrigerate for 30 minutes.

MEANWHILE, TO MAKE THE CREAMED POTATOES: Bring a large pot of salted water to a boil over high heat. Add the potatoes and cook until a fork easily pierces a potato, about 15 minutes. Drain the

GRILLED VENISON MEDALLIONS

(continued)

potatoes well, then return them to the pot. Add the cream and butter, and whip them until smooth and fluffy. Season the potatoes to taste with salt and pepper. Transfer the potatoes to a bowl, then cover the bowl and set it over a saucepan of simmering water to keep the potatoes warm.

TO GRILL THE VENISON: Prepare a barbecue grill for high heat. Remove the venison from the marinade, allowing the excess marinade to drip off; discard the used marinade. Grill the venison to desired doneness, about 5 minutes per side for rare or about 8 minutes per side for medium-rare. Transfer the venison to a carving board, tent with foil, and let rest for about 10 minutes.

MEANWHILE, TO MAKE THE REDUCTION SAUCE: Cook the bacon in a small, heavy-bottomed saucepan over medium heat until the fat is rendered and the bacon is crisp. Stir in the shallot and garlic, then add the mushrooms, bourbon, and reserved ½ cup marinade. Simmer until the sauce is reduced and thick enough to coat the back of a spoon, stirring occasionally, about 15 minutes.

TO MAKE THE SAUTÉED GREEN BEANS AND SHALLOTS: Blanch the green beans in a large pot of boiling salted water until bright green, about 2 minutes. Drain the beans in a colander, and transfer them to a bowl of ice water to stop the cooking, then drain well.

Melt the butter in a large, heavy-bottomed sauté pan over medium-high heat, then add the beans and shallots and sauté until the beans are crisp-tender, 2 to 3 minutes. Season to taste with salt and pepper and serve immediately.

TO SERVE: Place the potatoes and green beans on 4 plates. Cut the venison crosswise into 1-inch-thick medallions, and place the medallions alongside the potatoes. Spoon the sauce and mushrooms over the venison and serve immediately.

SERVES 4

Recipe courtesy of
MIKE HILL

RUSTIC ROASTED LEG OF RABBIT

WITH ROASTED CARROTS, HEN OF THE WOODS MUSHROOMS, AND RAMPS

The rabbit Mystery Box held ramps, carrots, fennel, chorizo, and maitake mushrooms. (It also contained, but Becky didn't use, ginger, cape gooseberries, Marcona almonds, and forbidden rice.) Becky's traditional preparation highlighted her chosen ingredients well without stretching them into anything improbable: Roasting carrots makes them incredibly sweet, just right for the intense flavors here, and the chorizo and ramps married beautifully. Becky reduced a rabbit broth, eventually using it as a concentrated base to moisten the shredded meat she'd removed from the rabbit while roasting the legs separately. The final dish is plated with roasted carrots, cooked ramps and mushrooms, a roasted leg, and that intense broth with the shredded meat. It's the essence of rabbit, a good way to taste it if you've never tried it before.

FOR THE BRAISED RABBIT AND BROTH

- 2 (2½-pound) rabbits
- 2 ounces Spanish chorizo, casings removed, cut into ½-inch pieces
- 5 cups chicken stock
- 2 cups water

  Kosher salt and freshly ground black pepper

FOR THE ROASTED RABBIT LEGS AND SAUCE

- 2 teaspoons caraway seeds
- 2 ounces Spanish chorizo, casings removed, cut into ½-inch pieces
- 2 tablespoons olive oil

- 6 ramps, bulbs and slender pink stems coarsely chopped
- 4 tablespoons (½ stick) unsalted butter

FOR THE MUSHROOMS

- 3 tablespoons unsalted butter
- 3 bunches (3½ ounces each) hen of the woods mushrooms (maitake mushrooms), base of stems trimmed, mushrooms separated but with caps and stems intact
- 6 ramps, bulbs and slender pink stems coarsely chopped

ROASTED CARROTS

- 3 small yellow carrots (about 5 ounces), peeled and quartered lengthwise
- 3 small orange carrots (about 5 ounces), peeled and quartered lengthwise
- 1 tablespoon extra-virgin olive oil

  Kosher salt and freshly ground black pepper

RUSTIC ROASTED LEG OF RABBIT

(continued)

TO MAKE THE BRAISED RABBIT AND BROTH: Cut each rabbit into 6 pieces so that you have 2 hind leg and thigh pieces, 2 front legs, and 2 saddle pieces from each rabbit. Cover and refrigerate the 4 hind leg and 4 thigh pieces.

Heat a large heavy pressure cooker over medium heat. Add the chorizo and cook until the fat is rendered, about 2 minutes. Working in batches, add the front legs and saddles, and cook until browned, about 8 minutes per batch. Add the chicken stock and water. Cover and seal the pressure cooker. Bring the pressure to 15 psi over high heat, then reduce the heat to medium-low and cook for 40 minutes. Turn off the heat and set aside for 10 minutes. Release the pressure from the cooker.

Transfer the rabbit to a bowl, and strain the broth into a skillet. Skim the fat off the top. Simmer the broth over medium-high heat until reduced to 3 cups, about 10 minutes. Set aside 1½ cups.

Remove the meat from the front legs and saddles and coarsely shred it. Add the shredded meat to the skillet and season to taste with salt and pepper.

TO MAKE THE ROASTED RABBIT LEGS: Preheat the oven to 400°F. Stir the caraway seeds in a small, heavy-bottomed sauté pan over medium heat until fragrant, about 2 minutes. Transfer to a spice grinder and grind into a powder. Sprinkle the ground caraway over the rabbit and season with salt and pepper. Set aside.

Cook the chorizo in a large, heavy-bottomed ovenproof skillet over medium-high heat until the fat is rendered, about 4 minutes. Using a slotted spoon, remove the chorizo. Add the oil, then lay the hind leg pieces, skin side down, in the skillet. Add the ramps and cook until the rabbit is browned on the bottom, about 5 minutes. Turn the rabbit over, transfer the skillet to the oven, and roast until an instant-read thermometer registers 160°F in the center of the thigh, about 10 minutes. Baste occasionally with the pan drippings.

Remove the skillet from the oven and set it over medium heat. Add 2 tablespoons of the butter, and cook until the butter begins to brown, basting the rabbit with the butter, about 2 minutes. Set the rabbit aside. Pour off any excess oil.

RUSTIC ROASTED LEG OF RABBIT

(continued)

Add the reserved 1½ cups of broth to the skillet and stir to deglaze the pan. Simmer over medium-high heat until reduced to ½ cup. Remove the skillet from the heat, then add the remaining butter and whisk to blend. Season to taste with salt and pepper.

TO MAKE THE MUSHROOMS: Melt the butter in a large, heavy-bottomed sauté pan over medium-high heat. Add the mushrooms and ramps and sauté until tender, about 3 minutes. Season to taste with salt and pepper.

TO MAKE THE ROASTED CARROTS: Preheat the oven to 500°F. Coat the carrots with the olive oil on a baking sheet and season with salt and pepper. Roast until they are crisp-tender and golden brown, turning as needed, about 15 minutes.

TO SERVE: Mound the mushrooms and ramps in the centers of 4 plates. Arrange the roasted carrots alongside the mushrooms. Using tongs, lift the shredded braised meat from the broth and mound it on top of the mushrooms. Set the roasted rabbit leg pieces on top. Spoon the sauce over and around the rabbit leg pieces and serve immediately.

SERVES 4

Recipe courtesy of
BECKY REAMS

 **WINE PAIRING**

A Pinot Noir is a classic match for the potent earthy flavors in rabbit. Choose a French Pinot Noir from the famed Burgundy region. These wines tend to have earthy and "barnyard" nuances that would pair perfectly with the distinct flavors of game meats, as well as the hen of the woods mushrooms and root vegetables.

PAN-SEARED RABBIT LEGS
AND MAITAKE MUSHROOM–GOOSEBERRY SAUCE WITH FORBIDDEN RICE AND ROASTED BRUSSELS SPROUTS

Mike Hill turned to the almost citrus-like flavor of cape gooseberries to brighten up his pan-seared rabbit. It helped sharpen the flavor of the ramps and slightly tamped down the earthiness of the mushrooms so the rabbit could really shine. Forbidden rice is a short-grained black rice, an heirloom variety that has far more vitamins and fiber than white rice. It's also called black rice or purple rice, cooks up dark purple, and has an appealingly nutty flavor that worked well with Mike's mushroom-gooseberry sauce.

FOR THE RABBIT

- 2 (2½-pound) rabbits
- 4 ounces Spanish chorizo, casings removed, finely diced (about ½ cup)
- 4 tablespoons olive oil
- 12 ramps, thinly sliced
- 1 fennel bulb, thinly sliced
- 2 carrots, peeled and thinly sliced
- 2 teaspoons caraway seeds
- 6 cups water
- Kosher salt and freshly ground black pepper
- All-purpose flour

FOR THE RICE

- 1 tablespoon unsalted butter
- 1 ounce Spanish chorizo, casings removed, finely diced (about 2 tablespoons)
- 10 ramps, bulbs and slender pink stems finely diced

- 1 cup forbidden black rice
- 1 teaspoon kosher salt
- ½ teaspoon freshly ground black pepper

FOR THE SAUCE

- 1 bunch (3½ ounces) hen of the woods mushrooms (maitake mushrooms), base of stems trimmed, mushrooms separated but with caps and stems intact
- 8 cape gooseberries, husks removed, diced

- ¼ cup finely diced ramps (bulbs and slender stems only)
- 2 tablespoons unsalted butter

ROASTED BRUSSELS SPROUTS

- 20 small Brussels sprouts, trimmed
- 2 tablespoons extra-virgin olive oil
- 1 tablespoon unsalted butter, melted
- Kosher salt and freshly ground black pepper

TO MAKE THE RABBIT BROTH: Cut each rabbit into 6 pieces so that you have 2 hind leg and thigh pieces, 2 front legs, and 2 saddle pieces from each rabbit. Cover and refrigerate the 4 hind leg and thigh pieces.

Heat a large heavy pressure cooker over medium heat. Add ¼ cup of the chorizo and cook until the fat is rendered, about 2 minutes. Add 2 tablespoons of the oil and then the ramps, fennel, and carrots, and sauté the vegetables until they soften slightly, about 5 minutes. Add the front legs and saddles and caraway seeds. Add the water. Cover and seal the pressure cooker. Bring the pressure to 15 psi over high heat, then reduce the heat to medium-low and cook for 30 minutes. Turn off the heat and set aside for 10 minutes. Release the pressure from the cooker.

Transfer the rabbit to a bowl, and strain the broth into an 8-cup bowl. Skim the fat off. Remove the meat from the front legs and saddles and reserve for another use; discard the bones and sinew.

TO MAKE THE RICE: Melt the butter in a large, heavy-bottomed saucepan over medium heat. Add the chorizo and cook until the fat is rendered, about 3 minutes. Add the ramps and sauté until they soften slightly, about 2 minutes. Stir in the rice, salt, and pepper and cook until fragrant, about 2 minutes. Add 2 cups of the rabbit broth and bring to a boil over high heat. Reduce the heat to medium-low, cover, and simmer without stirring until the rice is tender but still slightly chewy and the stock is absorbed, about 35 minutes.

TO MAKE THE RABBIT LEGS: Preheat the oven to 450°F. Season the rabbit with salt and pepper and dredge in flour.

Cook the remaining chorizo in a large, heavy-bottomed ovenproof skillet over medium heat until the fat is rendered, about 4 minutes. Using a slotted spoon, remove the chorizo. Increase the heat to high and add the remaining oil. Lay the hind leg pieces, skin side down, in the skillet and cook until browned on the bottom, about 4 minutes. Turn the rabbit pieces over, then transfer the skillet to the oven, and roast until an instant-read thermometer registers 160°F in the center of the thigh, about 10 minutes. Transfer the leg pieces to a plate, and return the skillet to the stove.

TO MAKE THE SAUCE: Heat the same skillet over medium-high heat. Add the mushrooms, cape gooseberries, and ramps, and sauté until they soften slightly, about 3 minutes. Add 2 cups of broth and stir to deglaze the pan. Simmer until the sauce reduces by half, about 5 minutes. Stir in the butter. Season the sauce to taste with salt and pepper.

TO MAKE THE BRUSSELS SPROUTS: Preheat the oven to 500°F. Cook the sprouts in a large saucepan of boiling salted water for 2 minutes. Drain, then place the sprouts in a bowl of ice water. Drain again, then cut the sprouts in half lengthwise.

Coat the sprouts with the oil and butter in a medium bowl. Season to taste with salt and pepper. Arrange the sprouts, cut side down, on a heavy baking sheet. Roast until crisp-tender and golden brown, turning as needed, about 15 minutes.

TO SERVE: Mound the rice in the center of 4 plates and arrange the Brussels sprouts cut side up around the rice. Place the rabbit legs on top of the rice. Spoon the mushroom sauce over and serve immediately.

Cover and refrigerate the braised meat and remaining broth for another use.

SERVES 4

Recipe courtesy of
MIKE HILL

STRAWBERRY SHORTCAKE

Strawberry shortcake was taken to a whole new level by Tali Clavijo, a musician from Chicago. His egg-enriched cakes with plenty of butter used half-and-half as the liquid, so they were about as "short," or fat-enriched, as they could be. The result was more nearly a scone than a biscuit, just right as the base for fresh sliced strawberries tossed with vanilla simple syrup. The berries stayed firm while still floating in juice, rather than taking on the sogginess that can come of leaving them to steep for too long in sugar.

Normally lightly sweetened whipped cream is the crowning touch on a good shortcake, but Tali surprised the judges with a wonderful strawberry foam, which is what turned this relatively simple dessert into a showstopper. It's pureed and strained berries that he poured into a whipped cream canister along with heavy cream. These containers, which much be charged with a nitrous oxide cartridge to make whipped cream, are easily acquired at cookware stores. The result is a bright pink, strawberry-flavored whipped cream that you can enjoy just as easily on a slab of pound cake.

FOR THE SHORTCAKES

- 2 large eggs
- 2 cups all-purpose flour
- 4½ tablespoons sugar
- 1 tablespoon baking powder
- ½ teaspoon salt
- ½ cup (1 stick) cold unsalted butter, diced
- ½ cup half-and-half

FOR THE VANILLA SIMPLE SYRUP

- 1 cup sugar
- 1 cup water
- 1 vanilla bean, split lengthwise

Fresh small mint leaves, for garnish

- 6 fresh strawberries, halved, for garnish

FOR THE STRAWBERRY FOAM

- 4 large fresh strawberries, diced
- ¼ cup Vanilla Simple Syrup
- ¾ cup chilled heavy cream

FOR THE CREAM

- 2 cups chilled heavy cream
- ⅓ cup confectioners' sugar

FOR THE STRAWBERRY FILLING

- 1 pound fresh strawberries, thinly sliced
- 6 tablespoons Vanilla Simple Syrup

TO MAKE THE SHORTCAKES: Preheat the oven to 425°F. Line a heavy baking sheet with parchment paper. Beat 1 of the eggs in a small bowl. Set aside.

Mix the flour, 3 tablespoons of the sugar, the baking powder, and salt in a food processor to blend. Add the butter and pulse until pea-size pieces of butter form. Whisk the half-and-half and remaining 1 egg in a medium bowl to blend. Gradually add the half-and-half mixture to the flour mixture, pulsing just until the dough comes together.

Transfer the dough to a floured work surface and pat it out into a 10 x 5-inch rectangle ½ inch thick. Fold the dough in half, forming a 5-inch square. Using a 2½-inch-diameter cookie cutter, cut out 6 biscuits, gathering and rerolling the dough scraps as necessary. Place the biscuits on the prepared baking sheet. Brush some of the beaten egg on top of the shortcakes, and sprinkle them with the remaining 1½ tablespoons of sugar. Bake until golden brown, about 18 minutes.

TO MAKE THE VANILLA SIMPLE SYRUP: Combine the sugar and water in a small, heavy-bottomed saucepan. Scrape the seeds from the vanilla bean into the saucepan, then add the bean. Simmer until a syrup forms and the syrup is reduced to about 1¼ cups, about 8 minutes. Remove the saucepan from the heat and set aside to cool completely. Discard the vanilla bean before using the syrup.

TO MAKE THE STRAWBERRY FOAM: Combine the strawberries and vanilla simple syrup in a medium, heavy-bottomed saucepan and bring to a boil over medium-high heat. Using an immersion blender, puree until smooth. Strain the puree through a fine-mesh sieve into a bowl. Set the bowl into another bowl filled with ice water and set aside to cool. Transfer the puree to a whipped cream canister. Add the cream. Charge the canister with 1 nitrous oxide cartridge. Refrigerate the mixture until ready to use.

TO MAKE THE CREAM: Using an electric mixer, beat the cream and confectioners' sugar in a large bowl until soft peaks form. Do not overmix.

TO MAKE THE STRAWBERRY FILLING: Toss the strawberries and vanilla simple syrup in a large bowl.

TO SERVE: Split the shortcakes horizontally in half and set the bottoms on 6 plates. Spoon a generous amount of the cream onto the bottoms of the shortcakes. Spoon the strawberry filling over the cream. Cover with the shortcake tops. Pipe the strawberry foam alongside the shortcakes. Spoon more cream on the plate. Garnish with more mounds of whipped cream, mint leaves, and halved strawberries.

SERVES 6

Recipe courtesy of
TALI CLAVIJO

CARAMEL-GINGER APPLE PIE

An Apple Pie challenge might be expected to produce a lot of crowd pleasers for this classic, easy, and all-American dessert. But the judges were amused that so many of the contestants, who'd already been busily flexing their culinary muscles with multi-part recipes, seemed to have such a tough time making a good apple pie! There's a reason that grandmothers and elderly aunts can be so famous for their pies: It takes a careful and patient (and cool) hand with the pastry to make a delicate, flaky crust. The apples shouldn't be overseasoned in order to let their tart flavors shine through, and the baking needs to be carefully timed so that the crust is golden brown, not burnt, while the apples are tender and toothsome. Judging from the pies that many of the contestants delivered up, this was no easy feat!

But Felix Fang got it just right and also managed to bring something new to the apple-pie canon with the addition of some candied ginger and a judicious sprinkle of red-pepper flakes. Part of the interesting technique that led to such a successful pie was that instead of tossing the raw apples with the sugar, she made a caramel sauce, thickened it very lightly with flour, and tossed the apple with that. The result was a pie that was tender, tangy, and fragrant, with the faint bite of ginger and red-pepper flakes complementing the tart apples perfectly.

FOR THE CRUST

- 2 cups all-purpose flour
- 1 tablespoon sugar
- ½ teaspoon salt
- 1 cup (2 sticks) cold unsalted butter, diced
- About 6 tablespoons ice water

FOR THE PIE

- ½ cup packed dark brown sugar
- ½ cup water
- ¾ cup heavy cream
- 4 (1 x 1-inch) pieces candied ginger, finely chopped
- Pinch of red-pepper flakes
- 1½ teaspoons all-purpose flour
- 4 large Granny Smith apples, peeled and cut into ¼-inch-thick slices
- 1 large egg, beaten

TO MAKE THE CRUST: Blend the flour, sugar, and salt in a food processor. Add the butter and pulse until pea-size pieces of butter remain, about 30 seconds. Drizzle the ice water over the mixture while pulsing until moist clumps form. Transfer the dough to a work surface and form the dough into 2 equal pieces. Form each piece into a ball and wrap separately in plastic. Refrigerate at least 30 minutes and up to 1 day.

TO MAKE THE PIE: Move the oven rack to the lowest position, then preheat the oven to 400°F.

Combine the brown sugar and water in a small, heavy-bottomed saucepan over medium-high heat and bring to a boil, stirring until the sugar dissolves. Gradually whisk in the cream and simmer until the mixture thickens slightly. Add the candied ginger and red-pepper flakes. Whisk 2 tablespoons of the caramel sauce with the flour in a small bowl to blend. Return the mixture to the remaining caramel sauce and bring to a boil.

Coat the apples with the caramel sauce in a large bowl.

Unwrap 1 dough ball and set it on a floured surface. Roll out the dough, rotating it and dusting the surface with flour to prevent it from sticking, until the dough is about 13 inches in diameter. Brush away the excess flour. Transfer the dough to a 9-inch-diameter glass pie dish and lightly press the dough into the dish. Trim the overhang to ½ inch. Chill the pie shell while rolling out the top crust. Roll out the second piece of dough on a lightly floured surface into a 12-inch round.

Transfer the apple mixture to the pie shell. Cover the pie with the top dough. Trim the overhang to ½ inch and press the edges together, then fold them under and crimp decoratively. Cut 4 steam vents in the top crust with a small sharp knife. Lightly brush the top of the pie with the egg.

Place the pie dish on the lowest rack of the oven and bake the pie until the crust is golden and the filling is bubbling, about 50 minutes. Transfer the pie to a rack and cool until warm.

Cut the pie into wedges and serve warm.

SERVES 8

Recipe courtesy of
FELIX FANG

DECADENT APPLE-CARAMEL SPICE CAKE

Decadent is the only name for this over-the-top cake. "Spice cake" alone would hardly indicate the riches inside. Once you cut into the towering, spice- and butter-enriched layers, you'll find a filling of tart Granny Smith apples cooked down with cinnamon, while the exterior is thickly coated with an incredibly rich cream cheese frosting that's spiked with the unusual (and delicious) addition of cream of coconut. Top it with caramelized pecans, spoon on a little salted caramel sauce, and you'll think you've found dessert nirvana. You may also think a thin slice is all you can manage . . . until you find yourself going back for just a little more.

To make a really professional-looking cake, pack the creamy frosting into a piping bag and pipe it all over the top and sides, or use a knife or offset spatula to slather it on in homemade swirls. You may find you have a couple extra tablespoons of apple filling—consider it a treat for the cook.

FOR THE CAKE

- 2½ cups all-purpose flour plus more for dusting
- 1 teaspoon baking powder
- 1 teaspoon baking soda
- 1 teaspoon salt
- 1 teaspoon ground cinnamon
- ½ teaspoon ground ginger
- ¼ teaspoon ground cloves
- ¼ teaspoon grated nutmeg
- ½ cup unsalted butter, at room temperature
- 1 cup granulated sugar
- ½ cup firmly packed light brown sugar
- 2 large eggs
- 1 teaspoon pure vanilla extract
- ½ cup buttermilk
- 1½ cups cinnamon applesauce

FOR THE FROSTING

- 3 (8-ounce) packages cream cheese, at room temperature
- ¾ cup (1½ sticks) unsalted butter, at room temperature
- ¾ cup canned sweetened cream of coconut
- 1½ teaspoons vanilla extract
- ¾ teaspoon princess cake and cookie flavor (optional)
- 3 cups confectioners' sugar

FOR THE FILLING

- 3 tablespoons unsalted butter
- 4 Granny Smith apples (about 1¾ pounds total), peeled, cored, and chopped
- 2 tablespoons granulated sugar
- ¼ teaspoon ground cinnamon

FOR THE CARAMELIZED PECANS

- 1 tablespoon unsalted butter
- 1 cup chopped pecans
- 2 tablespoons granulated sugar
- ⅛ teaspoon ground cinnamon
- ½ teaspoon vanilla extract

FOR THE SALTED CARAMEL SAUCE

- 1 cup granulated sugar
- ¼ cup water
- 6 tablespoons (¾ stick) unsalted butter
- ½ cup heavy cream
- 1 teaspoon vanilla extract
- About ½ teaspoon kosher salt

DECADENT
APPLE-CARAMEL
SPICE CAKE

(continued)

TO BAKE THE CAKE: Position the rack in the center of the oven and preheat the oven to 350°F. Coat three 8-inch round cake pans with nonstick cooking spray, then dust the pans with flour. Tap out any excess flour.

Sift the flour, baking powder, baking soda, salt, cinnamon, ginger, cloves, and nutmeg together into a large bowl. Using an electric mixer, beat the butter in another large bowl until creamy. Add the granulated sugar and brown sugar and beat until very well blended. Beat in the eggs one at a time, then beat in the vanilla. Continue beating on high speed until the mixture is light and fluffy, about 5 minutes. Reduce the mixer speed to low. Add the sifted dry ingredients to the butter mixture, alternating with the buttermilk, and mixing just until blended. Mix in the applesauce. Divide the batter between the prepared cake pans.

Bake the cakes until they spring back when lightly touched on top and a skewer inserted into the center comes out with some crumbs attached, about 30 minutes. Cool the cakes in the pans on a rack for 5 minutes. Invert the cakes onto the racks and cool completely. Turn the cakes over so the rounded sides are up. If time permits, wrap the cakes with plastic wrap and freeze for 10 to 15 minutes. Using a serrated knife, trim off the rounded tops of the cakes to level the tops.

TO MAKE THE FROSTING: Using an electric mixer, beat the cream cheese and butter in a large bowl until smooth, scraping down the sides of the bowl occasionally. Add the cream of coconut, vanilla, and princess flavoring, if using, and mix well. Add the confectioners' sugar, 1 cup at a time, and beat just until the frosting is smooth after each addition. Cover and refrigerate the frosting until it thickens slightly but is not hard, about 15 minutes.

TO MAKE THE APPLE FILLING: Melt the butter in a large, heavy-bottomed sauté pan over medium-high heat. Add the apples, sugar, and cinnamon and sauté just until the apples are crisp-tender and golden, about 18 minutes. Remove the pan from the heat and cool the filling to room temperature.

TO CARAMELIZE THE PECANS: Melt the butter in a medium, heavy-bottomed sauté pan over medium heat. Add the pecans and sauté for 1 minute. Add the sugar and cinnamon and cook, stirring constantly so that the pecans do not burn, until the sugar begins to caramelize, about 3 minutes. Remove the pan from the heat and mix in the vanilla. Transfer the pecans to a sheet of waxed paper and set aside to cool.

TO MAKE THE SALTED CARAMEL SAUCE: Stir the sugar and water in a medium, heavy-bottomed saucepan over medium-high heat until the sugar dissolves. Increase the heat to high and boil without stirring until the syrup turns a deep amber color, occasionally brushing down the sides of the pan with a wet pastry brush dipped into water and swirling the pan, about 7 minutes. Remove the pan from the heat and whisk in the butter. Slowly add the cream, whisking to blend. Whisk in the vanilla and ½ teaspoon of the salt. Season the sauce to taste with more salt, if desired. Cool the sauce completely, then store it in a sealed jar and refrigerate. Rewarm the sauce before serving.

TO ASSEMBLE THE CAKE: Place 1 cake layer, cut side up, on a platter. Spread ¾ cup of frosting over the top of the layer. Spoon half of the apple filling over the frosting, pressing it a bit into the frosting to adhere. Top with the second cake layer, cut side down, then cover with ¾ cup of frosting and the remaining apple filling. Top with the third cake layer, cut side down. Spread the remaining frosting decoratively over the top and sides of the cake. Sprinkle enough of the caramelized pecans over the top of the cake to cover it generously, then drizzle ⅓ cup of the caramel sauce over the top.

Cut the cake into wedges and serve with the remaining caramelized pecans and caramel sauce.

SERVES 12

Recipe courtesy of
AUDREY MCGINNIS

COCONUT AND TROPICAL FRUIT VERRINE

For the Michelin Star challenge, the Girls Team knew that only a highly refined dessert would do, and their verrine is a dream of fruit and cake. A verrine is any dessert or savory dish layered in a glass so the colors and textures are plainly visible, and Becky and Christine did not disappoint with a layer of glowing orange guava jelly, golden coconut cake, creamy white coconut cream, and a jewel-toned fruit compote. The coconut tuiles and mango slices for garnish added color and crunch, and the tiny verdant basil leaves threw the golden colors into sharp relief. You don't have to carefully layer this dessert into a glass like a multistarred chef in order to enjoy its haute cuisine flavors.

FOR THE GUAVA GELÉE

- ½ cup water
- 1 tablespoon agar agar
- 1 cup guava puree

FOR THE COCONUT CAKE

- 2 cups cake flour
- 1½ teaspoons baking powder
- ½ teaspoon salt
- ⅔ cup buttermilk
- 4 large egg whites
- ¼ teaspoon coconut extract
- 1⅓ cups granulated sugar
- 10 tablespoons unsalted butter, at room temperature
- ¼ cup shredded unsweetened coconut

FOR THE COCONUT CREAM

- 1¼ cups heavy cream
- ¼ cup canned sweetened cream of coconut
- ¼ cup confectioners' sugar
- ⅛ teaspoon coconut extract

FOR THE FRUIT COMPOTE

- 3 mangoes, peeled, pitted, and diced
- 2 bananas, peeled and diced
- 6 passion fruit, pulp and juice scooped out and reserved
- 2 teaspoons granulated sugar

FOR THE COCONUT TUILES

- ¼ cup light corn syrup
- ¼ cup granulated sugar
- ¼ cup (½ stick) unsalted butter
- ¼ cup shredded unsweetened coconut
- 1 tablespoon peeled, grated fresh ginger
- 1 tablespoon whole milk

- ⅓ cup micro Thai basil leaves, for garnish
- 8 small mango slices, for garnish

TO MAKE THE GUAVA GELÉE: Combine the water and agar agar in a small, heavy-bottomed saucepan and stir over medium-low heat until the agar agar dissolves, about 8 minutes. Transfer the agar mixture to a small bowl and stir in the guava puree. Set aside to cool completely, then whisk before using.

TO MAKE THE COCONUT CAKE: Preheat the oven to 350°F. Butter a 12 x 9 x 1-inch rimmed baking sheet, then line the pan with parchment paper.

Whisk the flour, baking powder, and salt in a medium bowl. Whisk the buttermilk, egg whites, and coconut extract in another medium bowl. Using an electric mixer, beat the sugar and butter in a large bowl until light and fluffy. Add the flour mixture to the butter mixture in 3 additions alternating with the buttermilk mixture in 2 additions. Beat to blend well between additions and occasionally scrape the bottom and sides of the bowl with a rubber spatula. Stir in the shredded coconut. Transfer the batter to the pan and spread evenly.

Bake the cake until the cake springs back when touched, about 20 minutes. Cool the cake completely in the pan on a rack. Using a 3-inch round cookie cutter (or another cutter that is just slightly smaller than the diameter of your dessert cups), cut out 8 rounds of cake.

TO MAKE THE COCONUT CREAM: Using an electric mixer, beat the heavy cream, coconut cream, confectioners' sugar, and coconut extract in a large bowl until very thick and soft peaks form.

TO MAKE THE COMPOTE: Toss together the mangoes, bananas, passion fruit, and sugar in a medium bowl.

TO MAKE THE COCONUT TUILES: Preheat the oven to 325°F. Line a large heavy baking sheet with a silicone baking mat.

Stir the corn syrup, sugar, and butter in a small, heavy-bottomed saucepan over medium heat until the butter melts. Stir in the coconut, ginger, and milk to blend. Remove from the heat.

Working in batches and using 1 teaspoon of batter for each tuile, spoon 6 pools of the batter onto the prepared baking sheet, spacing them evenly apart. Bake until the tuiles have spread and become deep golden brown, about 12 minutes. Cool completely. Transfer the cookies to a cooling rack lined with paper towels.

TO SERVE: Spoon the gelée into the bottom of 8 dessert cups. Set 1 cake round on top of the gelée in each cup. Spoon the fruit compote over the cake. Spoon the coconut cream over the fruit. Top with the tuiles, then garnish with a mango slice and basil leaves and serve immediately.

SERVES 8

Recipe courtesy of
THE GIRLS' TEAM
(Christine Ha and Becky Reams)

CARAMEL ROASTED PEACH
WITH TARRAGON CRÈME ANGLAISE AND SOUR CREAM–PEACH COMPOTE

Peaches weren't quite in season when Becky Reams opened the Mystery Box that also contained a steak, sour cream, fresh tarragon, watermelon, corn, and cabbage. Every other contestant used the steak in their box, but Becky was inspired by the fruit. She was the only contestant who made a dessert out of that particular Mystery Box and the only contestant who didn't use the steak. Instead, she solved the problem of not-quite-perfect fruit by roasting it, which made it juicy and sweet and caramelized the exterior sugars. She nestled the peaches in a pool of tarragon-infused crème anglaise and topped them with the caramelized peach juices from the pan. Then she brightened the plate and sharpened the flavors with a few dots of a tangy sour cream and peach compote. For plating during the competition, Becky only used a few dots of the colorful compote, but it's so delicious, you'll want to spoon it on with a more generous hand. Sugared tarragon leaves are delicious and beautiful, but you can easily skip them and you'll still enjoy this dessert immensely.

FOR THE CRÈME ANGLAISE

1½	cups whole milk
¼	cup fresh tarragon leaves, coarsely chopped
	Pinch of salt
6	large egg yolks
⅔	cup sugar

FOR THE SOUR CREAM–PEACH COMPOTE

2	firm but ripe peaches, peeled, pitted, and diced
6	tablespoons sugar
2	teaspoons fresh lemon juice
3	tablespoons sour cream

FOR THE ROASTED PEACHES

2	firm but ripe peaches, halved
½	cup sugar
½	cup water
2	teaspoons fresh lemon juice
	Pinch of salt

FOR THE SUGARED TARRAGON

10	to 15 fresh tarragon leaves
	About 2 tablespoons sugar

TO MAKE THE CRÈME ANGLAISE: Combine the milk, tarragon, and salt in a medium, heavy-bottomed saucepan and bring just to a simmer over medium-high heat. Simmer gently for 30 seconds, then cover and remove the saucepan from the heat. Steep for 5 minutes.

Whisk the egg yolks and sugar in a large bowl to blend, then gradually whisk in the hot milk mixture. Pour the mixture back into the saucepan, and stir constantly over medium-low heat until the sauce is thick enough to coat the back of a spoon, about 5 minutes. Strain the custard through a fine-mesh sieve into a bowl set over ice water, and stir until cool. Cover and refrigerate until cold.

CARAMEL
ROASTED PEACH

(continued)

TO MAKE THE COMPOTE: Combine the peaches, sugar, and lemon juice in a small, heavy-bottomed saucepan. Cover and cook over medium-low heat until the peaches are tender and the sugar is a rich caramel brown color, about 5 minutes. Cool slightly.

Add the sour cream to the cooled peaches. Using an immersion blender, puree the peaches until smooth. Thin the mixture to the desired consistency, if necessary, adding ½ teaspoon of water at a time. Cover and refrigerate until cold.

TO ROAST THE PEACHES: Preheat the oven to 400°F. Place 4 peach halves pit side down in a shallow glass baking dish and sprinkle with the sugar, water, lemon juice, and salt. Cover and roast until the sugar melts and forms a caramel syrup, about 15 minutes. Remove the dish from the oven and baste the peaches with the caramel, turn the peach halves over and remove the pits, if necessary. Roast until the peaches are tender but still hold their shape, basting occasionally with the caramel syrup, about 15 minutes.

MEANWHILE, TO MAKE THE SUGARED TARRAGON: Line a small baking sheet with parchment paper. Lay the tarragon leaves on the prepared baking sheet and sprinkle them with enough sugar to coat. Bake for 3 minutes. Turn the leaves over and bake until they are light and crisp, about 3 minutes. Set aside.

TO SERVE: Pour the crème anglaise into 4 shallow bowls. Place the roasted peaches cut side up in the bowls. Spoon some of the remaining caramel sauce from the baking dish into the pit indentations. Spoon small dollops of the peach compote around the peaches. Garnish with the sugared tarragon leaves and serve.

SERVES 4

Recipe courtesy of
BECKY REAMS

T he Soufflé challenge was one of the most difficult pressure tests ever on *MasterChef*. To succeed, one cook had to present three soufflés perfectly risen at the exact same moment that the time on the clock ran out. It was a task that even a seasoned pastry chef might find quite difficult. Joshua Marks, it must be said, rose beautifully to the challenge. His Cheddar Cheese Soufflés can be found on page 30. These fresh Raspberry Soufflés and his Dark Chocolate Soufflés (page 250) would both make a spectacular end to a meal. Don't feel you need to make them all at the same time.

RASPBERRY SOUFFLÉS

2 tablespoons (about) unsalted butter

3 tablespoons plus ⅔ cup granulated sugar

2 (6-ounce) containers plus ¾ cup fresh raspberries

3 tablespoons cornstarch

1½ tablespoons pectin

¼ teaspoon citric acid

4 large egg whites

Pinch of salt

Confectioners' sugar (optional)

Preheat the oven to 425°F. Butter eight 6-ounce soufflé dishes and sprinkle with 3 tablespoons of the granulated sugar, tilting the dishes to coat completely and tapping out any excess. Arrange the prepared soufflé dishes on a large baking sheet.

Puree the 2 containers of raspberries in a food processor. Strain the puree through a fine-mesh sieve into a medium, heavy-bottomed saucepan, pressing on the solids. Whisk the cornstarch, pectin, citric acid, and ⅓ cup of the granulated sugar into the puree to blend. Whisk over medium heat until the mixture boils and thickens to the consistency of pudding, about 3 minutes. Transfer the raspberry mixture to a large bowl and cool completely, stirring occasionally.

Using an electric mixer, beat the egg whites and salt in a large bowl just until frothy. Gradually beat in the remaining ⅓ cup of granulated sugar and continue beating just until stiff peaks begin to form. Fold one-fourth of the egg whites into the raspberry mixture to lighten, then fold in the remaining whites and ¾ cup of raspberries. Divide the batter among the prepared soufflé dishes, filling the dishes completely.

Bake until the soufflés puff and the tops feel firm, about 8 minutes. Dust the soufflés with the confectioners' sugar, if desired, and serve immediately.

Recipe courtesy of
JOSHUA MARKS

SERVES 8

DARK CHOCOLATE SOUFFLÉS

- **4 tablespoons (½ stick) unsalted butter**

- **5 tablespoons plus ¼ cup sugar**

- **5 ounces bittersweet chocolate (70% cacao), chopped**

- **2 cups whole milk**

- **½ vanilla bean, split lengthwise**

- **6 large eggs, separated**

- **¼ cup cornstarch**

- **Pinch of salt**

Preheat the oven to 425°F. Using 1 tablespoon of the butter, coat four 12-ounce soufflé dishes. Then sprinkle with 3 tablespoons of the sugar, tilting the dishes to coat completely and tapping out any excess. Arrange the prepared soufflé dishes on a large baking sheet.

Combine the chocolate, remaining 3 tablespoons of butter, and 1 cup of the milk in a medium, heavy-bottomed saucepan. Scrape the seeds from the vanilla bean, then add both the seeds and the bean to the milk mixture. Bring to a simmer over medium heat, whisking to dissolve the chocolate.

Meanwhile, whisk the egg yolks, cornstarch, salt, ¼ cup of the sugar, and the remaining 1 cup of milk in a large bowl to blend. Whisk the cornstarch mixture into the chocolate mixture and cook, whisking constantly, until the mixture thickens, about 5 minutes. Return the chocolate mixture to the large bowl and set aside to cool slightly, whisking occasionally. Discard the vanilla bean.

Using an electric mixer, beat the egg whites in another large bowl just until frothy. Gradually beat in the remaining 2 tablespoons of sugar and continue beating just until stiff peaks begin to form. Fold one-fourth of the egg whites into the chocolate mixture to lighten, then fold in the remaining whites. Divide the mixture among the prepared soufflé dishes, filling the dishes completely.

Bake until the soufflés puff and the tops feel firm, about 12 minutes. Serve the soufflés immediately.

SERVES 4

Recipe courtesy of
JOSHUA MARKS

Since she earned the title of MasterChef USA at the end of Season 2, Jennifer Behm's life has changed dramatically. Jennifer says, "I launched my catering company, Pink Martini Catering, and from its inception, it has been wildly successful both nationally and internationally. Among many exciting events, I had the honor to cook for the governor of Delaware, was awarded a special recognition from my hometown, have made numerous TV and radio appearances, and have cooked and hosted many other national events.

"My team and I are heading to India to cook three courses for 300 people in three different cities and we're doing a tasting event for 500 people. We are in talks with people in Australia and Hong Kong to create similar culinary events. I am developing my own line of products for the professional and home cook. I am also a founding member of the First State Bailliage of the Chaîne des Rôtisseurs. Most importantly, I got engaged to be married and yes, ironically, it is to a chef. I am excited about the opportunities that are to come in my culinary and professional future."

CHOCOLATE CRÈME BRÛLÉE
WITH RUM BANANAS

O n its own, Jennifer's chocolate crème brûlée would be a major treat. It's divinely rich, with the potent flavor of bittersweet chocolate backed up by the underlying tones of a vanilla bean. But she takes it a step further and tops each serving with bananas tossed with a sort of caramel-rum sauce. It's like Bananas Foster, but with crème brûlée instead of ice cream!

FOR THE CRÈME BRÛLÉE

- **3** cups heavy cream
- **6** ounces fine-quality semisweet chocolate, chopped
- **½** vanilla bean, split lengthwise
- **8** large egg yolks
- **⅓** cup plus 6 tablespoons granulated sugar

FOR THE RUM BANANAS

- **2** bananas
- **1** tablespoon unsalted butter
- **3** tablespoons packed light brown sugar
- **3** tablespoons light rum (preferably guava rum)

TO MAKE THE CRÈME BRÛLÉE: Preheat the oven to 300°F. Place eight 6-ounce custard cups in a shallow baking pan and set it aside.

Combine the cream and chocolate in a medium, heavy-bottomed saucepan. Scrape the seeds from the vanilla bean, then add the seeds and the bean to the milk and chocolate. Stir over medium heat until the chocolate melts. Remove from heat, cover, and infuse for 30 minutes.

Whisk the egg yolks and ⅓ cup of the granulated sugar in a medium bowl to blend. Gradually whisk in the hot chocolate cream. Strain the custard through a fine-mesh sieve into another bowl. Divide the custard among the cups. Set the baking pan in the oven, then add enough hot water to the pan to come halfway up the sides of the cups. Cover with foil and bake until the custards move slightly in the center when the cups are gently jiggled, about 35 minutes. Remove the cups from the water bath and refrigerate until cold. Cover and keep the custards refrigerated for at least 8 hours and up to 2 days.

Sprinkle the remaining 6 tablespoons of granulated sugar evenly over the crème brûlées. Using a kitchen torch, wave the flames over the sugar until it melts and caramelizes. Refrigerate about 30 minutes.

TO MAKE THE RUM BANANAS: Peel the bananas and cut them in half lengthwise, then cut them crosswise into ¾-inch pieces.

Heat a large, heavy-bottomed sauté pan over medium heat. Add the brown sugar and stir until it begins to melt. Add the rum and stir until the sugar dissolves and the sauce thickens slightly, about 1 minute. Add the butter. Add the banana slices and cook until heated through but not mushy, about 1 minute.

Garnish the crème brûlées with the bananas and serve immediately.

SERVES 8

"CLASSY CORN, TRASHY CORN" CORN PANNA COTTA
WITH RUM-CARAMEL SAUCE AND CHERRIES AND CARAMEL POPCORN

Becky's memorable recipe title sums up her clever dessert. The "classy" is a panna cotta, a softly set jelled cream infused with the flavor of fresh corn cobs, with the kernels themselves pureed and adding body to the panna cotta. The rum-caramel topping and the dark Morello cherries in syrup add a sophisticated edge to the sweet corn. But they're best complemented by the "trashy" part of the dessert: addictively tasty caramel corn, which Becky served up in a twist of brown paper on the side. You won't know which part to eat first.

FOR THE PANNA COTTA

- 3 tablespoons cold water
- 1 (¼-ounce) envelope unflavored powdered gelatin
- 3 ears fresh yellow corn, kernels cut off and reserved, cobs cut in half
- 2 cups heavy cream
- ½ cup sugar
- 1 vanilla bean, split lengthwise
- 1½ cups whole milk

FOR THE RUM-CARAMEL SAUCE

- 1 cup sugar
- ¼ cup water
- Pinch of cream of tartar
- ½ cup heavy cream
- 2 tablespoons dark rum
- Pinch of kosher salt

FOR THE CARAMEL POPCORN

- 1 tablespoon canola oil
- ⅓ cup yellow corn kernels, unpopped
- ½ cup cashews, toasted and coarsely chopped
- 2 teaspoons (or more) Maldon sea salt

FOR THE GARNISHES

- ½ cup dark Morello cherries in light syrup
- 1 tablespoon plus 1 teaspoon sugar
- ½ cup crème fraîche
- ¼ cup heavy cream
- Pinch of salt

TO MAKE THE PANNA COTTA: Place the water in a small bowl and sprinkle the gelatin over it. Set aside until the gelatin softens, about 15 minutes.

Combine the cobs, kernels, cream, and sugar in a large, heavy-bottomed saucepan. Scrape the seeds from the vanilla bean and add the seeds and bean to the corn mixture. Bring the mixture to a simmer over high heat, stirring to dissolve the sugar. Reduce the heat to medium-low and simmer until the kernels are tender and the cobs are hot through, stirring often, about 5 minutes. Discard the vanilla bean and set the cobs aside to cool. When the cobs are cool enough to handle, use a spoon to scrape the cobs and extract as much liquid as possible back into the remaining corn mixture, then discard the cobs. Whisk the softened gelatin mixture into the corn mixture to blend. Transfer the corn mixture to a blender and puree until nearly smooth. Strain the puree through a

fine-mesh sieve into a medium bowl. Whisk in the milk. Set the bowl in a larger bowl of ice water and stir until the mixture is cold but not set.

Pour the mixture into eight ¾-cup custard cups or soufflé dishes. Refrigerate uncovered until cold, then cover and keep refrigerated until the panna cotta is set, at least 8 hours or overnight.

TO MAKE THE RUM-CARAMEL SAUCE: Stir the sugar, water, and cream of tartar in a medium, heavy-bottomed saucepan over medium-high heat until the sugar dissolves. Increase the heat to high and boil without stirring until the syrup turns a deep amber color, occasionally brushing down the sides of the pan with a wet pastry brush dipped into water and swirling the pan, about 7 minutes. Slowly add the cream, whisking to blend. Stir in the rum and salt. Set aside to cool the sauce completely.

TO MAKE THE CARAMEL POPCORN: Preheat the oven to 350°F. Line a large heavy baking sheet with parchment paper. Heat the oil in a large pot over high heat. Add the oil, then the popcorn kernels. Cover and shake the pot constantly until all the popcorn has popped, about 3 minutes. Transfer the popcorn to a second baking sheet and set aside to cool slightly.

Toss the popcorn, cashews, and ½ cup of the caramel sauce in a large bowl to coat. Spread the caramel corn over the lined baking sheet and sprinkle with 1 teaspoon of the salt. Bake until the caramel is a shade darker, stirring after the first 10 minutes, about 20 minutes total. Cool completely on the baking sheet. (The caramel corn will become crisp when cool.)

Fold 8 small sheets of parchment paper into cones. Sprinkle the caramel corn with 1 teaspoon salt and fill the cones with the caramel popcorn.

TO MAKE THE GARNISHES: Combine the cherries and their syrup with 1 tablespoon of the sugar in a small, heavy-bottomed saucepan and bring to a simmer over medium-high heat. Reduce the heat to medium-low and simmer until the liquid has reduced and become syrupy, about 5 minutes. Set aside.

Whisk the crème fraîche, heavy cream, the remaining 1 teaspoon of sugar, and a pinch of salt in a medium bowl until creamy and thick.

TO SERVE: Set the cups of panna cotta on a larger plate. Spoon the cherries on top of the panna cotta. Drizzle some of the caramel sauce over. Spoon a small amount of the whipped cream alongside the cherries on top of the panna cotta. Set the cones of caramel popcorn alongside the panna cotta and serve.

SERVES 8

"CLASSY CORN, TRASHY CORN" CORN PANNA COTTA
(continued)

Recipe courtesy of
BECKY REAMS

MEYER LEMON TIRAMISU

Tiramisu has had its day, and serious foodies tend to think it's passé. But Frank Mirando made it into something exciting and new again, a dessert you'll be thrilled to eat. Frank's deft hand with Italian food had been well noted by the judges and his fellow competitors, and, frankly, everyone expected his tiramisu to win anyway. What nobody expected was the unusual twist of using Meyer lemon, which turned it from tired to terrific. A cross between a lemon and an orange, a Meyer lemon has a thin, aromatic skin and sweet, mildly acidic juice that's very fragrant. If you thought you were tired of tiramisu, try this version. It's a whole new lease on the life of a favorite old dessert.

½ cup sugar

3 large egg yolks

1 tablespoon finely grated Meyer lemon zest

¼ cup Meyer lemon juice

3 tablespoons hazelnut liqueur (such as Frangelico)

2 tablespoons orange liqueur (such as Grand Marnier or Cointreau)

1 tablespoon Marsala

8 ounces mascarpone cheese, at room temperature

¾ cup chilled heavy cream

About 40 (from two 3.5-ounce packages) crisp ladyfingers (Boudoirs, Champagne biscuits, or savoiardi)

About 1 cup freshly brewed espresso, chilled

About 2 tablespoons unsweetened cocoa powder

Whisk the sugar, egg yolks, lemon zest, lemon juice, hazelnut liqueur, orange liqueur, and Marsala in a double boiler over simmering water until pale, fluffy, and doubled in size, about 4 minutes. Transfer to the bowl of a stand mixer fitted with the whisk attachment. Mix on medium speed until the custard is pale, creamy, and cool, about 5 minutes. Add the mascarpone cheese and beat just until blended (do not overmix or the mixture will curdle).

Beat the heavy cream in another large bowl until soft peaks form. Fold the whipped cream into the mascarpone mixture.

Working with 1 ladyfinger at a time, submerge the ladyfingers in the espresso, turning to coat. Arrange a single layer of the soaked ladyfingers in the bottom of a 9 x 5 x 2¾-inch loaf pan. Spread one-third of the lemon cream (about 1 cup) over the ladyfingers. Dust the cream with cocoa powder. Repeat layering more soaked ladyfingers, lemon cream, and cocoa powder 2 more times. Cover and refrigerate for at least 2 hours.

SERVES 8

Recipe courtesy of
FRANK MIRANDO

CORN BUDINO
WITH CHOCOLATE SAUCE AND CANDIED CORN AND PINE NUTS

Budino is Italian for "pudding," but it's generally not the type of creamy, fluffy pudding that Americans usually mix up out of a box with some milk. Some budinos are firmed up with the very Italian addition of semolina, while others are more like a baked custard. Frank Mirando took his in the custard direction, with the sweetness of pureed fresh corn, which marries so well with sugar, eggs, and milk. The bittersweet chocolate sauce is a master stroke, cutting the sweetness of the corn, and the "candied corn"—literally corn kernels (and pine nuts) in caramelized sugar—adds a little humor along with some crunchy texture.

FOR THE BUDINO

About 1 tablespoon unsalted butter

3 ears yellow corn, kernels cut off and reserved, cobs cut in half

2 cups whole milk

½ cup sugar

4 large eggs

¾ teaspoon kosher salt

¼ teaspoon vanilla extract

FOR THE CHOCOLATE SAUCE

4 ounces bittersweet chocolate (70% cacao), chopped

½ cup whole milk

FOR THE CANDIED CORN AND PINE NUTS

¼ cup pine nuts

¼ cup fresh yellow corn kernels

1 tablespoon sugar

TO MAKE THE BUDINO: Position a rack in the center of the oven and preheat the oven to 300°F. Lightly butter six ¾-cup custard cups or soufflé dishes. Set the cups in a 13 x 9-inch baking dish.

Pulse the corn kernels in a food processor until their juices are released. Transfer the corn kernel mixture to a medium, heavy-bottomed saucepan. Add the cobs and milk and bring to a simmer over high heat. Remove the saucepan from the heat, then cover and steep for 15 minutes. Remove the cobs from the corn mixture and set them aside to cool. When the cobs are cool enough to handle, use a spoon to scrape the cobs and extract as much liquid as possible back into the remaining corn mixture, then discard the cobs. Strain the corn mixture through a fine-mesh sieve into a medium bowl, pressing on the solids to extract as much liquid as possible. Discard the solids.

Whisk the sugar, eggs, salt, and vanilla in a large bowl until the sugar dissolves. Whisk in the strained corn mixture. Pour the custard into the prepared cups. Set the baking dish in the oven, then pour enough hot water into the baking dish to come halfway up the sides of the custard cups. Cover the baking dish with foil and bake the custards until they move slightly in the center when the cups are gently jostled, about 55 minutes. Chill the custards uncovered until cold, at least 4 hours or overnight.

TO MAKE THE CHOCOLATE SAUCE: Stir the chocolate in a double boiler until melted. Stir in the milk. Set aside and keep warm.

TO MAKE THE CANDIED CORN AND PINE NUTS: Heat a medium, heavy-bottomed sauté pan over medium heat. Add the pine nuts and stir until they are golden brown, about 4 minutes. Transfer the pine nuts to a plate. Add the corn kernels to the pan and cook until golden brown, about 4 minutes. Return the pine nuts to the pan and sprinkle the sugar over. Cook until the sugar melts and caramelizes, tossing to coat the nuts and corn, about 2 minutes. Set aside.

Run a knife around the sides of the custard cups to loosen the custards. Invert the custards onto plates. Spoon the chocolate sauce around the custards. Garnish with the candied corn and pine nuts and serve immediately.

SERVES 6

Recipe courtesy of
FRANK MIRANDO

EXOTIC FRUIT TART

T wo contestants who had been eliminated got one chance to fight their way back into the challenge, so the competition surrounding this pretty fruit tart was extremely intense. With his supremely elegant version, made in the classic French style, Joshua Marks got a new white apron and the chance to compete again. The lightly sweetened pastry cream and the crisp buttery crust make this a delightful dessert, but it's the spiraling arrangement of the beautifully cut fruit that make it a work of art. It's not difficult, but it does take care and precision. Most important of all is the glaze, the final touch that will make your tart glow like a jewel. Load a pastry brush heavily with the glaze and dab it gently on the fruit rather than trying to actually brush the fruit, which may disturb the pattern.

FOR THE PASTRY CREAM

½ cup sugar

¼ cup cornstarch

2 cups whole milk

5 large egg yolks

1 teaspoon vanilla extract

FOR THE CRUST

2 large egg yolks

¼ cup ice-cold water

2½ cups all-purpose flour

¼ cup sugar

½ teaspoon salt

1 cup (2 sticks) cold unsalted butter, diced

FOR THE GLAZE

4 tablespoons apricot nectar

1 teaspoon cornstarch

¼ cup fresh pomegranate juice (from about ½ pomegranate)

1 passion fruit, halved

2 tablespoons sugar

2 teaspoons corn syrup

FOR THE FRUIT TOPPINGS

¼ small pineapple, peeled, cored, and thinly sliced

1 mango, peeled, pitted, and sliced

2 kiwifruit, peeled and sliced

6 fresh strawberries, sliced

¼ cup fresh blueberries

TO MAKE THE PASTRY CREAM: Whisk the sugar and cornstarch in a medium, heavy-bottomed saucepan to blend. Gradually whisk in the milk, then the yolks. Whisk over medium heat until the pastry cream thickens and boils, about 7 minutes. Whisk in the vanilla. Strain the pastry cream into a small bowl; press plastic wrap directly onto the surface. Refrigerate until cold, at least 2 hours and up to 2 days.

TO MAKE THE CRUST: Lightly beat the yolks with the ice water in a small bowl to blend.

Pulse the flour, sugar, and salt in a food processor to blend. Add the butter and pulse until the mixture resembles a coarse meal and pea-size pieces of butter still remain. Add the yolk mixture and pulse just until a dough begins to form. Transfer the dough to a floured work

EXOTIC FRUIT TART

(continued)

surface and gather the dough into a ball, then flatten it into a 7-inch disk. Wrap in plastic and refrigerate for 30 minutes.

Place the oven rack in the middle position and preheat the oven to 350°F.

Roll out the dough into a 15-inch round on a lightly floured surface using a floured rolling pin. Transfer the dough to an 11-inch-diameter tart pan. Fit the dough into the pan, pushing the edge of the dough to ⅛ inch above the rim. Trim the dough and save some scraps to repair any cracks in the partially baked shell, if necessary. Freeze the shell until firm, about 10 minutes.

Line the shell with parchment paper or foil and fill with pie weights. Bake until the edge is golden and the bottom is set, about 20 minutes. Carefully remove the pie weights and parchment (or foil) and gently pierce any bubbles with a fork to release the air, if necessary. Continue baking without the weights or paper until the bottom is pale golden, about 15 minutes. Cool completely.

TO MAKE THE GLAZE: Whisk 2 tablespoons of the apricot nectar with the cornstarch in a small bowl to blend. Set aside.

Combine the remaining 2 tablespoons of apricot nectar, pomegranate juice, passion fruit pulp and juice, and sugar in a small, heavy-bottomed saucepan and bring to a boil over high heat. Reduce the heat to medium-low and whisk in the cornstarch mixture. Bring to a simmer, then simmer until the mixture thickens, stirring often, about 2 minutes. Stir in the corn syrup, then strain the glaze into a small bowl. Cover and cool.

TO ASSEMBLE THE TART: Spoon the chilled pastry cream into the cooled tart shell. Arrange the fruit toppings decoratively over the pastry cream. Brush enough of the glaze over the fruit to coat it, and serve.

SERVES 8

Recipe courtesy of
JOSHUA MARKS

CHOCOLATE MOUSSE WITH
POMEGRANATE-LEMON SAUCE AND CANDIED LEMON ZEST

The chocolate mousse that Joshua Marks made might have been too much: It's about as rich as it could possibly be. But Joshua saved it from being cloying by studding the top with zesty strips of candied lemon peel, and pouring around it a tart red syrup of pomegranate juice and lemon. Chocolate and lemon aren't typical, but they have a real affinity, particularly in rich desserts like this, where the sharpness of the lemon cuts through the creamy flavors to really help the chocolate shine through.

FOR THE CHOCOLATE MOUSSE

- **6 ounces bittersweet chocolate (70% cacao), chopped**
- **6 tablespoons (¾ stick) unsalted butter**
- **6 large eggs, separated**
- **¾ cup sugar**
- **⅓ cup heavy cream**

FOR THE CANDIED LEMON ZEST

- **½ cup sugar**
- **½ cup water**
- **Julienned zest of 1 lemon**

FOR THE POMEGRANATE-LEMON SAUCE

- **½ cup fresh pomegranate juice (from about 1 pomegranate)**
- **2 tablespoons fresh lemon juice**
- **¼ cup sugar**
- **¼ cup water**

Recipe courtesy of
JOSHUA MARKS

TO MAKE THE MOUSSE: Stir the chocolate and butter in a large bowl set over a saucepan of simmering water until melted. Set aside until cool to the touch, about 10 minutes.

Using an electric mixer, beat the egg yolks and ½ cup of the sugar in a medium bowl until light and airy. Using clean beaters, beat the egg whites with the remaining sugar in another large bowl until soft peaks form.

Using a silicone spatula, fold the egg yolk mixture into the chocolate mixture. Fold in half of the egg white mixture to lighten the chocolate, then fold in the remaining egg white mixture.

Beat the cream until thick soft peaks form. Fold the cream into the chocolate. Cover and refrigerate at least 1 hour and up to 1 day.

TO MAKE THE CANDIED LEMON ZEST: Line a baking sheet with parchment paper. Combine the sugar and water in a small, heavy-bottomed saucepan over high heat and bring to a boil, stirring. Add the lemon strips and bring to a simmer. Reduce the heat to medium-low and simmer until the strips are tender, about 5 minutes. Transfer the strips to the baking sheet and cool; discard the syrup.

TO MAKE THE POMEGRANATE-LEMON SAUCE: Meanwhile, combine the pomegranate juice, lemon juice, sugar, and water in a small, heavy-bottomed saucepan over medium-high heat. Simmer until the sauce is reduced by half and slightly syrupy, about 7 minutes. Cool.

TO SERVE: Spoon the mousse into 6 to 8 bowls. Pour the sauce around the mousse. Garnish with the candied lemon zest and serve.

SERVES 6 TO 8

WHITE CHOCOLATE MOUSSE
WITH POACHED RHUBARB AND STRAWBERRIES, ROASTED STRAWBERRY PUREE, AND STRAWBERRY DUST

Because this dessert was created as part of the Michelin Star challenge, Frank and Joshua plated it with all the extreme formality you'd expect from haute cuisine, including piping the mousse into a row of beautifully rounded nests, holding a spoonful of the roasted strawberry puree, on a long rectangular serving dish. For home cooks, it's much more practical to spoon out little rounds of the mousse on individual plates, adding a spoonful of the poached rhubarb on the side and sprinkling on the strawberry dust. However, if you want to try the more high-end version they made, finish the plate with a few drops of 25-year aged balsamic vinegar and a drizzle of basil oil. You can make the latter by blanching ½ cup of basil leaves in boiling water for 10 seconds. Rinse them in cold water, pat dry, and puree in a blender with ¼ cup olive oil. The result will remain bright green.

FOR THE POACHED RHUBARB AND STRAWBERRIES

- ¾ cup water
- ½ cup granulated sugar
- 1 tablespoon verjus
- 1 vanilla bean, split lengthwise
- 3 thin rhubarb stalks (about 8 ounces total), cut into 3 x ½-inch batons
- 8 ounces fresh strawberries (about 2 cups), halved

FOR THE ROASTED STRAWBERRY PUREE

- 8 ounces fresh strawberries (about 2 cups), quartered
- 2 tablespoons granulated sugar
- 1 teaspoon fresh lemon juice

FOR THE MOUSSE

- 6 ounces good-quality white chocolate, chopped
- 1¼ cups cold heavy cream
- 1 gelatin sheet
- 2 large egg whites
- 2 tablespoons granulated sugar

FOR THE STRAWBERRY DUST

- ½ cup puffed rice cereal
- 2 tablespoons cake flour
- 2 tablespoons confectioners' sugar
- 1½ tablespoons unsalted butter
- 2 teaspoons strawberry powder
- Pinch of red sea salt

TO POACH THE RHUBARB AND STRAWBERRIES: Combine the water, sugar, and verjus in a medium, heavy-bottomed sauté pan. Scrape the seeds from the vanilla bean, then add the seeds and bean to the sugar mixture. Bring to a simmer over medium-high heat, stirring to dissolve the sugar, then simmer until a thin syrup forms, about 2 minutes. Remove the pan from the heat and add the rhubarb and strawberries. Set aside until the rhubarb and strawberries are tender but still hold their shape, about 5 minutes. Transfer the mixture to a baking sheet to cool completely.

WHITE CHOCOLATE MOUSSE

(continued)

TO MAKE THE STRAWBERRY PUREE: Preheat the oven to 450°F. Toss the strawberries, sugar, and lemon juice in a medium bowl to coat. Set aside until juices begin to form, about 2 minutes. Transfer the mixture to a small heavy baking sheet and roast until the strawberries begin to release their juices and the juices begin to caramelize, about 8 minutes. Transfer the mixture to a fine-mesh sieve and, using a ladle, press the mixture through the sieve and into a medium bowl. Transfer the puree to a squeeze bottle and refrigerate until cold.

TO MAKE THE MOUSSE: Combine the white chocolate and ¼ cup of the cream in a large metal bowl. Set the bowl over a saucepan of simmering water (do not allow the bottom of the bowl to touch the water) and stir until the chocolate is melted and smooth.

Meanwhile, soak the gelatin sheet in a bowl of cold water until softened, about 5 minutes. Drain well, then add the gelatin to the white chocolate and stir until melted. Remove the bowl from over the simmering water and set the bowl aside to cool until the chocolate mixture is lukewarm, whisking occasionally, about 10 minutes.

With an electric mixer, beat the remaining 1 cup of cream in a large bowl until very thick and soft peaks form. Using clean dry beaters, beat the egg whites with the sugar in a medium bowl just until moist, semifirm peaks form. Fold the whites into the chocolate mixture, then fold in the whipped cream. Cover and refrigerate immediately until set, at least 4 hours.

TO MAKE THE STRAWBERRY DUST: Preheat the oven to 400°F. Combine the cereal, flour, confectioners' sugar, butter, strawberry powder, and salt in a small food processor and blend until a cornmeal consistency forms. Spread the mixture onto a small heavy baking sheet and bake until golden brown, about 8 minutes. Cool completely. Return the mixture to the food processor and pulse until a powder texture forms.

TO SERVE: Spoon the mousse onto 6 plates. Spoon the poached rhubarb and strawberries alongside. Drizzle droplets of the strawberry puree around the mousse. Garnish with the strawberry dust and serve immediately.

SERVES 6

Recipe courtesy of
THE BOYS' TEAM
(Frank Mirando and Joshua Marks)

BANANA-AND-PEANUT-STUFFED PUFF PASTRY
WITH SWEET MASCARPONE CHEESE

In the Mystery Box that contained duck and a banana, there were, among other things, mascarpone, peanuts, puff pastry, Fresno chile, and marjoram. Monti Carlo took a noticeably unorthodox approach to her ingredients by focusing on the banana. She quartered it, then sautéed it in butter flavored with Fresno chile. Then she slathered squares of unbaked puff pastry with a little mascarpone, sprinkled on peanuts, and rolled a piece of fried banana inside each square. Basted with an egg wash and baked till golden and puffy, sprinkled with diced Fresno chile and fresh marjoram leaves, it was . . . interesting looking. Pretty and golden, but with no indication what was inside. Don't worry, just take a bite while it's still warm. The banana and mascarpone meld into a creamy filling, the Fresno chile adds a mildly fruity kick, and the peanuts add crunch and an earthier flavor. It's an unexpectedly good dessert from a jumble of Mystery Box ingredients, and no one was more surprised at its success than Monti herself!

¾ **cup sugar**

6 **tablespoons (¾ stick) unsalted butter**

1 **Fresno chile pepper, finely diced (wear plastic gloves when handling)**

4 **bananas**

1 **sheet frozen puff pastry (half of 17.3-ounce package), thawed and chilled**

  All-purpose flour

¾ **cup mascarpone cheese, at room temperature**

¼ **cup shelled peanuts, toasted and finely chopped**

3 **teaspoons finely chopped fresh marjoram**

1 **large egg, beaten**

Preheat the oven to 375°F. Line a heavy baking sheet with parchment paper, then sprinkle ¼ cup of the sugar evenly over the paper and bake until the sugar is melted and deep golden brown, about 15 minutes. Cool the sheet of caramelized sugar completely (it will become brittle when cooled). Leave the oven on, but increase the temperature to 425°F.

Meanwhile, combine the butter and half of the Fresno chile in a small, heavy-bottomed saucepan. Cook over low heat until the butter melts but does not boil. Remove the pan from the heat and set aside to infuse for 15 minutes. Strain the chile butter and set aside. Discard the chile.

Peel and quarter the bananas crosswise. Heat the chile butter in a large, heavy-bottomed sauté pan over medium-high heat. Add the banana pieces and cook until they soften slightly and begin to brown but do not become mushy, about 2 minutes. Transfer the banana pieces to a plate and cool completely.

Roll out the pastry sheet on a lightly floured surface to a 14-inch square. Cut the pastry into four 7-inch squares. Spread 3 tablespoons of mascarpone cheese over the center of each piece of pastry. Sprinkle each with 1 tablespoon of the sugar. Sprinkle the peanuts over each,

then sprinkle each with ½ teaspoon of the marjoram. Arrange the bananas in the center. Sprinkle each with 1 tablespoon of sugar. Roll up the bananas in the pastry, folding in the sides and pressing them to seal just before rolling up the pastry completely, as if making a burrito. Brush the egg over the seam and press to seal. Transfer the pastries to a baking sheet. Bake until the pastries are golden, about 25 minutes. Cool for 10 minutes.

Transfer the pastries to 4 plates. Crumble the sheet of caramelized sugar and sprinkle the pieces over the pastry. Sprinkle the remaining marjoram and chile over the pastry and serve immediately.

SERVES 4

BANANA-AND-PEANUT-STUFFED PUFF PASTRY
(continued)

Recipe courtesy of
MONTI CARLO

ITALIAN TRIFLE:
BALSAMIC-BASIL STRAWBERRY PRESERVES, MASCARPONE LEMON CURD, AND AMARETTO CREAM

Frank Mirando turned everyday Italian tiramisu on its head with Meyer lemon (see page 256), but Stacey Amagrande took that idea one step further. She turned a typical English trifle on its head by making it Italian! Trifle in its most basic form is cubes of sponge cake topped with a little sherry, fruit, custard, and whipped cream. It's a good solid sweet in the English tradition, yes, but not exactly exciting. Italian trifle, on the other hand, is a taste sensation. Ladyfingers topped with homemade strawberry preserves with a hint of balsamic vinegar for tanginess. Instead of custard, a lemon curd made with eggs, butter, lemon juice, and zest, and mascarpone for creaminess. And the master stroke is Stacey's almond cream—whipped cream flavored with Amaretto, an almond-flavored Italian liqueur.

FOR THE STRAWBERRY PRESERVES

- 12 medium fresh strawberries (about 7 ounces)
- ⅓ cup plus 1 teaspoon sugar
- 3 teaspoons fresh lemon juice
- 1 teaspoon aged balsamic vinegar
- 1 tablespoon fresh basil chiffonade

FOR THE MASCARPONE LEMON CURD

- 3 large eggs
- ½ cup sugar
- 1 tablespoon grated lemon zest
- 6 tablespoons fresh lemon juice
- 6 tablespoons unsalted butter
- ¼ cup mascarpone cheese

FOR THE AMARETTO CREAM

- ¾ cup chilled heavy cream
- 1½ teaspoons sugar
- 1 teaspoon Disaronno Amaretto or other almond liqueur

FOR THE TRIFLES

- 4 ladyfingers, cut into bite-size pieces
- 3 tablespoons sliced almonds, toasted
- 4 small fresh basil leaves, for garnish

TO MAKE THE STRAWBERRY PRESERVES: Quarter 8 of the strawberries and combine them with ⅓ cup of the sugar, 1 teaspoon of the lemon juice, and the balsamic vinegar in a small, heavy-bottomed saucepan. Cook over medium heat, stirring until the sugar dissolves and the syrup comes to a simmer. Reduce the heat to medium-low and simmer until the berries are very tender and the syrup thickens, stirring often, about 5 minutes. Cool slightly. Using an immersion blender, puree the strawberry mixture until smooth. Transfer the puree to a bowl and cool completely, about 20 minutes.

Meanwhile, dice the remaining 4 strawberries and combine them with the basil and the remaining 1 teaspoon of sugar and 2 teaspoons of lemon juice in a small bowl. Marinate for 10 minutes. Fold the marinated strawberry mixture into the cooled strawberry puree. You should have about ¾ cup of strawberry preserves. Cover and refrigerate until cold.

TO MAKE THE MASCARPONE LEMON CURD: Combine the eggs, sugar, lemon zest, and lemon juice in a large bowl, then set the bowl over a saucepan of simmering water and whisk constantly until the mixture thickens, about 3 minutes. Remove the bowl from the heat and whisk in the butter. Strain the custard into a bowl. Whisk in the mascarpone and refrigerate until cold.

TO MAKE THE AMARETTO CREAM: Whisk the cream, sugar, and almond liqueur in a large bowl until soft peaks form.

TO ASSEMBLE THE TRIFLES: Place the broken ladyfingers in the bottom of 4 individual (8-ounce) trifle dishes or dessert dishes. Divide the strawberry preserves among the dishes and lightly tap the dishes to spread the preserves evenly. Spoon the mascarpone lemon curd on top and then top with the almond cream. Garnish with toasted almonds and basil leaves and serve.

SERVES 4

Recipe courtesy of
STACEY AMAGRANDE

MOLTEN LAVA CAKE

T his style of cake is a quickly baked chocolate dessert whose center remains uncooked so that it pours forth a stream of hot chocolate sauce when you press in your spoon. It was invented by Chef Jean-Georges Vongerichten, but versions of it can now be found on restaurant menus around the world. And many of them are subpar—if the cakes are overbaked, there's no molten stream. If they're too underbaked, you get a stream of something more akin to cake batter than chocolate sauce. Quite simply, Anna Rossi nailed it with her Molten Lava Cake. Presented with gorgeous red citrus lightly poached in a spicy syrup and a few candied pistachios that brought color and crunch, it was a dish that wowed the judges, who roundly agreed that Anna's version was restaurant-worthy—perhaps better! If you're in doubt about your cakes, always err on the side of underbaked. Fluted ramekins make for a glamorous presentation, but you can bake these in plain ramekins or even rounded custard cups.

FOR THE CANDIED PISTACHIOS

- ½ cup raw shelled pistachios
- ¼ cup sugar
- 2 tablespoons water

FOR THE CITRUS SAUCE

- 1 ruby grapefruit
- 1 blood orange or Valencia orange
- ½ cup sugar
- ½ cup water
- 2 star anise
- 1 cinnamon stick
- 2 teaspoons cardamom pods

FOR THE CAKES

About 2 tablespoons plus ½ cup (1 stick) unsalted butter

About ¼ cup unsweetened cocoa powder

- 4 ounces high-quality bittersweet chocolate (65% cacao), chopped
- 2 large eggs
- 2 large egg yolks
- ¼ cup sugar

  Pinch of salt
- 2 teaspoons all-purpose flour

TO MAKE THE CANDIED PISTACHIOS: Stir the pistachios in a medium, heavy-bottomed sauté pan over medium heat until toasted, about 5 minutes. Transfer to a medium bowl and set aside to cool.

Stir the sugar and water in a small, heavy-bottomed saucepan over medium-high heat and bring to a boil, stirring just until the sugar dissolves. Simmer without stirring until the syrup thickens enough to coat a spoon, about 3 minutes. Pour over the pistachios and stir to coat. Set aside to cool.

TO MAKE THE CITRUS SAUCE: Cut the top and bottom ½ inch off the grapefruit and the orange. Stand each on 1 flat end. Following the contour of the fruit, cut off all the peel and white pith. Working over a

MOLTEN LAVA CAKE

(continued)

bowl, cut the fruit between the membranes, releasing their segments into the bowl. Squeeze the segmented grapefruit and orange to extract as much liquid as possible from the membranes. Remove the segments from the juice and set them aside.

Combine the reserved juices, sugar, water, star anise, cinnamon stick, and cardamom pods in a small, heavy-bottomed saucepan and bring to a simmer over high heat, stirring just until the sugar dissolves. Reduce the heat to medium-low and simmer until the syrup is reduced to about ½ cup, about 15 minutes. Strain the syrup.

TO MAKE THE CAKES: Preheat the oven to 450°F. Coat four 4-ounce ramekins with about 2 tablespoons of the butter, then coat with cocoa powder. Tap out the excess cocoa.

Stir the chocolate and the remaining ½ cup butter in a bowl set over a saucepan of simmering water until the chocolate and butter melt and the mixture is smooth. Remove the bowl from the heat.

Using an electric mixer, beat the whole eggs, egg yolks, sugar, and salt in a large bowl until the mixture is pale yellow and thick. Fold the yolk mixture into the chocolate mixture. Gently fold in the flour. Divide the batter equally among the prepared ramekins, filling them about three-fourths full. Bake until the tops are just set but the centers are still fluid, 5 to 8 minutes.

TO SERVE: Immediately run a thin knife around the edges of the ramekins to loosen the cakes. Invert the ramekins onto the centers of 4 plates and let sit for 10 seconds in the ramekin, then lift and remove the ramekins. Spoon the candied pistachios on top. Pour the syrup around the cakes. Arrange the citrus segments around the cakes and serve.

SERVES 4

Recipe courtesy of
ANNA ROSSI

Acknowledgments

The *MasterChef* family would like to thank our partners at Fox, The Shine Group, Shine America, and One Potato Two Potato, and give a very special thanks to our world-class judges Gordon Ramsay, Graham Elliot, and Joe Bastianich.

Many thanks, too, to Ben Adler, David Anderson, Robin Ashbrook, Monica Austin, Sandee Birdsong, Gillian Blake, Laura Caccavo, Amy Cohen, Mike Darnell, Carl Fennessy, Wenda Fong, Paul Franklin, Jeff Friedman, Eden Gaha, Linda Giambrone, Melissa Gold, Lori Heiss, Nicole Iizuka, Sabrina Ishak, Edwin Karapetian, Ozen Kazim, Ben Liebmann, Elise Lineberger, Pat Llewelyn, Yeesum Lo, Bobby Luedtke, Alex Mahon, Elisabeth Murdoch, Mark Nash, Adam Neal, Kelly Perron, Peter Rice, Lee Rierson, Franc Roddam, Adeline Ramage Rooney, Alyssa Sales, Joe Schlosser, Tom Sheets, Kate Shields, Steve Shikiya, Armando Solares, Kelia Tardiff, Laurie Tixier, Korrin Tarle, Rochelle Palermo Torres, Triple 7 Public Relations, Ivana Zbozinek, the *MasterChef* contestants past and present, and, of course, the entire *MasterChef* crew. Without everyone's hard work, this project would not have been possible. Thank you for inspiring the MasterChef in all of us.

Index

Underscored page references indicate sidebars.
Boldface *references indicate photographs.*

E